Contemporary Islamic Law in Indonesia

Exploring Muslim Contexts

Series Editor: Farouk Topan

Ethnographies of Islam:
Ritual Performances and Everyday Practices
Edited by Badouin Dupret, Thomas Pierret, Paulo Pinto and Kathryn Spellman-Poots

The Challenge of Pluralism:
Paradigms from Muslim Contexts
Edited by Abdou Filali-Ansary and Sikeena Karmali Ahmed

Cosmopolitanisms in Muslim Contexts:
Perspectives from the Past
Edited by Derryl MacLean and Sikeena Karmali Ahmed

Genealogy and Knowledge in Muslim Societies:
Understanding the Past
Edited by Sarah Bowen Savant and Helena de Felipe

Development Models in Muslim Contexts:
Chinese, 'Islamic' and Neo-liberal Alternatives
Edited by Robert Springborg

Contemporary Islamic Law in Indonesia:
Sharia and Legal Pluralism
Arskal Salim

www.euppublishing.com/series/ecmc

Contemporary Islamic Law in Indonesia

Sharia and Legal Pluralism

Arskal Salim

EDINBURGH
University Press

IN ASSOCIATION WITH

THE AGA KHAN UNIVERSITY
(International) in the United Kingdom
Institute for the Study of Muslim Civilisations

To my beloved parents Abdul Muin Salim and Arhamy Dappung

Edinburgh University Press Ltd
The Tun – Holyrood Road
12 (2f) Jackson's Entry
Edinburgh EH8 8PJ
www.euppublishing.com

Typeset in 10.5/13 Goudy by
Servis Filmsetting Ltd, Stockport, Cheshire,
and printed and bound in Great Britain by
CPI Group (UK) Ltd, Croydon CR0 4YY

A CIP record for this book is available from the British Library

ISBN 978 0 7486 9333 7 (hardback)
ISBN 978 0 7486 9348 1 (webready PDF)
ISBN 978 1 4744 0342 9 (epub)

Contents

Figures, Diagrams and Table

Figures

Diagrams

Table

Acknowledgements

This is the first of two books that I planned to emerge from my long fieldwork in the post-tsunami Aceh from 2007 to 2008 and frequent visits thereafter. I am greatly indebted to so many people in Aceh who have introduced me to various local (legal) concepts and provided me with information about their life experiences within and beyond courtrooms. Most of them have even been so kind as to offer assistance, guidance and sustenance in one way or another. Without the direction and support I received from many people in Aceh, I would probably have not been able to write this present book.

I would like to first acknowledge Rusjdi Ali Muhammad for his endless support since my first step on Aceh's soil. He has helped me in ways that I cannot forget. He represents a caring father as well as a welcoming host whenever I visit Aceh. He kindly facilitated my first trip and my accommodation when I came to Aceh during the civil emergency status and before the 2004 tsunami. Secondly, I must acknowledge the tremendous support I gladly received from John Bowen of Washington University. Working closely with him over the past five years on various projects, he not only guided me through ways of navigation in the field of legal anthropology, but he also provided me with stimulating ideas for research and publication, including this present book.

The idea for this book in particular stemmed initially from my three-year engagement (November 2006–October 2009) as a postdoctoral fellow at the Max Planck Institute (MPI) for Social Anthropology, Halle, Germany. My special thanks go to this scientific research institution, most notably to the leaders of Legal Pluralism Project Group, the late Professor Franz von Benda-Beckmann and Professor Keebet von Benda-Beckmann, who had offered their generous support in many ways. Franz in particular read a few chapters (in their preliminary and rough versions) of this book and provided me with written comments. I have benefited enormously from the spirit of collegial exchange that exists among all members of the project group (Bert, Martin, Jutta, Judith, Caroline, Fadjar), who created a stimulating intellectual atmosphere during my three-year stay in Germany. A monthly 'theory evening' at the apartment of Franz and Keebet in Halle, and a yearly retreat to Westensee, six-hour drive from Halle, where Franz's and Keebet's holiday home is located, will always remain in my memory.

While conducting fieldwork in Aceh, a great number of interviewees and colleagues were so helpful and made my work a lot easier. I would like to express my thanks to all my interviewees who serve as judges at the different sharia courts of Aceh for devoting their time and effort to this research. They include Soufyan Saleh, Jufri Ghalib, Rosmawardani, Marluddin, Rafiuddin, Armiya Ibrahim and Zubaedah Hanoum. I also owe special thanks to the professors and academics of the Ar-Raniri State Islamic University of Banda Aceh (Rusjdi Ali Muhammad, Hamid Sarong, Al Yasa Abubakar, Syahrizal, Yusny Saby, Hasbi Amiruddin, Farid Wajdy, Warul Walidin, Badruzzaman Ismail, Safir Widjaya, Ismail Muhammad, Amirul Hadi, Eka Srimulyani, Kamaruzzaman and Aslam Saad), who discussed various socio-religious issues in Aceh with me and provided valuable insight. My thanks also go to colleagues at the Law Faculty of Syiah Kuala University of Banda Aceh (Muzakkir Abubakar, Saleh Syafei, Saifuddin Bantasyam, Taqwaddin, Nurdin Husein) for offering information and analysis on legal political developments in Aceh.

My gratitude also goes to my Acehnese friends at PKPM (Mujiburrahman, Muslim Zainuddin, Hasnul Arifin, Abidin Nurdin, Ridha, Sayuthi, Mahmuddin, Nazir and Khairizzaman) all of whom helped me enormously when living in Aceh (March 2006–August 2006, September 2007–June 2008). My PKPM friends, people at the Aceh Institute (Alkaf, Saiful Akmal, Chairul Fahmi, Teuku Jafar), partners at the ICAIOS (Saiful Mahdi, Reza Nurdin, Rizanna, Sehat Ihsan) and Supriadi Adiguna were so helpful in giving me a sense of being at home whenever I came to Aceh. Many thanks for this friendship throughout the last years.

The research for this book could not have been completed without the financial support provided by different institutions. The MPI for Social Anthropology provided funding for most fieldwork that led to this book. In addition, I am grateful for the British Academy Small Research grant in 2010 that enabled me to investigate a variety of contested norms and practices relating to the aftermath of triple divorce in Aceh. The findings of this research appear as Chapter 9 of this book. I am also thankful for a three-month fellowship offered by the Asia Research Institute at the National University of Singapore that allowed me to revise some chapters and restructure the shape of this book as it is now. I was fortunate to receive suggestions from Michael Feener on revising some parts of the earlier draft while staying in Singapore between August and October 2011. Likewise, I thank Aga Khan University, Institute for the Study of Muslim Civilisations, London, and Syarif Hidayatullah State Islamic University, Jakarta, Indonesia, for granting me teaching absences over certain periods that I was away on fieldwork research between 2007 and 2010.

I owe much gratitude to all my fieldwork assistants in Aceh (Zarkasyi, Masrijal, Dafiuddin, Ernita, Haura, Reza) and local researchers (Nanda Amalia, Abidin Nurdin, Al Chaidar, Marzi Afriko) who offered information in various ways that helped me to complete the field research. I sincerely thank them for their efforts in various data collection tasks, including arranging visits to meet interviewees, discussing and analysing cases, newspaper clippings, taking pictures of events and transcribing most parts of recorded interviews. Additional support was provided by a number of close friends in different ways. Nadirsyah Hosen has been a great friend. I thank him for not only providing me with enthusiastic conversations during the many virtual or real discussions we have had since we were PhD students, but also for having shared strategies and tips that greatly helped me stay on an international academic track. Adlin Sila has been a genuine friend who always shares his intellectual fervour and anthropological research with me. I thank him for every endeavour he made to show me what truthful yet academic friendship is.

I feel so fortunate to be part of University of Western Sydney (since late 2012), and to have received a great deal of support and helpful input on various academic matters, especially from colleagues at the Religion and Society Research Centre (Adam Possamai, Eva Garcia, Julia Howell, Bryan Turner, Jan Ali and Steven Drakeley). Adam has been a great mentor. He not only strongly supports the publication of this book, but he always encourages me to publish more works out of my research.

I am very grateful to various people for helping me in the preparation of this book. My sincere thanks go to Rhubarb Academic Editing, who looked closely at the final manuscript for English style and grammar, correcting both and offering suggestions for clarity and improvement. I also thank Abidin Nurdin and Siska Novirianti, who respectively assisted me by preparing appendices and glossary. A number of editors at the Aga Khan University and Edinburgh University Press (Charlotte Whiting, Farouk Topan, Sikeena Ahmed, Michelle Houston and Nicola Ramsey) have helped me in one way or another in publishing this book. Their professional and careful assistance are gratefully acknowledged.

I feel a deep sense of gratitude to my mother, Arhamy Dappung, and my late father, Abdul Muin Salim, who passed away in May 2011. I am dedicating this present book to both of them as a symbol of my love for guiding me in life through many of their prayers. Last but not least, I am very deeply grateful to my wife (Maya) and my three children (Akmal, Maykal and Marsal) for the support and loving encouragement they have offered me over the course of my years of work and research. I truly admire the sacrifices they have made to follow behind my steps and to move across countries (Indonesia, Australia, Germany, the United Kingdom and then Australia again) over the past twelve years. Their incredible patience and understanding, for I had to travel to visit research sites, deliver papers at conferences and devote long hours to reading and writing, are far too huge to acknowledge in full. With my most heartfelt thanks, I must say that without them the present book may not have been written.

Finally, Some of the material included in this book was derived from my previous publications as follows:

1. An earlier draft of Chapter 2 appeared in the form of an article: 'Dynamic Legal Pluralism in Indonesia: Contested Plural Legal Orders of Contemporary Aceh', *Journal of Legal Pluralism* 61 (2010): 1–30.
2. Some sections in Chapter 5 have been published in: 'Politics, Criminal Justice and Islamisation in Aceh', *Islam, Syari'ah and Governance Background Paper Series* (2009), 3, University of Melbourne, Australia.
3. Several paragraphs in Part One of this book were fragments of an article: 'Shari'a from Below in Aceh (1930s–1960s): Islamic Identity and the Right to Self-determination with Comparative Reference to the Moro Islamic Liberation Front (MILF)', *Indonesia and Malay World* 32 (2004): 80–96.

I thank the editors (Melanie Wiber, Tim Lindsey and Ben Murtagh) of the respective journals and publications for permission to reproduce them in more refined analyses in this book.

Note: In this book specialist non-English terms are italicised at first instance only.

Map 1 Aceh, Indonesia

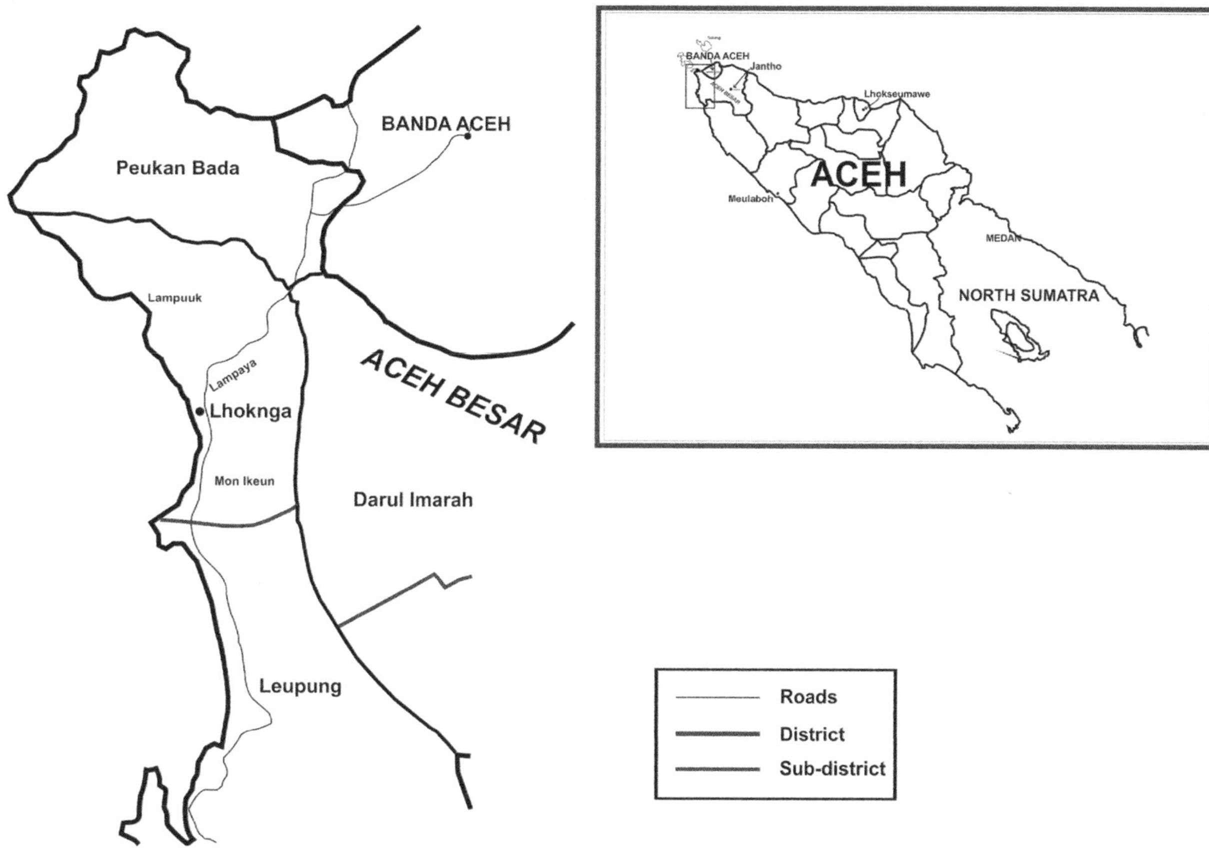

Map 2 Research sites in Aceh

Introduction

The tsunami and the recovery effort have rearranged
the lives and political organization of people,
bringing about changes in cultural practices and settlement patterns,
the end of secessionist conflict and a fledging peace process,
as well as allowing new political voices and power-based relationships to emerge.

Grigorovich (2009: 155)

I went to Aceh, Indonesia, for the first time when I was a PhD student. I was looking at the way in which a programme of Islamisation of the law was being introduced by the government (by incorporating certain aspects of sharia religious law into regional regulations, known locally as *qanun*) and implemented in this province. For many years, travel to this part of Indonesia, which is located at the northern tip of the island of Sumatra, was restricted. Since 1976, Aceh had been an area of prolonged conflict between the Indonesian military and the Aceh independence movement (GAM). While this had begun with heavy armed fighting and killings in several specific districts, from 1999 onwards there was escalation of the conflict and clashes occurred in almost every district, including the capital of the province, Banda Aceh.[1]

It was late May 2004 when I first stepped on Aceh's soil. The 'military emergency' status in Aceh had ended just a couple of weeks before and had changed to 'civil emergency'. The Garuda Indonesia airplane that flew me from Jakarta landed at noon, and, along with other passengers, I walked into the terminal building. At the entrance doors of the Blang Bintang airport building, I was stunned to see so many soldiers standing around with weapons in their hands. They may have just been doing their job, yet, as a native Indonesian originally from a different island (South Sulawesi) and having often travelled to a number of cities in Indonesia without ever encountering this type of situation, I quickly felt that there was something different in and about Aceh and I realised that this province was not comparable to the others. During this first experience of visiting Aceh (for almost a week) I was overwhelmed with anxieties and fears. Five months later, I returned to Aceh during the Ramadan fasting month (October 2004), two months before the Boxing Day tsunami. This time, although I became used to seeing the same scene, I still experienced the same feelings as before.

In June 2005, six months after the devastating earthquake and tsunami disaster, I returned to Aceh. This was not a pre-planned PhD fieldtrip, because all my PhD research fieldwork had been completed in 2004. My PhD supervisor, Professor Tim Lindsey of Melbourne University, encouraged me to visit Aceh once again to investigate the extent to which the post-tsunami conditions had affected the Islamisation of law in the region. It was a coincidence that at the time of my return to Aceh, the punishment by caning of a number of offenders was about to take place. From the beginning of the process of introducing sharia law, the inclusion of the caning penalty into Aceh's regional regulation has sparked debate among lawyers and jurist scholars in Indonesia, and has attracted severe criticism from the wider international community. Despite this, on 25 June 2005, after the Friday prayer, the first implementation of this punishment – the caning of more than twenty offenders (most of whom were charged with violating the qanun on gambling) – eventually took place in the district of Bireun (four hours' drive from the capital of the province). With the assistance of a local youth organisation based in Banda Aceh, I was able to videotape the first 'Islamic' punishment[2] officially imposed in a territorial part of the secular republic of Indonesia.

Legal Changes

The swift and dramatic changes in the legal systems of Indonesia in general, and of Aceh in particular, have taken place in less than ten years. In 1999, following the collapse of the authoritarian Suharto regime in May 1998, Aceh was awarded autonomous status, with special privileges in some social, legal and cultural spheres. Two years later, the implementation of sharia in Aceh was officially declared and a distinctive court (*Mahkamah Syar'iyah*) was established to examine offenders against Islamic criminal law. In 2002 and 2003, relevant institutions, rules and punishments were stipulated in regional regulations (known locally as qanun) and passed by the provincial legislature. Although legislation on Islamic punishments were introduced in 2002, the legislature did not immediately instigate rigorous implementation of sharia in the region. In October 2002, the chairman of the Aceh *ulama* council (MPU) declared that Muslims who violated Islamic rules stipulated in the qanun would be lashed. By early 2004, the *Syar'iyah* Court had sentenced some offenders to the caning penalty. However, up to the time when Aceh was hit by the earthquake and tsunami in December 2004, not a single person had been punished this way. It was only six months after this disaster that the punishment of public caning finally took place.

Was the earthquake and tsunami disaster a crucial factor that made possible and promoted the implementation of the caning penalty? As I have pointed out elsewhere (Salim 2008: 163–4), many people in Aceh considered this calamity a spiritual test or even a punishment from God. In the first months following the disaster, religious sermons delivered on many occasions and at various places centred on this matter. In fact, every evening, at the time of the after-sunset prayer, the *Wilayatul Hisbah* (religious enforcement officers) marched from one mosque to another to echo and spread this message to the participants in the prayer. It was believed that through this disaster, God had communicated with the Acehnese, advising them to stop committing sinful deeds, to reconcile with each other and comply with sharia rules. It was further understood that the tsunami was God's message to the government to enforce sharia in the province in earnest.[3]

Some people, however, were unconvinced that the tsunami was God's punishment for the Acehnese. To these people, the protracted armed conflicts in Aceh from 1976 onwards, which had caused the deaths of many innocent people, as well as mental and physical wounds, had already been punishment enough. In their view, the large-scale earthquake that led to the disastrous tsunami was merely tectonic activity under the earth, which they regarded as *sunnatullah* (a natural process). For them, this had nothing to do with whether or not sharia was implemented in Aceh. In fact, the argument continued, as Aceh is located in a geologically unstable area, where earthquakes often occur, there is no guarantee that a future tsunami will not hit Aceh even if sharia were applied fully. For them, the disaster is one thing and the implementation of sharia is another, separate thing,[4] and, in short, the disaster was not an escalating factor for the implementation of sharia in Aceh. Nevertheless, in my view, it would be hasty to say that the disaster had no significance in the various legal and political transformations in Aceh.

Perhaps the most far-reaching change that the disaster brought about in Aceh was the acceleration of the peace process. On 15 August 2005, eight months after the disaster, through the support of the international mediator, the Crisis Management Initiative (led by Martti Ahtisaari, the former president of Finland), both the government of Indonesia and the Free Aceh Movement (GAM) finally signed the Helsinki Agreement and ended the prolonged bloody conflict in the province (Aspinall 2005). Although this complicated peace process had commenced several years earlier, the post-disaster conditions created a particular context in which both parties to the conflict felt the urgency of taking a major step forward and speeding up the peace process (Husain 2007). Given the previous intricate processes involved in this agreement, it was unimaginable that the Helsinki Agreement would have been so promptly signed without such a huge-scale disaster having preceded it.

The Helsinki Agreement served as a legitimate basis for the transformation of the legal political system in Aceh, which led to the issuance of Law 11 of 2006 on the Governance of Aceh. This law provides Aceh with a stronger framework that affects changes in the existing legal constellation in Aceh in many ways. This legislation contains explicit provisions on plural legal orders by formally recognising *adat* (customary) institutions as well as Islamic legal institutions in matters of dispute resolution in their respective jurisdictions. The law has not only reinforced the status of adat institutions[5] in Aceh, but has also filled gaps and eliminated ambiguities in the previous regulations in relation to the application of sharia in Aceh.[6] The legitimacy of sharia rules and the status of the Mahkamah Syar'iyah and its jurisdiction have been strengthened and widened. In fact, the 2006 Law on the Governance of Aceh is considered to have elevated the status of the Mahkamah Syar'iyah to a more eminent position.[7]

This book is an ethnographic account of legal pluralism in Aceh, Indonesia, in what is, simultaneously, a post-conflict and post-disaster situation. A number of significant changes in the legal and political structures of Aceh that have taken place, concurrently, since the demise of the New Order regime, have led to the deepening of legal pluralism in Aceh. Legal pluralism is practically understood here as 'the co-existence of more than one legal order (or mechanism) in the same socio-political field' (F. Benda-Beckmann 2006: 58). While these dynamics of plural legal orders began with the emergence of a new democratic state of Indonesia through the decentralisation policy, it was the post-tsunami recovery processes that accelerated and consolidated the presence of plural legal orders in Aceh.

Some scholars have explained the changes in legal systems that have taken place elsewhere and at other times. A prominent legal anthropologist, June Starr (1992), explained that changes in Ottoman and Turkish law in the nineteenth and twentieth centuries were due to the roles of, and competition between, state elites. Contextualising her field research on law within a theory of cultural, societal and legal change, Starr (1992: xviii) considered both that law is 'a process and that it is shaped by rules and a cultural logic', and 'a discourse fought over by very real agents with different political agendas'. Starr's conclusion was that legal changes in modern Turkey were mostly directed by the secular elites who succeeded in the contest, leaving only a few spaces for the traditional Islamic elites who were politically marginalised. Accordingly, the Ottoman Turkish legal system, from the Tanzimat era in the nineteenth century until the 1970s, was almost completely secularised.

In the same vein, Franz von Benda-Beckmann and Keebet von Benda-Beckmann (2013) discussed political and legal transformation in the relationship between different legal orders in West Sumatra, Indonesia. In their recent book, both writers discussed the transformation of traditional village polity (*nagari*) from the Dutch colonisation period to the post-Suharto decentralisation programme; namely, from 1999 onwards. In the light of this framework and timeline, the authors analysed changes and continuities within village government through the ever-changing relationship between the three major bodies of law based in state government, religion and *adat* (custom). Contestation between these different legal realms, especially among their respective supporters (state officials, religious clerics and adat leaders), has helped to (re)shape the existing local structure and legal practice over time.

The above-mentioned anthropological studies conducted by Starr (1992) and F. and K. von Benda-Beckmann (2013) on legal changes were based on a long-term historical perspective. They therefore cannot avoid the prevailing political factors, competition between elites in particular, that (re)shape the final outcome of legal transformation. A shift resulting from political contestation helps to explain why a transformation as well as a reconfiguration occurs in any given legal system. While this book shares this premise, it contends that it is not only competition among elites, but also certain major key events that seem to effect pertinent changes in a legal system. In fact, rapid legal changes cannot be well understood only by looking at a shift in social and political settings, which often takes place gradually. Rather, one has to consider some emerging and inevitable conditions, which are not necessarily political, that have allowed, encouraged and even forced state elites to make rapid changes in norms, institutions and procedures of law.

For this reason, the present book ponders three particular key events that have profoundly affected rapid changes in Indonesia's legal system in general and contemporary Aceh's legal structure in particular: (1) the 2004 Boxing Day tsunami disaster that severely damaged most coastal areas of Aceh; (2) the August 2005 Helsinki Peace Agreement that ended the protracted armed conflict between the Indonesian military and the Free Aceh Movement; and (3) the presence of many international agencies involved in rebuilding Aceh in the post-conflict and post-disaster recovery processes from 2005 onwards. All these key events have ushered in many new initiatives and programmes of rapid legal transformations both at national level and, even more so, at the local level.

Although the origins of these changes can be traced back to several years before the end of the Suharto regime, the impetus of all this rapid transformation in Aceh was provided by certain key events that ensued following the 2004 Boxing Day earthquake and tsunami.

This book provides a study of probably the fastest changing legal system in the Muslim world. This change has occurred largely because of post-tsunami and post-conflict recovery processes. The post-tsunami rehabilitation process is at the centre of all these transformations, since it not only drove the efforts to end the long-standing Aceh conflict, but also accidentally unlocked Aceh from international isolation with the arrival in the province of numerous global aid agencies. Taken together, the post-tsunami recovery process, the accompanying internationalisation of Aceh, and the development of peace following the Helsinki Agreement have each in their own ways stimulated legal and political transformations that affect the social structure and communities of Aceh. By examining relevant legal knowledge and practice in villages, courts and political spaces, this book demonstrates that the post-conflict and post-disaster recovery processes have hastened changes in legal norms, institutions and procedures.

The book deals with various changes in both the national legal system of Indonesia and the regional legal structure in its province of Aceh. It seeks to complement numerous existing works[8] on Islam and law in Aceh by offering a legal pluralist perspective. The focus of this book is the encounter between diverse patterns of legal reasoning advocated by multiple actors or put forward by different institutions (be they local, national and international, official and unofficial, or judicial, political and socio-cultural) attendant to a vast array of issues arising in the wake of the December 2004 earthquake and tsunami in Aceh. The book not only studies disputes about rights to land and other forms of property, but it also investigates other types of dispute in a wider sense. It concerns disputes about power relations, conflict of rules, gender relationships, the right to make decisions and prevailing norms. This book presents disputes contested on multiple levels and in diverse forums, either through negotiation or adjudication, and regardless of whether or not they have been settled. These disputes include cases in which various actors from villages, courts, the provincial government and the legislature, the national Supreme Court and even the central state have become closely involved.

WHAT IS LAW?

This study asks the questions 'what is law?' and 'what does law do?' Moreover, 'what does law do after a natural disaster as a community recovers and rebuilds?'. It not only addresses legal problems and disputes that took place in the tsunami-affected areas, but also examines how different actors selectively and interchangeably use particular norms in various cases and forums to secure, or to defend, their interests. The book includes a range of socio-legal issues from the dispute over jurisdiction between (legal) institutions, competing sources of legal rules and the emerging challenges of pre-existing local norms, as well as transnational legal issues. For this venture, I would like to consider three main approaches in legal anthropology, as described below.

Law as Culture

The 'law as culture' thesis initially emerged from the debate between Gluckman (1955) and Bohannan (1957) on the issue of whether or not the legal logic and the process of reasoning in dispute settlements are present in all societies in the same way. The work of Clifford Geertz (1983) shed light on this debate. Geertz considered that norm or value should be called 'law' if rooted in the collective resources of culture rather than in the separate capacities of individuals. This was because, for Geertz (1983: 215), 'law is local knowledge'. Geertz (1983: 218, 232) thus argued that law is 'a species of social imagination', in which it 'is constructive of social life, not reflective, or anyway not just reflective, of it', and, hence, different cultural traditions maintain different legal sensibilities. Lawrence Rosen, who studied an Islamic village court in Morocco, echoed Geertz's conception of law as an expression of culture. In one of his books, Rosen (2006) argues that law is actually part of culture's way of expressing its sense of the order of things. Rosen (2006: 7) suggested that law must not be seen simply as a mechanism for attending to disputes or enforcing decisions, not solely as articulated rules or as evidence of differential power, but as a framework for ordered relationships. Law, in Rosen's understanding, cannot be detached from an orderliness that is itself dependent on its attachment to all the other realms of its adherents' lives.

The theory of law as culture, especially in the sense of Rosen's legal definition, is characterised as ordered relations. This is quite problematic in the sense that it is more often than not that law produces inequalities as well as discrimination among members of a community. This approach to law tends to fail largely because it often ignores not only the diversity within one specific culture, but also political and economic contexts in which norms are invoked, challenged and restated. What is more, the cultural system does not always work to influence subjects' legal actions. Instead, what become the main factors that drive people's legal movements, as pointed out by Starr and Collier (1989), are asymmetrical relationships between different (legal) orders and differences among people's access to resources.

Law as Domination

Sally F. Moore (2005) noted that 'law as domination' has been one of a number of popular approaches employed by legal anthropologists. What is central in this approach is the 'elite interest' argument, where law is purported to serve the cause of the more politically powerful parties. A part of this theory is 'law as a tool for social engineering'. As a result, instead of the norm, it is power that determines the outcome (Gulliver 1963, 1969). The 'law as domination' theory is problematic for two reasons. The first, as pointed out by Lazarus-Black and Hirsch (1994), is that this line of argument does not adequately consider that law is both the vehicle for material domination and cultural reproduction, and the site for local opposition to that domination and the struggle over cultural meaning. Thus, law not only consolidates and legitimates power positions, but it also serves as a resource for less powerful individuals or population groups in their struggle against domination as well as exploitation (F. and K. Benda-Beckmann 2001). The second reason is that the 'law as domination' thesis does not adequately take the disputing processes into account. It lacks the notion that disputing is, as Merry (1990: 5) put it, 'a process of meaning making, or, more precisely, a contest over meanings'. The process of dispute is not only an arena for securing justification for the claimed interests, but also a site for meaningful construction that can be mobilised to contest for domination as well as against subordination.

Law as Contested Field

June Starr and Jane F. Collier (1989) observed that there has been a shift in the main concern of the anthropology of law, from seeing a dispute as something to be resolved at the local level towards seeing local disputes as embedded in larger, often dialectic, conflicts between different interests. In light of this, the framework preference of this book is centred on the interests of different actors in the disputing processes. My study is particularly interested in seeing law as a means, in a great variety of ways, by which people, groups or the state act in their own interests. In this case, 'law offers a legitimate frame of reference in which political, economic and legal interests are defended' (K. von Benda-Beckmann 2001b: 44). Thus, this book considers law as a contested field, in which, as pointed out by F. von Benda-Beckmann (2002) and K. von Benda-Beckmann (2001a), not only may different legal norms exist parallel to and in competition with each other, but also various legal orders may challenge one another, often with none being self-evidently superior to the others.

My objective in this study is to explain law as a contested field; I agree with both Starr and Collier (1989), who conceptualise law as embedded in, and created by, particular historical circumstances and by interrelationships between local, national and international elements. This book therefore examines legal changes in contemporary Indonesia, in Aceh in particular, by addressing local meaning and also history and power (Starr and Collier 1989). It not only discusses legal changes, political contestation or village disputes as something to be resolved locally, but it also considers, most importantly, all those legal and political transformations as embedded in larger, often dialectic, conflicts between different actors, interests and values. Law thus becomes a showground where not only may separate legal orders compete or co-exist, but where numerous, yet different, legal subjects and norms may also challenge one another. This book is, therefore, not mainly the ethnography of Acehnese society, rather, it is the ethnography of legal disputes, practice and institutions. Its central concerns are the relations of individual actors to various legal forums and traditions as seen from outside formal legal institutions.

Background and Islamic Context of Aceh

By the end of 2012, Indonesia had thirty-four provinces. Earlier, during the late New Order period, Indonesia had twenty-seven provinces, including East Timor. After East Timor became an independent state in 1999, Indonesia acquired some new provinces by way of splitting up those provinces that had large land areas or big populations. The eight new provinces of the post-New Order are North Molucca (1999), Banten (2000), Bangka Belitung (2000), Gorontalo (2000), West Papua (2001), Riau Island (2002), West Sulawesi (2004) and North Kalimantan (2012). Of the thirty-four provinces of Indonesia, five have special status in that they are allowed to make some governmental arrangements in particular aspects of government. These provinces include Aceh, Jakarta, Yogyakarta, Papua and West Papua. However, Aceh is the only province granted special autonomy in the implementation of sharia.

Aceh is located at the northern tip of Sumatra. Following the decentralisation policy in the aftermath of the centralised Suharto regime, there are now five municipalities and eighteen regencies in this province. Banda Aceh is its capital. Along with a provincial legislature, a governor, with his lower administrative staff (mayors and heads of districts), holds full responsibility for governing the province. Unlike the *Dinas Syariat Islam* (Islamic Sharia Department) that constitutes the provincial government structure, the police, military, public prosecutor and courts (both civil and religious) of this province are all branches of, and subordinate to, their central government offices in Jakarta. These branches are not only available at the provincial level, but also exist at the district regional level. In fact, as in other places in Indonesia, the police station is present in each of the sub-district areas in Aceh.

According to the 2010 census, the population of Aceh was about 4.5 million people. The previous census, in 2000, was not properly conducted due to security issues. It was estimated, however, that Aceh then had more than 4 million people. So, within ten years, there had been an increase of more than 10 per cent. There was little accurate information as to how many people were in Aceh before and after the December 2004 tsunami disaster. Nevertheless, the Central Agency on Statistics (BPS) of Aceh issued an estimate that in 2003 the population of Aceh was 4,218,500. This figure decreased to 4,075,500 in 2004, and decreased even further in 2005 to 4,031,600. In 2006, the population increased to 4,153,600.[9] No detailed explanation was offered as to why the size of the population of Aceh had changed in this way over this period of time. Many are sure, however, that the fluctuation had to do with the devastating catastrophe and the ensuing recovery processes.

As far as socio-political categorisation in the pre-modern history of Aceh is concerned, there were at least four distinct groups: (1) the *uleebalang* (aristocrats), who were self-governing rulers and controlled most of the trade (including that with the Dutch) and collected taxes in their respective authorities; (2) the sultan, who tried to restrict the uleebalang's autonomy and competed with them to control trade internally and externally; (3) the ulama (religious leaders/scholars), who were isolated at Islamic *dayah* (learning institutions) and led the struggle against the Dutch who befriended the uleebalang; and (4) ordinary people, such as peasants or small landowners, who comprised the majority of Acehnese (Schröter 2010).

In the twentieth century this categorisation totally changed. The first two groups were gone by the middle of the twentieth century: the Dutch abolished the sultanate of Aceh in the first decade of the twentieth century; and the ulama attacked and killed many uleebalang figures in the 1948 Cumbok massacre (Syamsuddin 1985). A new social group emerged during the New Order period (1966–98), namely, the technocrats. This group was a combination of academics, military officers and bureaucrats in the regional government. In the view of Morris (1983), the technocrat was regarded as a 'new uleebalang', who worked cooperatively with the New Order government.

In the aftermath of the New Oder period, especially after the 2005 Helsinki Peace Agreement, the social composition within Acehnese society changed once again. This change was triggered by the recent emergence of former elites and members of the Free Aceh Movement (GAM) into the political arena as a result of occupying important bureaucratic positions in Aceh's provincial government and gaining a majority of seats at the local legislature (Stange and Patock 2010; Ansori 2012). In fact, some of them have been involved in major development projects in the province and have become (un)official business counterparts of the government (Aspinall 2009b). This new development has not only reconfigured the social composition of the Acehnese, but it has also created a need to redefine who are the uleebalang and which group aptly represents them in the contemporary context of Aceh.

Given that Islam came to Indonesia for the first time through Aceh,[10] the Acehnese are proud of having accepted Islam earlier than other Muslim ethnic groups in Sumatra or the other islands of Indonesia. Muslims are the majority population in Aceh. According to the 2010 census, they make up 98.81 per cent of the total population of this province. The rest of the population (1.19 per cent) is a mix of other religions, such as Christians, Buddhists, Catholics, Hindus and Confucians (see Appendix 1). As pointed out by Schröter (2010), while the Acehnese are widely considered the staunchest Muslim adherents among Muslim ethnic groups in Indonesia, the population is far from homogeneous. Instead, they are not only culturally and ethnically diverse, but also their religious practice is fundamentally plural (Bowen 1993, 2003).

Islam and politics in modern Aceh have been characterised by the competing roles of, and the contested power between, the ulama, on the one hand, and other political entities, on the other. For many decades, the ulama sought to actively mobilise the expression of Islamic identity in this region and to influence its society by a number of means.[11] In the first years after Indonesia's independence, they were able to control the local government in Aceh. Nonetheless, they encountered some difficulties in reconciling the Acehnese Islamic identity with Indonesia's religiously neutral ideology, Pancasila. The organisation of the Acehnese ulama (Persatuan Ulama Seluruh Aceh – PUSA), under the leadership of Teungku Daud Beureu-eh, eventually declared the secession of Aceh from Indonesia in 1953, and became part of the Negara Islam Indonesia (Islamic State of Indonesia) led by Sekarmadji Maridjan Kartosuwiryo in West Java (van Dijk 1981; Syamsuddin 1985). However, as this revolt was brought to a stop in the early 1960s, the power of the ulama declined across the whole province.

Forming an alliance with the Indonesian military, the ulama of Aceh had another chance to return to the local political arena following the banning of the Indonesian Communist Party and the downfall of President Sukarno in the mid-1960s. Working closely together during this political transition, the ulama received the green light from the military to reorganise themselves under a new organisation of ulama (*Majelis Permusyawaratan Ulama* – MPU). In spite of this, there was a suspicion that the new organisation of ulama would resemble the earlier rebellious PUSA. For this reason, the military directed the organisation to carry out its programmes generally to maintain local security and political stability rather than enhancing religious awareness among Muslims. The resulting coalition between the ulama and the military was thus superficial and, in fact, proved to be the first step in a process by which many ulama were co-opted by the incoming military-backed government (Salim 2008: 144–6).

During the more than three decades of the New Order (1966–98), the ulama were provided with a respectable status and generous incomes by the government. They were not only offered positions in the ulama organisation, but also positions as judges in the religious courts, as lecturers and professors at the State Institute for Islamic Studies (IAIN Ar-Raniry), as teachers in the state or private Islamic *madrasa* (schools) or as chiefs of the offices of religious affairs in each city and regency in Aceh. Only a few ulama (who lived in rural areas in particular) could escape this political co-optation. These ulama devoted their energies to religious education in their respective dayah, thus allowing them to maintain moral authority and integrity among the people of Aceh (Salim 2008: 149–50). As they were isolated from many of the government's development programmes, on legal development in particular, the legal views of the rural ulama remained conservative and for numerous cases they preferred to apply only traditional Shafi'i jurisprudence. By ignoring most of the Islamic injunctions that had been incorporated into some national legislation, they sought to portray themselves as the guardians of an authentic identity of Islam in Aceh.

In the post-New Order era (from 1998 onwards), the ulama were once again offered a key political role. This offer was not intended solely to provide the ulama with a greater role thanks to two national laws (Law 44 of 1999 and Law 18 of 2001) that granted Aceh special autonomy to apply sharia comprehensively. Instead, the offer was mainly directed towards helping to restore the declining position of the technocrats' leadership in Aceh following gross human rights violations and economic exploitation in Aceh during the New Order period. By way of bringing the ulama and the technocrats to work jointly for the implementation of sharia in Aceh, it was expected that the technocrats' political legitimacy would be strengthened and therefore able to counter the increasing popularity of the separatist movements and other opposition groups in Aceh (Salim 2008: 152–3). This ultimate objective, however, was not achievable.

The role of the ulama in the post-tsunami and post-conflict recovery processes remains marginal. The power they acquired based on a series of national laws has been mainly symbolic or rhetorical in the current political atmosphere in Aceh. Their influence upon a variety of policy-making processes in the post-tsunami situation remains relatively weak. The way they engaged in formulating the blueprint for the rebuilding and reconstruction of Aceh demonstrated their weaknesses. Although the MPU had officially requested that the government listen to its voice, the contribution by the ulama to the blueprint formulation was not favourably considered. For this reason, they were mostly unhappy with the blueprint. The ulama, who mostly came from rural areas, organised a meeting to criticise the blueprint as lacking sufficient religiosity. At this meeting, they once again insisted that the government must engage in consultation with them in forming any policy to redevelop Aceh. National or international aid agencies seeking to support the redevelopment of Aceh should also consult them. These demands by the ulama, however, have not had much impact (Salim 2008: 166).

SOURCES AND APPROACHES

After fieldtrips to Aceh for my PhD research in 2004 and 2005, I had an opportunity to return to Aceh in 2006 and stay quite a lot longer. From March to September 2006, I was hired by the International Development Law Organisation (IDLO) to produce legal documentation compiling legal principles and processes relating to land, guardianship and inheritance, with particular reference to women's involvement (Salim 2006). For this, I made observations and interviewed village elders of the tsunami-affected villages located in Banda Aceh and Aceh Besar. I also met with judges of sharia courts in both areas and discussed relevant legal issues with them. From the legal documentation a number of law manuals and a legal documentary film were then generated, which have been useful as legal resources and as an information service to assist (female) tsunami survivors in claiming (back) their rights in the aftermath of the disaster. For six months living in Aceh, I not only studied a vast array of local knowledge, customary principles and institutions, but also extended my networking and interaction with numerous important local figures from academia, the judiciary, the bureaucracy, civil society and international aid organisations.

As part of my postdoctoral research fellowship, funded by the MPI for Social Anthropology, I conducted lengthy fieldwork and lived, from August 2007 to May 2008, in a village of Lhoknga sub-district, Aceh Besar. This village is not far (about 18 km) from the capital of the province, Banda Aceh. However, it is much farther from the capital of Aceh Besar district, Jantho, where both the district sharia and civil courts are located. It was almost 50 km and there was no regular or direct public transport from Lhoknga sub-district to Jantho city. Many ideas and much of the material for this book derived from my ten months of fieldwork in Aceh Besar district. The last four chapters, in fact, comprise case studies that mostly took place in this region.

Through daily interaction with people in the village and its neighbouring communities, I was able to comprehend why and how legal pluralism has been at the heart of the Acehnese understanding. For many Acehnese, Islam and local custom are not different entities. There is a widely shared proverb among the Acehnese: *agama ngon adat han jeut cre, lagee zat ngon sifeut* (religion and adat cannot be separated, both are like the substance of something and its attribute). Various practices within the local community are therefore considered naturally religious as well as customary.

For the first half of my stay in Aceh, I looked at how religion was employed by people who became involved in disputes. It was not easy to detect whether each of the contending parties invoked religious ideas, norms or motivations in their claims as well as argumentations. What often appeared on the surface in many disputes was economic, financial or social and political interest. For this reason, I decided not to investigate the basis of the claim or legal reasoning in order to locate the role of religion in the disputation processes. Rather, I looked at a concept that leads to ending a dispute – *musyawarah mufakat*, a traditional mechanism of mutual consultation to reach consensus or agreement among contending parties with the help of elders or third parties. This is the way many Acehnese seek to make sense of their social world. For the Acehnese, peaceful consultation is one of their fundamental principles, in which the unity of both adat and religion can be secured. This unity does not become a primary reference only in community life, but also reflects the critical role of religion in dispute-management processes in Aceh.

In connection with the unity of religion and adat in Acehnese society, a very popular Acehnese aphorism (*hadih maja*) is worth mentioning here: *meunyoe buet ka mupakat, lampôh jirat jeut ta peugala* (if a consensus is to be achieved, even the cemetery park can be pawned). This aphorism maintains that for the purpose of achieving social agreement, the Acehnese would even compromise sacred property. Some outsiders may observe that the Acehnese do like to have disagreements or tensions in their practical interaction with one another. Yet it must be borne in mind that the Acehnese are always very fond of ending conflicts and achieving a consensus. For them, a peaceful settlement through any means is the key to terminating every kind of dispute. Nevertheless, not every dispute can end peacefully. In fact, a failure of mutual consultation takes place when either of the contending parties senses injustice or experiences oppression. The principle of the unity of religion and adat thus collapses.

While living and studying in the village during my long stay in Aceh, I paid numerous visits, on a regular basis, to civil and sharia courts in both Banda Aceh and Jantho. At the courts, I looked at legal dossiers and archives of decisions. These are good sources for finding summaries of court cases and include a variety of information. Although these sources alone cannot be taken to reflect actual social practices, they help to illustrate what has happened between parties contracting a marriage, seeking grounds for divorce, establishing claims of rights to particular properties, and presenting evidence and legal reasoning before the judges. They also show the considerations of the judges and their final decisions. In short, the summaries of court cases do attract further analysis and discussion on contested claims, competing norms or conflicting rules.

To accomplish the archival study of court cases, I also had discussions with relevant people, including chiefs of court, judges, clerks, both parties to litigations and their respective lawyers. With the permission of the participants, many of these interviews were taped. The interviews normally took between half an hour and two hours, depending on the time available to the interviewee. Some people were interviewed more than once to ensure their views had been accurately recorded. The interviews focused on a range of aspects, such as knowledge about a case in question, claims made by both contending parties, evidence brought before the judges, legal reasoning put forward to support claims, and views on, and positions regarding, the particular case. By comparing and contrasting data resulting from different interviews and investigative processes, I was able not only to better understand the part or role played by each individual actor in a case in question, but I could also cross-check each source of information against others to identify whether there were incorrect or one-sided accounts.

On some occasions, I was invited to sit with the Higher Sharia Court's judges in Banda Aceh and listen to their discussion on certain appealed cases that they were examining. Hearings and evidence presentation were no longer necessary at this level of adjudication. The judges were evaluating the decision issued by the lower courts and assessing whether legal substance, or its procedure, had been upheld correctly and consistently. At the first instance level, the composition of judges comprises a panel with one chair and two members. The panel at the appellate level, likewise, has three judges. The court's unanimous decision is, therefore, not always guaranteed. Some judges were keen to apply the black-letter law in a given issue. Yet there were others who sought to go beyond the legal text and make a reinterpretation in the light of analysis of gender issues or socio-cultural changes.

One of the cases discussed by the judges at such a meeting was a dispute over an inherited land parcel, involving a daughter who had lost both her parents in the tsunami disaster while a sibling of her father's still survived. Basing its decision on the Compilation of Islamic law (KHI Article 176) as well as the general practice in many places in Aceh, the lower court had decided to give a half share to the daughter. When the case reached the Higher Sharia Court, the appellate judges were in disagreement. One of them concurred with the lower court's decision. However, the other two judges were against the decision and instead viewed the daughter as the sole heir, who would therefore be entitled to receive all the land. According to a senior judge, the decision to allocate all the inheritance estate to the only surviving daughter has become a *yurisprudensi tetap* (consolidated jurisprudence), which means an established decision that is repeatedly applied by the Supreme Court to similar cases that they examine.[12]

The jurisprudence of the Supreme Court on inheritance disputes has been important for two reasons in particular. First, no single provincial qanun (regulation) exists to deal exclusively with Islamic inheritance law. Secondly, the

Compilation of Islamic Law (a legal handbook that includes inheritance issues and is to be used by Indonesian religious courts) is a non-imperative guide. Despite the fact that Indonesia is not a purely common law country (in fact, it is a country with a civil law tradition), the jurisprudence on inheritance cases becomes crucial, since it acts as a precedent, dictating that all judges acknowledge it as a valid and superior reference. Failure to comply with this convention will have no formal sanction, but judges who do not comply will be considered less capable of correct adjudication.

Many studies[13] on the ways in which judges in Islamic courts make their decisions have inspired the approach of this book. Some of those works paid particular attention to gender equality in the courtrooms, while others focused on contending argumentation between different norms in the disputes examined in the religious courts. Following their approach, I have studied plural legal reasoning inside and outside courtrooms, not only by investigating conflict or disagreement about claims to rights to various forms of assets, but also by analysing gender relationships and, more importantly, contested norms in the disputing processes.

As this study considers law as a contested field, it looks at what kind of norm is applied or adhered to (that is, *fiqh* (Islamic jurisprudence), adat principles, provincial regulations or qanun, national legislation and international norms), and how much it has been taken into account by the various individual actors (be they rural villagers, tsunami survivors, landowners, heirs, local religious leaders, officials or politicians and judges) in making their claims and justifying their arguments in the dispute processes, over a range of legal issues in the post-conflict and post-disaster period. This study is particularly interested in analysing disputes and how various actors, directly or through their institutions (village meeting, sub-district religious office, civil or sharia court, the national Supreme Court, the provincial government and the central state), refer to and use, selectively and interchangeably, particular norms in various cases and different forums to secure, or to defend, their rights, as well as to uphold justice and restore order. Relationships among these actors, or their institutions, have never been monolithic. They are often characterised by internal contradiction and external conflict. Actors, or their institutions, may independently co-exist, either within or outside a particular hierarchy level. Their stances, aims and jurisdictions may overlap or be in competition. Actors and institutions may not only work together to strengthen, or to give a higher priority to, a particular norm, but they may also attempt, either jointly or separately, to exclude a single norm or provision for a shared aim or for their own particular purpose. Given this intricate constellation, it is hard to imagine that there would be a single unitary dominant rule or norm that prevails at all times and in all places.

An Overview of the Book

This book uses case studies to examine plural legal constellations of customary rules, religious norms, state laws and international conventions formed as a result of historical circumstance and conflict between the legal reasoning of different actors in disputes. In addition, it will focus not only on individuals and groups who use laws and legal processes to pursue their own ends, but will also pay attention to local and national socio-political processes, international dimensions that (in)directly affect local people, issues and norms that affect legal subjects as representative of particular socio-economic interests, and principles that represent different ideological positions. The discussion therefore includes a range of socio-legal issues, from the dispute of jurisdictions between (legal) institutions, competing sources of legal rules and the emerging challenges of pre-existing local norms, to transnational issues.

This book has three parts. Part One looks at the changes in the legal system that have taken place over more than a decade in Aceh, during which a special autonomous status was formally granted enabling Aceh to implement sharia. Considering a number of factors that caused changes, such as the collapse of the New Order regime in 1998, the 2004 tsunami tragedy and the 2005 Helsinki Agreement, this part discusses how such changes have affected existing legal orders and made shifts in jurisdictions. After the notion of legal pluralism is unpacked in Chapter 1, to show how this book employs it as an analytical tool, Chapter 2 presents a case showing the increasing jurisdiction of Aceh's sharia courts, on the one hand, and the declining authority of civil courts in present-day Aceh, on the other. The chapter seeks to offer an explanation of how a shift, as well as contestation, was taking place in the plural legal orders of Aceh. By presenting this case, the chapter not only shows that elements in plural legal orders actively interact and even contest one another, but it also unveils a shift in legal pluralism through its description of distinct social fields that have different sources of content and legitimacy for the plural legal orders that belong to a single legal system. The various changes in the legal status and designation of sharia courts in Aceh demonstrate one of the tensions between legal centralism and legal pluralism in the country's history.

Chapter 3 elaborates and clarifies the extent to which the jurisdiction of Aceh's sharia courts has expanded in a real sense. This chapter demonstrates that the state's offer of increasing jurisdiction to the sharia courts did not practically translate into widely broadened scope and strengthened authority. In fact, the ambiguity, as well as the contestation, resulting from the condition of plural legal orders was observable in a number of ways. This chapter presents several cases to demonstrate overlapping or competing jurisdictions between different state legal institutions in Aceh (civil and sharia courts). As proved through a number of property ownership disputes brought before different courts in Aceh from the early 1980s until as recently as 2012, the extent to which Aceh's sharia court is able to exercise broader jurisdiction remains mostly on paper. In fact, the civil courts have clearly resisted the expanding jurisdiction of sharia courts.

Part Two presents implications of legal transformation that resulted in asymmetric legal pluralism, modified processes of local legislation and enhanced understanding of rights among different actors. Chapter 4 highlights a salient feature of the unequal legal options available for Muslim litigants. The 2006 law on the governance of Aceh has reinforced this legal configuration. This law enforces the principle of personality, rather than the territorial principle, implying that the state has created a legal distinction between its citizens based on their religion. A sub-section in this law provides non-Muslims citizens with legal choices in some penal offences (such as alcohol consumption and gambling). Instead of going to the civil court, non-Muslim offenders are allowed to opt for adjudication and sentencing by the sharia court. The choice of court is not available to Muslim offenders. Although legal pluralism has been a key feature in Islamic legal thought and practice, Muslims in Aceh do not have the right to move across different legal orders and jurisdictions.

Chapter 5 focuses on the struggle between different groups contesting social and political control in Aceh. Dealing with the legislation of the controversial stipulation of *rajam* (stoning to death) in the local qanun of *jinayat* (Islamic penal law), this chapter explains how recent political changes have redirected the trajectory of the Islamisation of law in Aceh towards stagnation. Furthermore, by describing the tension between the executive and legislative branches of the Aceh government concerning this issue, the chapter demonstrates how various (in)formal sources of law (such as historical legal fact, Islamic legal jurisprudence, international human rights conventions and the Indonesian national constitution) are invoked and are highly contested.

Chapter 6 concerns various guidelines for land dispute settlement and asks to what extent Islam plays a role in this. As Muslims constitute the majority population and because Islamic sharia has been officially implemented in Aceh, a very crucial issue in this regard is whether religion plays a role in land disputes and how much disputants draw on religious reasoning? This chapter presents a case examined at the Jantho civil court concerning disputed land claims to argue that Islam's role appears to be that of marginal rhetoric and that 'discourse shopping' is evident among disputants. This chapter therefore illustrates how widespread legal pluralism has become.

Part Three addresses norms and practices contested between Aceh's villages and courtrooms. In particular, it deals with legal cases on property ownership, inheritance, insurance benefits, remarriage and divorce. Chapter 7 investigates whether orphaned grandchildren may replace their predeceased parent(s) as the substitute heirs. This chapter demonstrates how differences between the living Muslim law and the state's compilation of Islamic law often involve diverse legal reasoning and interpretations that come from different sources of law and are introduced by various agencies, including international NGOs.

Drawing on the decisions of sharia courts in Aceh and appellate courts at both provincial and national levels, Chapter 8 seeks to discover why insurance benefits are or are not considered a part of a bequest. This chapter identifies the norms that are often referred to and contested in the courts, and also reveals how different legal norms may exist parallel to, and in competition with, each other. Above all, this chapter highlights the legal paradoxes of the implementation of sharia in post-tsunami Aceh. Ironically, many judges of sharia courts rely on secular-national jurisprudence rather than giving priority to a local norm considered more in line with Islamic jurisprudence.

Chapter 9 focuses on the legality or validity of (re)marriage. It sheds light on a variety of legal norms and practices involved in saving a marriage after triple *talaq* (divorce) among the people of Aceh. Studies of modes of divorce pronouncement and its ensuing legal implications have received little scholarly attention.[14] Although there are some studies on triple divorce in Islam (Mahmood 1992; Al-Azri 2011), an ethnographic study on the subject in question is truly rare, let alone one that employs a legal pluralist framework. By comparing court adjudications and village practices concerning marriage and divorce, this chapter discovers diverse ways of reconciling divorced couples, and inconsistent legal reasoning for keeping marriages in place. This chapter not only explores how legal scholars and jurists from diverse backgrounds perceive this problem, but also answers the questions: whose decision is legitimate?; is state legality considered subordinate to religious validity or vice versa?; would social acceptance of villagers, concerning a decision made either by the state or by religious authorities, be taken into account in determining its legality or legitimacy?

NOTES

1. For further details on the Aceh conflict, see Kell (1995); Reid (2006); Miller (2009); Aspinall (2009a).
2. The proponents of sharia in Aceh consider the caning penalty as a kind of law of God. As it is mentioned in the Qur'an a couple of times, this penalty is believed to be an authentic punishment of Islam. On the contrary, the penalty of imprisonment is not only regarded as a man-made law, but is also seen as a Western secular product. By enforcing caning as one of the applicable punishments in Aceh, the proponents of sharia could claim to have legitimately implemented sharia in this region in a real sense.
3. For more on this particular issue, see Idria (2010); Wierienga (2010).

4. Interview with Hamid Sarong, 14 June 2005; interview with Safir Wijaya, 17 June 2005.
5. See Articles 96–99 of Law 11 of 2006.
6. See sharia-related provisions in this law, such as on the application of Islamic sharia (Articles 125–127), the sharia court (Articles 128–137), the MPU or *ulama* council (Articles 138–140), the Police Force (Article 207(1) and (4)), the Public Prosecutor (Articles 208(2) and 210) and Human Rights (Article 227(1c)).
7. See Articles 69(c) and 70(c) of Law 11 of 2006.
8. See, for instance, Ismuha (1978, 1980); Sarong (2002); Bowen (2003); Muhammad (2003); Syahrizal (2003, 2004); Abubakar (2004, 2008); Hadi (2004); Ichwan (2007); Lindsey *et al.* (2007); Lindsey (2012); Feener (2013).
9. This information is available online at http://aceh.bps.go.id/?r=data/dinamis&id=3&id2=14, accessed 7 April 2014.
10. For more discussions on the arrival of Islam in Aceh and other islands of Indonesia in general, see Ricklefs (2001); Azra (2006).
11. For more studies on Acehnese ulama, see Baihaqi (1983); Ismuha (1983); Alfian (1985); Saby (2001); Amiruddin (2004).
12. Interview with Rafiuddin, the former chief of Jantho district Syar'iyah Court, 27 April 2006.
13. For instance, Moors (1995); Bowen (1998b, 2003); Hirsch (1998); Tucker (1998); Peletz (2002).
14. Numerous works pay attention to historical as well as legal perspectives of divorce in Islam (Amira El Azhary 1996; Sonbol 1996; Ahmad 2003; Rapoport 2005; Omar 2007). Other works pay particular attention to divorce case studies at courts in different places and at different times (Layish 1991; Shaham 1994; Stiles 2003). In addition, there are several authors who examine formal mechanisms and types of procedures required for a valid divorce in different Muslim contexts (Carroll and Kapoor 1996; Carroll 1997; Bowen 2003; Kusrin 2006; Nakamura 2006; Cammack *et al.* 2007).

Part One

Between Orders and Jurisdictions

Chapter 1

Unpacking Legal Pluralism

Adat bak Po Teumeureuhom (Adat is referred to the sultan)
Hukom bak Syiah Kuala (Law is referred to the supreme judge)
Qanun bak Putroe Phang (Qanun is referred to the queen consort)
Reusam bak Lakseumana (Reusam is referred to the admiral]
Leumoh Adat jahee raja (Weak Adat makes for a cruel ruler)
Leumoh Hukom diatoe lee pangkat (Weak Law is controlled by the powerful)
Leumoh Qanun tinggai bak kalam (Weak Qanun remains on the paper)
Leumoh Reusam gadoh budaya (Weak Reusam causes a loss of culture)

A hadih maja of Aceh

The notion of legal pluralism has attracted wide scholarly interest since the early twentieth century. It has become an increasingly important topic given the prevalence of legal modernisation during the nineteenth and twentieth centuries, which laid great emphasis on both legal centralism and legal positivism. These two approaches elevated the importance of the legislative and judicial bodies of the state in law (decision) making, and rejected the authority of any law from a source outside the state, unless it was given the force of law by the state. Legal pluralism thus arose as an alternative to legal centralism. While the modern nation-state's legal centralism considers only one uniform law for all subjects, legal pluralism is a situation characterised by the co-existence of two or more laws that interact within the processes of modernisation programmes in nation-states (Hooker 1975).

Legal pluralism in some contexts is often justified as a technique of governance on pragmatic grounds (Griffith 1986: 5). It is also often understood as a special legal arrangement where different groups of the population are defined in terms of their respective ethnicities, religions or other categorisations. In the view of Woodman (1999: 10), this is a situation of 'state law pluralism' where different bodies of law are branches of one larger body of norms. This type of legal pluralism is identified as 'weak' legal pluralism, as opposed to 'strong' legal pluralism. In strong legal pluralism, different legal orders exist together and do not necessarily have to recognise or negate each other (Moore 1978). Strong legal pluralism is characterised by situations in which law is neither all state law nor administered by formal state institutions. Rather, it presents the co-existence of different legal orders that do not belong to a single system (Griffith 1986: 8), and where all these different bodies of law have separate and distinct sources of content and legitimacy (Woodman 1999: 10).

Researchers, be they anthropologists, sociologists, jurist scholars or political scientists, have, however, never reached a consensus in understanding legal pluralism. Although some categories have been produced by different anthropologists and legal scholars for use in describing legal pluralism (as expressed in terms of binary oppositions, such as strong versus weak, classic versus new, early versus late, juristic versus sociological, and state law pluralism versus deep legal pluralism), there have been on-going efforts to scrutinise it further and to employ it as an effective analytical tool in various research contexts. This study, therefore, aims to investigate not whether or not legal pluralism exists, but rather what form legal pluralism takes.

Legal pluralism has informed my study in many ways. My initial research interest in studying legal pluralism started in 2006 when, as a postdoctoral research fellow, I joined the Legal Pluralism Research Group (now the Department of Law and Anthropology) at the MPI for Social Anthropology, Halle, Germany. Under the leadership and supervision of internationally renowned scholars Professor Franz von Benda-Beckmann and Professor Keebet von Benda-Beckmann, the group comprised legal scholars and anthropologists from a number of countries, including Germany, the Netherlands, Denmark and Indonesia.

My experience of working with this group for three years, and especially the interaction with both professors F. and K. von Benda-Beckmann and the influence of their publication, steered me towards a close scrutiny of plural legal orders. A situation of plural legal orders occurs where two or more legal institutions co-exist, separately or interdependently operating within the same legal system. Plural legal orders may comprise civil magistrates, religious courts, village tribunals and other forms of institutional adjudication. As these orders may be hierarchical, parallel to, or independent of each other, the relationship between them can be either complementary or competitive, often with no single legal order self-evidently superior to the others (F. von Benda-Beckmann 2002; K. von Benda-Beckmann 2009).

My comprehension of legal pluralism was extended further through numerous encounters with Professor Werner Menski of the School of Oriental and African Studies Law School, London. When living in London from 2009 to 2012, I often met him at some scholarly event held by university centres or institutes around Bloomsbury, London. In addition, Professor Menski kindly invited me to deliver a guest lecture for his students each semester. The subject was 'Legal Systems of Asia and Africa', and I was encouraged to approach and analyse my presentation topic, Indonesia's legal system, from the perspective of legal pluralism.

Through such academic interaction and through his works, Professor Menski introduced me to two very important points in his thoughts on legal pluralism. The first is a quadrangle of law. For quite a long time several scholars (Chiba 1986; Buskens 2000; F. and K. von Benda-Beckmann 2006a) had been portraying post-colonial legal pluralism in many Asian and African countries as having a triangle of law: state law, religion and local customs. Although there has been awareness lately that international and transnational norms (on such issues as human rights, gender equality, indigenous peoples and nature conservation) have become more important elements in the construction of the law, it was Menski who systematically revised those three-level systems of law and extended the 'triangle' into his 'kite model' (see Diagram 1.1). In this model,

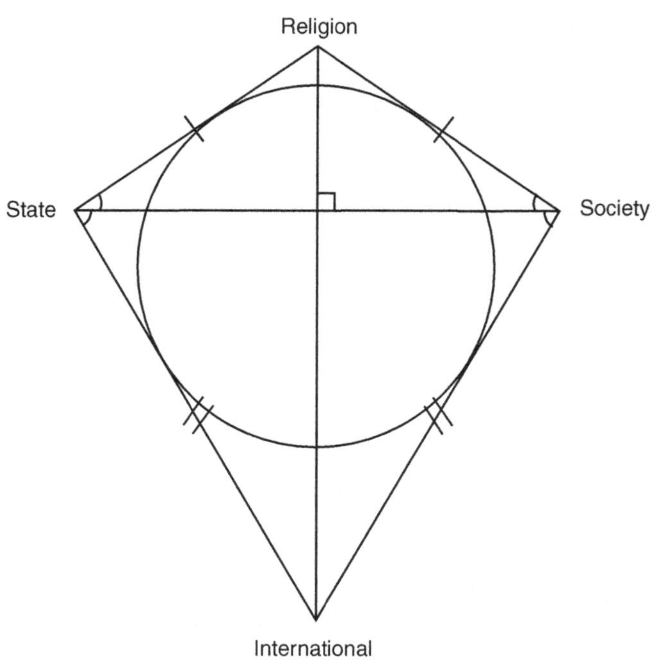

Diagram 1.1 Menski's kite model

Menski (2011) identified four key elements of legal pluralism: state, society, religion and international norms.

The second point is plurality of pluralities. This means that each of the four elements of law identified above has internal plurality as well. According to Menski (2010), plurality of pluralities is an obvious characteristic of legal pluralism anywhere in the world. Notably, nowhere can one find only a single type of state law or international law. Equally, neither custom nor religion has just one identifiable form. For Menski (2011: 14), all four of these legal orders identifiable within legal pluralism are 'deeply plural entities in themselves, with their own internal conflicts and tensions'.

Menski's kite model was, however, criticised because the position of the legal subject in his theory is unclear. The position of the legal subject is considered important because, when situations of legal pluralism occur, or are imposed, people would not necessarily and spontaneously become passive beneficiaries of different regulations. Instead, they may be active actors who consciously choose to commit to a particular legislation from the diversity of available laws (Jackson and Gozdecka 2011: 103).

Contextualising legal subjects in their interactions among plural legal orders, as well as among plural legal norms, is therefore crucial. The relevant question here is not which legal orders have jurisdiction over, or which legal provisions (legislation) should be applied to, a particular legal subject at any given time and place. Rather, it is why and how does a legal subject (1) encounter and contend with the jurisdiction of different legal orders, (2) distinguish and justify various forms of legal evidence, and (3) support or defend a claim according to diverse legal provisions?

My insight into this particular issue of the legal subject in legal pluralism was shaped and enhanced through my communication with Professor John Bowen of Washington University (St Louis). Professor Bowen was one of my PhD examiners and, since first communicating with him in 2005, I have established a strong intellectual connection with him. Professor Bowen's interest in the legal ethnography of Muslim societies and his distinct approach to considering contemporary Islamic legal practice has greatly inspired me. In his work on the anthropology of public reasoning in Indonesia, in Aceh in particular, Bowen (2003) discussed various local attempts, within Muslim communities in Aceh, to reconcile different sets of social norms and laws, including those derived from Islam, from local custom, and from contemporary ideas about gender equality.

I was further exposed to his distinct frameworks on plural legal reasoning in disputing processes when we became part of an international collaborative research team working on an anthropological study project, Andromaque, funded by the French National Research Agency over three years (2011–13). Focusing on women, and their property rights and legal disputes in Islamic courtrooms as well as within Muslim communities in Aceh and South Sulawesi, Indonesia, we looked at multiple actors (judges, litigants, lawyers, village leaders and women) and how they developed their respective legal reasoning, consisting of different ways of justifying their claim, and various forms of interpretation and argumentation to support or defend it.

Muslim Legal Pluralism

Legal pluralism is an inevitable historical fact in any of the religious legal traditions, including Islam. One of the sources of this legal pluralism in Islam, according to Arabi (1999), is the contrast between sharia, as God's ideal law, and fiqh, as human understanding attempting to discover that law. As I have explained elsewhere (Salim 2008: 12), while sharia comes from God through those verses of the Qur'an which do not need further clarification, fiqh (which literally means understanding) is the interpretation by human beings of those Qur'anic legal verses that have imprecise or multiple meanings. Likewise, because sharia was revealed, it takes only one form, while fiqh varies according to different individuals' reasoning. As a consequence, manifestations of legal pluralism in Islam abound in fiqh. Thus, when Muslim legal pluralism is mentioned, it has more to do with fiqh (as a product of thoughts by Muslim individuals) rather than with sharia.

A plural legal form was the main feature of Islam. This can be traced back to the Prophetic tradition. It was recorded in Sahih al-Bukhari (the most credible collection of Prophetic traditions among Sunni Muslims) that the Prophet Muhammad (d. 632 CE) instructed Muslims who went out to the battle of Bani Qurayza to only perform the *salat al-'Asr* (the late-afternoon prayer) in Bani Qurayza. Some understood this instruction literally and did not observe the prayer at the usual time, but performed it later when they reached their destination, despite its appropriate time having lapsed. Others took the Prophet's instruction to mean that they should move quickly and perform the prayer at the correct time, in spite of not having reached the end of their journey. Later, when the Prophet learned of this he did not object to either course of action (Kamali 2003: 66).

The most striking aspect of legal pluralism in Islam is seen in a response by Malik b. Anas (d. 795 CE), the founder of the Maliki school of Islamic jurisprudence based in Medina, to a request by the Abbasid caliph, Al-Mansur (d. 775 CE). Through his secretary, Ibn al-Muqaffa', Caliph Al-Mansur asked Malik to allow his (Malik's) legal treatise, *al-Muwatta'*, to be adopted as the sole law of the state. Al-Muqaffa' said to Malik:

> [It is] decided to take your book, *al-Muwatta'*, so that copies of it are made, and to send a copy to each district of Muslims, ordering them to abide by its

> content to the exclusion of any other, and to forsake anything else of this new science; for I am convinced that the knowledge of the people of Medina and their science are the root of this new science. (Arabi 1999: 64)

Replying to this request, Malik answered:

> Don't do this! People had received sayings and heard traditions and related incidents, and each party accepted what they had received, and ruled by it, and believed it – traditions going back to the Companions of the Messenger of God and others. Forcing them to renounce what they believed is hard; so let people follow their ways and what the inhabitants of each part choose for themselves. (Arabi 1999: 64)

It could be said that what is considered religious law within Muslim legal practice has never been a single monolithic conception. In fact, the first three centuries of Islam (from the seventh to the tenth centuries) saw private groups of autonomous jurists developing the law, working independently of any state intervention, which resulted in a plurality of Islamic legal views and practices in various regions (Vikør 2005: 89–113). Diversity in legal norms and rulings arose among the four major Sunni schools (Hanafi, Maliki, Shafi'i and Hanbali) and within each school.[1] A Muslim is thus able to choose a specific legal opinion outside the realm of his or her own legal school (Arabi 1999). This condition in turn generated *takhayyur*, a doctrine of selection among different legal opinions within those schools. In his study on Muslims living in England, Yilmaz (2005) demonstrated the contemporary practice of takhayyur in which Muslim individuals navigate across legal opinion and schools. For this reason, Jackson (2006: 166–7) aptly argued that, 'Islamic law was not grounded in any commitment to any strict dictates of legal centralism, certainly not in the sense of any state monopoly over law.'

Plural legal norms, as well as plural legal reasoning, were the initial forms of legal pluralism in Islam. Plural legal orders as the next form of legal pluralism came only in the thirteenth century. In 1265, the Mamluk sultan Baybars decided to appoint four chief judges in each Mamluk town and city. This was done first in Cairo and Damascus and then in other cities such as Aleppo, Tripoli, Hama, Safed, Jerusalem and Gaza. Each had its own quadruple judicial system (Escovitz 1982; Rapoport 2003). This system of adjudication by four chief judges, popularly known as the millet system, continued up to the Ottoman period. The millet system administered legal pluralism not only internally to Muslim subjects, it also organised the different religious ethnic groups under its rule in accordance to their respective legal systems (Karpat 1982). Each religious community, other than Islam (such as Jews and Christians), had the right to preserve its own courts, to appoint judges and to apply legal principles for the use of co-religionists. The Ottoman Empire, as an Islamic central authority, exercised overall control, but did not interfere in the internal functioning of the respective religious authorities (Quataert 2000).

Under the millet system, although Muslims could pick and choose among judges belonging to different schools of Islamic jurisprudence, they were still restricted to attending an Islamic court.[2] Non-Muslim subjects, however, were entitled to a choice of law (Kuran 2004: 484–8). This right provided a choice of legal forums to non-Muslims who were conducting commercial business with other non-Muslims. They could go to the Islamic court instead of going to their own religious courts. But for criminal offences, they were restricted to adjudication by the Islamic court. According to Kuran (2004: 484), the earliest basis for this kind of legal pluralism, in which non-Muslims had a choice of jurisdictions in civil matters, was an intercommunal arrangement known as the *'Ahd 'Umar* (Pact of Umar). This pact instructed, among other things, that 'Christians and Jews were subject to Islamic law in all commercial and financial dealings involving Muslims. In interacting with other non-Muslims, however, they were free to choose among jurisdictions' (Kuran 2004: 485). A case involving this choice of jurisdiction in Aceh, concerning not a civil matter, but a criminal offence, will be outlined in Chapter 4.

In the post-colonial Muslim communities of the modern nation-states emerging in the twentieth-century Muslim world, plural legal orders have been a core feature (Hooker 1975). As noted in the study by the International Council on Human Rights Policy (2009: 11–12), there are four reasons why plural legal orders have been observable in a country's legal system: (1) they are a result of conflict or a legacy of post-conflict processes of reconstruction; (2) they are part of an attempt to prevent conflict between the state and its citizens or between different groups of citizens; (3) they are established because of the transnationalisation of law via the imposition, or the importation, of legal concepts from other states, multilateral bodies or international NGOs; and (4) they are introduced for the reason of identity politics.

Whether they like it or dislike it, most Muslims living in this era of nation-states have to experience legal pluralism in many ways (although some may not encounter plural legal orders because they do not live in a post-colonial Muslim state or because the law of their country enforces Islamic law only through a single Islamic legal institution). However, as Hallaq (2004: 243) observed, Muslims experiencing legal pluralism may have in mind two different perceptions of legal sovereignty, one emanating from the legal centralism of the nation-state and the other from the internal legal coercion of religion. As a result, when encountering a variety of legal problems in social life, they may often wonder whether state legality is subordinate to religious validity or vice versa.

Indonesia's Legal Pluralism

Plural legal orders in Indonesia are a legacy of the Dutch colonial legal structure, which was based mostly on racial or ethnic groups. The Dutch colonial administration treated diverse groups of the Netherlands East Indies population differently, according to their racial classification (Fasseur 1994). These plural legal systems continued even after Indonesia's independence in 1945.

In post-independence Indonesia, the colonial policy continued with some modifications. While adat legal institutions (*peradilan desa*) were largely eliminated in the 1950s for the sake of Indonesian unity and judicial integrity, adat norms were retained and continued to be applied by the state *pengadilan negeri* (civil courts). At the same time, some particular areas of sharia law were applied by an Indonesian system of state *pengadilan agama* (religious courts).[3] With such arrangements, Indonesia developed a complex system of legal pluralism that allowed a variety of legal sub-systems operate in the realm of a single sovereign state power (Lubis 2003).

However, the religious bureaucracy of Indonesia, the Ministry of Religious Affairs, which was founded early in 1946, modified this system by initiating attempts to develop a new legal arrangement that differentiates citizens according to their religion. Extracting some functions related to Islam from other departments, such as the religious courts, education department and information services, the ministry sought to transform the Ottoman millet system into a new Indonesian version (Salim 2008). The newly independent state of Indonesia has thus revised the Dutch legacy of a plural legal system not necessarily in an attempt to prevent conflict between different religious groups, but mostly in order to acknowledge Indonesia's diversity, as well as the distinctiveness of Muslims as the majority religious group in Indonesia.

It is for this reason that, since the early 1990s, the Indonesian government has introduced a new legal policy aligned to the so-called 'legal distinction'. This new legal framework provides particular religious groups with specific laws exclusively applicable to them (Salim and Azra 2003). This has resulted in a clear demarcation between citizens based on their religious adherences. In the final analysis, where the colonial legal policy led to discrimination according to race, the Indonesian legal system has been equally prone to discriminate against citizens according to religion. Current legal transformation in Aceh has intensified this trend of differentiation between Muslims and non-Muslims.

Legal Pluralism in Aceh

The issue of legal pluralism is not new in Aceh. Bowen (2003) discussed local struggles to reconcile different sets of social norms and laws, including those derived from Islam, local custom and contemporary ideas about gender equality in Aceh, as well as elsewhere in Indonesia. Bowen paid attention mostly to interpretations, different ways of justification, and contending argumentations about religion and social norms in the disputes among Muslim people in Aceh, the Gayo in particular. However, the explanation of how change, as well as contestation, has taken place in post-tsunami Aceh remained beyond his scope.

Plural Legal Orders

Plural legal orders in Aceh have been present since before Indonesia's independence in 1945. During the era of Aceh's Islamic kingdom (1700–1900), sharia religious law and local customary laws (*adat*) co-existed and at times were hardly distinguishable. The Dutch colonial presence in Aceh at the turn of the twentieth century, however, contributed to sharper demarcations between sharia and adat. Dutch policies tended to support adat institutions and adat leaders to the detriment of specifically Islamic interests in Aceh. Dutch agendas of co-optation, as well as 'divide and rule' tactics, further exacerbated tensions between the uleebalang and the ulama as representatives of increasingly distinct spheres of adat and Islam, respectively (Syamsuddin 1985).

The presence of the sharia court in Aceh can be traced as far back as the office of the Qadi Malik al-Adil in the sixteenth century (Hadi 2004). During the Dutch colonial time, however, this court was restricted and replaced by the *musapat* tribunals, which were established by the Dutch to uphold justice for the Acehnese (Angelino 1931). Later, under the Japanese occupation (1942–5), Islamic religious courts were given the Japanese name *syukyo hoin*, and had limited jurisdiction, mostly over matters of personal status (Ismuha 1980).

The relationship between Aceh and the national government in Indonesia's formative early years was crucial to the initial development of Aceh's plural legal orders. The first years of Indonesia's independence found the Acehnese ulama in control of key political positions in the regional government. For the ulama, it was now time to realise 'their primary aim [which] was to apply as much Islamic law as possible in Acehnese society' (Syamsuddin 1985: 111). Because the majority of the population in the other regions of Indonesia was Muslim, the new republic of Indonesia was considered to share an Islamic identity with the Acehnese. It was the belief of the ulama that establishing Aceh as an independent Indonesian state would allow the Acehnese to formally implement Islamic law, and they therefore demanded the establishment of an autonomous religious court (Mahkamah Syar'iyah) as a separate institution from the general civil judicature (Salim 2004).

In 1947, the governor of Sumatra, Teuku Mohammad Hasan, approved the inauguration of religious courts in Aceh. However, not long after that, the

Indonesian central government overrode that decision. Partially in response to the frustration of Islamic interests in Aceh, a rebellion, led by Teungku Daud Beureu-eh, arose in the 1950s proclaiming Acehnese independence from Indonesia. This movement was connected to a rebellious movement in West Java for the establishment of an Islamic state, or *Darul Islam*, led by Kartosuwirjo, who regarded himself as head of this Islamic state of Indonesia (Syamsuddin 1985).

In an attempt to end this armed conflict, Government Regulation 29 of 1957 was issued, acknowledging the foundation of sharia courts in Aceh. Even then, however, their jurisdiction remained limited in ways similar to colonial times (Lev 1972: 81–3). Further persuasive efforts in 1959 aimed at Aceh achieving 'special region' status had no substantial legal effect in strengthening sharia courts in the province. According to Boland, the Indonesian central government held the view that permitting such institutions would threaten the power of the unitary Indonesian state (Boland 1982: 185). Thus, it was not surprising that, on the grounds of 'unity and the unitary nation', the New Order regime later reinforced legal centralism by issuing Law 5 of 1974 on Regional Government, which effectively abolished the special status of Islamic religious courts in the province of Aceh (Salim 2004). In 1989, with the passing of the Religious Judicature Act, the sharia courts in Aceh were re-designated as pengadilan agama in a further step towards unifying the structure and the status of the Islamic courts throughout the country (Cammack 2003).

The current formal implementation of sharia in Aceh has been a complicated process. It was achieved through various local efforts. Following the collapse of the centralistic Suharto regime in 1998, strong demands for decentralisation provided a chance for the implementation of sharia in Aceh through special autonomy. Through a series of special autonomy laws,[4] sharia was formally applied and sharia-supporting institutions were reinforced (Lindsey *et al.* 2007; Feener 2013). For instance, the local ulama council returned to its previous name, the Majelis Permusyawaratan Ulama (MPU), but now with legislative authority purportedly equal to that of the provincial legislature. Additionally, a new structure was established within provincial, as well as district, bureaucracy to manage the implementation of sharia in Aceh, namely, Dinas Syariat Islam. And last, but not least, the special autonomy of Aceh also allowed the local pengadilan agama to return to its earlier name of Mahkamah Syar'iyah, but now with more jurisdiction than other religious courts outside Aceh enjoy. This latter issue will be discussed in detail in Chapter 2.

Plural Legal Provisions

Given that Islamic sharia has now been officially implemented in Aceh and that its supporting institutions have been strongly established, one may expect that Islamic sharia norms would have a higher status than, and be given priority over, other types of rules. However, this is not always the case. One should remember that what is conceived as an Islamic norm in Aceh is not a singular construction. In fact, the meaning and the scope of (Islamic) law among Aceh Muslim communities differs from time to time and from one place to another. It might refer to: (1) a classical fiqh of Shafi'i juristic tradition, which is still widely held in rural areas; (2) a legal rule formulated in qanun passed by provincial legislature; (3) a judgment conferred by judges of the sharia courts; (4) a decision based on musyawarah mufakat in a meeting attended by village leaders; (5) a provision stated in the Compilation of Islamic Law (KHI), which remains nationally applicable for settling Muslim family issues in Indonesia, including in Aceh. In light of this, Islamic legal reasoning in Aceh bases itself on a vast array of understandings of Islam, combined at the same time with conceptions based on custom, tradition and state legislation.

Since it was codified and enacted in 1991, the KHI has been the Islamic legal handbook referred to by judges at Islamic courts (including Aceh's sharia court) in settling various Muslim family disputes in Indonesia. The book covers three main topics of family law: marriage, inheritance and *wakaf* (land endowment). Although the KHI is a non-binding manual, it is considered the Indonesian version of Islamic law, which synthesises different norms, mainly derived from Islamic jurisprudence or fiqh, customary rules and national laws, the latter being, in general, a Dutch colonial legacy. It is for this reason that some scholars (Bowen 2003; F. and K. Benda-Beckmann 2006a) have argued that Indonesia's legal system has three sources of law, namely, Islam, custom and national legislation. These three types of legal source explain the historical interests and foundations of law in Indonesia, but, moreover, this variety of legal sources reflects three different ways of thinking about laws, norms and the state itself.

Inheritance provisions in the KHI are the best illustration of how it simultaneously accommodates the three sources of law listed above. This codification has included customary rules, such as the stipulation concerning *gono-gini* (joint marital property), which was widely practised by many ethnic groups in Indonesia. The KHI is certainly Islamic law, not only because of its label, but, more importantly, because a number of its stipulations were adopted directly from Islamic legal traditions. Of course, it need not be reiterated that this legislation clearly constitutes a national regulation, which was made legally official via a modern system of state legal processes.

However, in current Indonesian legal contexts, a fourth source of law should be added to the list: international law. For the last couple of decades, issues of human rights and gender equality have been widespread in Indonesia, and attract the attention of a large number of people from diverse backgrounds. Not only were these principles of international law ratified and incorporated into a number of state national legislations,[5] but they are also invoked by contending parties to defend particular positions and interests in various legal forums. In fact, as pointed out by K. von Benda-Beckmann (2001b), even cases where an existing legal system does not allow or recognise those international laws, claimants or NGO activists often invoke and refer to norms of human rights and gender equality to support their claims against the state and against other, non-state, actors. For them, international norms are considered important not only as legal rules, but also as a normative framework that gives meaning to social relationships and hence to conflicts.

This is especially true for the post-disaster and post-conflict recovery processes in Aceh. The physical constructions and continued efforts to build and maintain peace attracted worldwide attention, and exposed Aceh to a massive influx of international humanitarian agencies that came to help to reconstruct its infrastructure, including its legal order. The presence in post-tsunami Aceh of various international actors meant that new values, as well as social change, were introduced through their humanitarian assistance. The international donor agencies have been closely involved in providing or facilitating dispute management at the village level. Legal assistance provided by international actors is likely to convey certain principles of international law, resulting in, and perhaps even further deepening, legal pluralism in Aceh.

These international actors not only interacted with state representatives, but also directly with their new partners at the local level. Through cooperative works with local NGOs,[6] some global aid agencies, such as the International Development Law Organisation (IDLO), The Asia Foundation (TAF) and Humanistisch Instituut voor Ontwikkelingssamenwerking (HIVOS), support gender-mainstreaming activities and provide female tsunami survivors with legal information and assistance. In this case, it is important to recall what Turner (2006) has observed in Morocco: on the one hand, there is always a contest among international actors for the opportunity to implement their respective legal standards, and, on the other hand, there might be local resistance to programmes carried out by those international institutions. It must be admitted that some sections of Acehnese communities, particularly some figures connected with traditional Islamic dayah, have opposed gender equality and human rights-related programmes launched by international NGOs. This is mostly due to their fear that such programmes may aggravate the situation and threaten the formal implementation of sharia in the region.

These international agencies therefore infiltrate principles of international laws into the Acehnese community by way of national Islamic legislation, the KHI in particular. While the notion of gender equality and concepts of human rights could not be introduced blatantly, as this would only invite widespread criticism and open resistance from the Acehnese,[7] the Compilation of Islamic law is familiar and its contents acceptable to some groups of people in Aceh, especially religious judges and legal academics. For this reason, some relevant provisions in the KHI that support gender equality have been given emphasis. These include those alluding to the position of the wife in relation to joint marital property (Article 97), rights and access to inheritance for orphaned granddaughters (Article 185), and property ownership in relation to women in general (Articles 176, 178, 180). A number of religious judges and legal academics were recruited to inform elders and heads of villages about Islam and justice by disseminating these selected contents of the KHI, which are strongly oriented to perspectives of gender equality and human rights (Salim 2006; Salim *et al.* 2009). Chapters 7 and 8 will refer to this issue in detail.

Plural Legal Processes

The expansion of the jurisdiction of religious norms and institutions (for example, sharia courts and the ulama council) in contemporary Aceh does not necessarily translate into the marginalisation of adat. Adat has, in fact, played a key role in many ways, including in dispute settlements. In the last decade, adat has become much more officially recognised and increasingly important in the daily lives of villagers. As is happening in other parts of Indonesia, and as a result of legal and political reform through a series of special autonomy laws granted to Aceh (Davidson and Henley 2007), there has been noticeable adat revivalism. The resurgence of adat gives more emphasis to local norms in dispute settlements and land management (Bowen 2003).

Adat currently remaining in use in Aceh is not necessarily a set of traditional rules handed down from one generation to the next in a verbatim form. As Moore (1986) suggested in her study on Tanzania (Kilimanjaro), custom must be seen as negotiated elements in on-going social change and political order. The recent development of adat in Aceh was facilitated by the issuance of a series of national and regional regulations in the post-New Order era, including Bylaw 7 of 2000 on the Administration of Adat Life, which details the structural arrangements, as well as functional jurisdictions, of customary village structures of community justice. The institutionalisation of the adat (legal) system was furthered by several provincial regulations enacted following the Helsinki Peace Agreement, such as Qanun 9 of 2008 on Cultivation of Adat Life and Adat Istiadat (custom), Qanun 10 of 2008 on Adat Institutions, and Qanun 8 of 2012 on Wali Nanggroe (Regional-Cultural Leadership).

In fact, the post-disaster and post-conflict situations have stimulated the rise of adat institutions into the public sphere. Following the December 2004 tsunami tragedy, many cases that needed to be decided by the sharia courts could not be immediately responded to and resolved. This was partly because most court buildings in the affected tsunami regions (such as those in the cities of Banda Aceh, Meulaboh, and Calang) were damaged, and some of their judges and employees were missing or had died. As appropriate human resources and infrastructure were not present, adat or local practice appeared to help many tsunami survivors manage their own legal problems. This situation encouraged the village authorities to assume some legal duties related to the post-tsunami recovery process. Many cases of remarriage, for instance, were not brought to the courts to procure an authorised confirmation that the previous spouse of an applicant was missing or had died because of the disaster. In fact, a number of remarriages between those whose spouses were lost took place without judicial declaration from the courts. These remarriages occurred after the *'idda* (waiting period) of 130 days had elapsed for the women whose husbands had died. This practice was based largely on religious knowledge and has long been commonly applied at the local level.

The re-emergence of adat-based dispute settlement in this context, as another means of resolving legal problems in contemporary Aceh, has been the main concern of several international agencies. The IDLO, for instance, has compiled customary local principles, as well as nationally applicable rules, that comparatively delineate stipulations on land issues, matrimonial property, inheritance, guardianship and provisions for orphans. In addition, the United Nations Development Programme (UNDP) has published a handbook to guide village elders in settling disputes in their respective regions. Moreover, with the support of various international actors, village leaders in Aceh were given particular training to educate them on how to mediate effectively between contending parties. The question of whether the post-tsunami and post-conflict recovery processes created a special momentum for wider recognition of the customary judicature at the village level, and thus deepened and led to another shift in Aceh's plural legal orders, deserves further scrutiny in the future as this remains an on-going process.

Finally, the following questions emerge: which source of law is superior and which is subordinate?; and what could one learn from a range of different institutions and competing norms in contemporary Aceh?

Just how many components of each of the previously mentioned sources of law are accommodated in the development of the national legal system in Indonesia or the regional legal structure in Aceh is a difficult question. Although Islamic law and adat justice have now been given special status and international norms have gained currency in Aceh's public sphere in recent years, one should not be hasty and argue that the state national law has become ineffective. Indeed, it must be borne in mind that it is 'state law pluralism' (Woodman 1999) that is taking place, where the national state sanctions and organises those diverse authorities, and acknowledges various sources of law and gives direction on how they should be properly applied in Aceh.

Although an increasing number of legal changes have been possible in the aftermath of the tsunami disaster, as well as compromise resulting from political struggles after the prolonged armed conflicts in the region, competition among multiple sources of law has, in its turn, given rise to different points of view with respect to people's aspirations for the particular forms of law they want to see implemented.

NOTES

1. For studies on Islamic legal schools, see Melchert (1997); Vikør (2005); Hallaq (2005).
2. It must be noted, however, that in the sixteenth century the Ottomans began to change the former condition of total equality between the Hanafi and Shafi'i law courts by adopting a policy of bias towards the Hanafi, the official *madhhab* of the Ottomans (Gerber 1999).
3. Despite not being an Islamic state, Indonesia has a religious jurisdiction that now operates throughout more than thirty provinces, under the name pengadilan agama. Based on Law 7 of 1989 on the Religious Court, the jurisdiction of these courts includes mostly Islamic family issues, such as marriage, divorce, inheritance, guardianship and *wakaf* (charitable trusts/endowments).
4. See Law 44 of 1999 on the Special Status of Aceh; Law 18 of 2001 on the Special Autonomy for Aceh; and Law 11 of 2006 on Governing Aceh.
5. See Law 7 of 1984 on the Ratification of the UN Convention on the Eradication of Discrimination against Women; Law 8 of 1998 on the Ratification of the Convention Against Torture and Other Cruel, Inhuman or Degrading Treatment or Punishment; Law 29 of 1999 on the Ratification of the International Convention on the Elimination of All Forms of Racial Discrimination; Law 12 of 2005 on the Ratification of the International Covenant on Civil and Political Rights; Law 11 of 2005 on the Ratification of the International Covenant on Economic, Social and Cultural Rights; Presidential Decree 36 of 1990 on the Ratification of the Convention on the Rights of the Child.
6. These NGOs, among others, are Putroe Kandee, Beungong Jeumpa and KKTGA.
7. Interview with Lies Marcos, The Asia Foundation's Senior Programme Officer, 18 March 2008.

Chapter 2

Shifting Legal Orders

> The year 2001 saw the formal establishment of the Syar'iyah Court;
> the year 2002 witnessed the enactment of the Qanun on the Syar'iyah Court;
> the year 2003 welcomed the formal inauguration of the Syar'iyah Court;
> the year 2004 saw the formal transfer of some minor criminal jurisdiction (jinayat) to the Syar'iyah Court;
> and the year 2005 watched the execution of caning imposed by the Syar'iyah Court
>
> Al Yasa Abubakar, chairman of the Provincial Sharia Office of Aceh (2000–10)

Could sharia law be implemented under the nation-state legal system? Since the last century this question has attracted many scholars, including Muslim intellectuals, who have provided either affirmative or negative answers (Taji-Farouki 1996; Brown 1997; Vikør 2000; Zubaida 2003; An-Na'im 2008; Hallaq 2009). Unlike these authors, who have only published their ideas about the position of sharia law and its application in the era of contemporary nation-states, Al Yasa Abubakar, professor of sharia law at Ar-Raniry Islamic University in Banda Aceh, has been enthusiastically endeavouring both to write about it and to bring sharia law into the legal system of the state.[1]

Having trained in Islamic jurisprudence in Cairo, Abubakar has a great interest in classical Islamic legal interpretation. Yet, interestingly, his legal views do not necessarily reflect the obsolete interpretation of Islamic injunctions. In fact, he embraces modern legal views that ponder social and historical contexts for the implementation of sharia laws in particular local settings (Bowen 2008).

Professor Abubakar is one among the few key actors in Aceh who are closely involved in drafting sharia law and making it a reality. In his capacity as chief of the Provincial Office of Islamic Sharia for ten years (2000–10), Abubakar not only managed to initiate a number of Islamic legislations into Aceh's regional regulations, but also empowered the position of the religious court (Syar'iyah Court) of Aceh in Indonesia's legal system.

In Indonesia, a nation-state whose majority population is Muslim, two separate legal national sovereignties co-exist: one emanating from the state and the other from religion (Hallaq 2004). Abubakar is fully aware that classical sharia law and the law of the nation-state are separate systems, but this does not mean that they are mutually exclusive. In Abubakar's view, while it was possible to practise sharia law under caliphate or Muslim kingdoms, the current implementation of sharia law by a nation-state is a new experience. According to Abubakar (2008: 63–4), the changing social culture needs to be taken into account when the state wants to apply sharia law. It was for this reason, that Abubakar (2008: 39), among others, was keen to suggest the conversion of the existing Religious Court, rather than the Civil Court, into the Syar'iyah Court.

This chapter provides a narrative of the shift in the plural legal orders of Aceh. It discusses the way in which a legal institution that specifically upholds the implementation of sharia in Aceh (Syar'iyah Court) was locally initiated and its jurisdiction expanded. This demonstrates that changes in Aceh's plural legal orders are not necessarily connected with the nation-state's offer of the formal implementation of sharia in the region. In fact, situations that have ensued from conflict and environmental disaster have hastened these changes in the local legal constellation.

The Shift in Aceh's Plural Legal Orders

Like elsewhere in Indonesia, Aceh has two parallel state courts (civil and religious) that co-exist in every district or municipal region. For an appeal, respective higher courts of both state courts are present at the provincial level. Further appeals must go to the Supreme Court in Jakarta, which exercises the powers of cassation. Both state courts operate in different domains. While the Religious Court exercises its jurisdiction mostly in family matters (marriage, divorce, inheritance and child guardianship), the Civil Court examines a broad range of legal matters, such as family issues of non-Muslims and commercial, land and labour disputes, as well as criminal offences. In fact, for more than four decades, the Religious Court remained subordinate to the Civil Court, a condition that was generally observable in other provinces of Indonesia also. Civil and Religious courts had equal status only when the Indonesian legislature passed the 1989 Law on the Religious Court (Cammack 2003).

Later, in the post-Suharto period (from 1998 onwards), the jurisdiction of the Religious Court changed, raising it to a higher position than that of the Civil Court. Following the political peace process that ended the prolonged and bloody conflict in Aceh between the Independent Aceh Movement (GAM) and the Indonesian army, the name of Aceh's Religious Court was amended to 'Syar'iyah Court', and its jurisdiction was expanded beyond that of the Civil Court, which gradually decreased.[2] By way of the 2006 Law on the Governance of Aceh, some penal jurisdictions were confirmed for Aceh's religious court. This gives Aceh's Religious Court wider jurisdiction than that of religious courts in Indonesia's other provinces.

The shift in plural legal orders in Aceh is the outcome of complex legal and political changes, especially during the post-New Order era. One important factor in the creation of plural legal constellations is 'resistance from the periphery or challenge of the local' (Yilmaz 2005: 26–7). The current plural legal situation in Aceh is the accumulated result of a protracted struggle by the 'periphery' against the dominant central state (Morris 1983).[3] The willingness of the central government to allow more legal pluralism in Aceh appeared to be an initial step towards the political peace process. The central government believed that greater local authority over religion, customs and education would overcome the widespread problems that had resulted from the bloody conflict in Aceh, which had re-emerged after Hasan Tiro established the GAM in 1976 (Kell 1995; Aspinall 2002; Smith 2002).

For the 'centre', which aspires to 'legal modernity', legal pluralism was seen as threatening the authority, integrity and sovereignty of the modern nation-state. By contrast, the 'periphery' often viewed the state's homogenising project as a threat to its distinct identity and, in response, strove to preserve the institution of a distinct system of sharia courts. In some cases, the centre has eventually acknowledged and accommodated the periphery's demands more and more by formally incorporating certain aspects of local law and its institutions into the official legal system.

For this reason, the Habibie government (1998–9) enacted Law 44 of 1999 on the Special Status of the Province of Aceh. Two years later, the implementation of the sharia in Aceh was officially declared through Law 18 of 2001 on the Special Autonomy for the Province of Nanggroe Aceh Darussalam. Among other things, this law entailed the (re-)establishment of a special court, the Syar'iyah Court. Additionally, only five years later, a statute (Law 11 of 2006 on the Governance of Aceh) was passed to reconfirm the jurisdiction of the Syar'iyah Court.

This local development of Islamic institutions in Aceh has been fostered in various ways by the power of the Indonesian central government. The Indonesian Supreme Court, in particular, has been leaning towards extending the assistance it gives to the plural legal institutionalisation at the periphery. This has a lot to do with the internal dynamics of the Indonesian legal system in the post-New Order period (Salim 2003), among them the growing Islamisation within the Supreme Court,[4] and was especially so following the passage of Law 35 of 1999. This particular law is the amendment to Law 14 of 1970 on the Fundamental Rules of Indonesian Judiciary. The main aim of this amending law was to integrate and manage different courts (which were previously supervised by different ministries) under the auspices of the Supreme Court.

'Special autonomy' for Aceh was part of a series of enactments in the post-authoritarian Suharto regime, in which not only were adat institutions revived and recognised, but sharia-supporting bodies were established and reinforced. The local ulama council was transformed into the Majelis Permusyawaratan Ulama (MPU), holding legislative authority that would come to be seen as equal to that of the provincial legislature. Additionally, a new provincial bureaucracy, the Dinas Syariat Islam, was established to manage the implementation of the sharia in Aceh. And, most important to the subject of this chapter, Acehnese 'special autonomy' also allowed for the transformation of local pengadilan agama into their new form as the Syar'iyah Court, with wider jurisdiction than that of other religious courts outside Aceh.

Stepping to the Shift

The expansion of the Syar'iyah Court's jurisdiction began with legislative discussions of Law 18 of 2001 on the Special Autonomy for the Province of Aceh. One of the key topics covered was the form and limits of authority of the proposed Syar'iyah Court. The provisions of this law (Articles 25 and 26) did not specify whether it would be part of the existing religious judicature (pengadilan agama) or the general civil judicature (pengadilan negeri). This led to debates among Acehnese legislators. Some wanted the Syar'iyah Court to replace the existing religious courts. Under this scheme, the structure and personnel of the pengadilan agama would be transformed into that of the Syar'iyah Court, but with a wider jurisdiction that included certain criminal acts. By transforming the existing religious courts into the Syar'iyah Court, some proponents of the formal implementation of the sharia thought that they could thereby revive their historical authenticity as well as a unique Acehnese identity.

Others, however, proposed that the Syar'iyah Court should serve, instead, as an over-arching rubric for various kinds of existing state courts (including the Civil Court, the Religious Court, the Military Court and the Administrative Court) in Aceh. Each of those courts would thus continue to handle litigation in accordance with their respective jurisdictions, but now under the name and ultimate authority of the Syar'iyah Court. In addition, the jurisdiction over any new provision enacted in the regional regulation, known locally in Aceh as qanun, would be allocated in accordance with each court's respective authority. Under this model, for example, the offence of gambling would be dealt with by the civil courts rather than by the religious courts. In this sense, the Syar'iyah Court would not be a physical entity, but an ad hoc institution that organised judges from various courts and facilitated their settlement of disputes and litigation arising from the enactment of the qanuns in Aceh. In other words, this model of the Syar'iyah Court would not require the establishment of a new court, but would merely complement and 'Islamicise' the rules and procedures of the existing courts, consistent with the implementation of the sharia in the region (Sarong 2002). However, this idea was not well received as it was considered too simple and not sufficiently prestigious for the special autonomy of Aceh.

Ambiguous or Limited Jurisdiction?

Many proponents of the sharia in Aceh were already predisposed towards viewing the central government with considerable scepticism. This was mainly due to the ambiguous jurisdiction granted to Aceh's Syar'iyah Court. Law 18 of 2001 stated that the Syar'iyah Court's jurisdiction was subordinated to the prevalent national legal system. The text of Article 25(2) of this Law stated:

> The jurisdiction of the Syar'iyah Court . . . is based on the Islamic sharia within the national legal system, which will be further arranged through the Qanun of the Province of Nanggroe Aceh Darussalam.

As seen in this provision, two phrases seem to contradict each other. On the one hand the first phrase, 'Islamic sharia within the national legal system', emphasises that the jurisdiction of the Syar'iyah Court over sharia matters should be solely and completely within the scope of the secular Indonesian legal system. This implies that the national legal system must be given priority over the Islamic sharia. On the other hand the phrase in that provision, 'which will be further arranged through the Qanun', suggests that the jurisdiction of the Syar'iyah Court should be based on the Acehnese provincial qanun.

Under the first phrase ('Islamic sharia within the national legal system'), the limit of the jurisdiction is the national legal system itself. This means that as long as the national legal system has accommodated the implementation of particular aspects of the sharia, these aspects are under the jurisdiction of the Syar'iyah Court. However, because the national legal system has not recognised many aspects of the sharia, this jurisdiction is very limited. Under the second clause, however, the limit of the jurisdiction of the Syar'iyah Court is set by provincial legislature enactments in the form of the qanun. This provision would conversely have the effect of broadening the Syar'iyah Court's jurisdiction to cover any sharia rule, provided it was enacted locally in the form of the qanun.

The ambiguity of the Syar'iyah Court's jurisdiction under Law 18 of 2001 is only the beginning of the problem. Debates over such issues continued and, in 2003, President Megawati issued Presidential Decree 11 of 2003 to 'further regulate' the operation of the Syar'iyah Court.[5] This regulation, however, was viewed by many Acehnese as contradicting Article 31 of Law 18 of 2001, which states that any further rules are to be implemented by a government regulation if they are related to the authority of the central government, and in the form of a qanun provided that they concern the authority of the Aceh government. Opposing this presidential decree, Abubakar (2004: 43–4) argued:

> If the establishment of the Syar'iyah Court is regarded as within the authority of the central government, then [it] must be enacted in the form of a government regulation . . . On the other hand, if [the foundation of the Syar'iyah Court is] considered within the authority of the Provincial Government, [the Syar'iyah Court] should be ratified by the Qanun.

The form of legal enactment is also crucial, because the higher the position of a regulation in the formal legal hierarchy, the broader its scope, and the more authority and influence it entails (see Diagram 2.1). The fact that the Syar'iyah Court was regulated by a lower status instrument (presidential decree) was thus seen as detracting from its importance in the implementation of the sharia in Aceh.

If Law 18 of 2001 made the jurisdiction of the Syar'iyah Court vague, Presidential Decree 11 of 2003 went even further. This latter regulation diminished the broad jurisdiction of the Syar'iyah Court as stipulated in Qanun 10 of 2002 on Islamic Sharia Justice. Article 49 of this qanun stated that the jurisdiction of the Syar'iyah Court includes *ahwal al-syakhshiyyah* (personal matters), *muamalat* (trade and commerce) and jinayat (criminal acts). This qanun was enacted partly to clarify the ambiguity of the Syar'iyah Court's jurisdiction in Law 18 of 2001. However, Presidential Decree 11 of 2003, which was issued five months after the enactment of that qanun, limited the jurisdiction of the Syar'iyah Court to 'that of the religious court plus any other legal authority that relates to social life in rituals [*ibadah*] and activities that glorify Islam [*syiar Islam*] as stated in the qanuns'.[6]

Given that the presidential decree has a higher legal status than the qanun (which is a regional regulation) and in view of the fact that the Syar'iyah Court's jurisdiction over criminal acts was not mentioned in the presidential

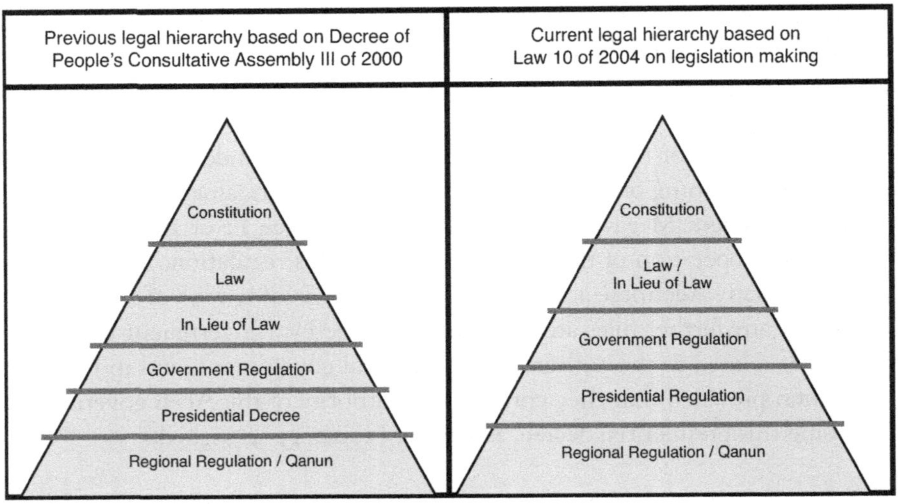

Diagram 2.1 The sources of law and the hierarchy of regulations in Indonesia

decree, it is reasonable to infer that the decree was intended to invalidate the penal jurisdiction of the Syar'iyah Court as prescribed in Qanun 10 of 2002. This particular episode and the following discussion clearly show how the central government was reluctant to concede the consolidation of plural legal orders in Aceh, despite support for the institutionalisation of Islamic law in Aceh from other sectors.

The presidential decree not only blurred the jurisdiction of the Syar'iyah Court, it also lacked any provisions for, or explanation of, the role of other important legal institutions, such as the police and the *kejaksaan negeri* (public prosecutor), and how they should work with the Syar'iyah Court. Their involvement was necessary for the Syar'iyah Court to function in exercising its new additional penal jurisdiction (Abubakar 2004). Likewise, the presidential decree lacked a provision that regulated the transfer of penal jurisdiction from the civil judicature to the Syar'iyah Court. This was necessary to determine which cases should come under the jurisdiction of the Syar'iyah Court and which should remain with the Civil Court. A provision of this kind was obviously needed to resolve disputes relating to jurisdiction between the respective state courts in the future.

Clarifying the Syar'iyah Court's Penal Jurisdiction

Given these impediments to the Syar'iyah Court in the exercising of its additional jurisdiction as granted by the qanun, subsequent efforts have been made by the supporters of the implementation of sharia in Aceh to confirm the new jurisdiction of the Syar'iyah Court over criminal acts. Included in these efforts has been the attempt to arrange for the active involvement of the police and the prosecutor's office with the Syar'iyah Court in dealing with penal cases. This attempt was facilitated by the preparation of a draft Government Regulation (*peraturan pemerintah*) on the Application of Islamic Sharia Justice, intended to implement Law 18 of 2001 on the Special Autonomy of Nanggroe Aceh Darussalam.

However, this effort failed, as a senior official in Megawati's cabinet refused to validate it.[7] In correspondence with the Coordinating Minister of Politics and Security and the governor of the Province of Nanggroe Aceh Darussalam,[8] the Cabinet Secretary stated that the draft had been refused on the grounds that the essence of the provisions in the draft were already dealt with in Article 15(2) of Law 4 of 2004 on the Judicial Power. It states:

> Islamic sharia justice in the province of Nanggroe Aceh Darussalam is executed in a special court within the structure of the religious court, as long as its jurisdiction relates to the jurisdiction of the religious court, and it is a special court within the structure of the general state court, as long as its jurisdiction involves the jurisdiction of the general state court.

This brief provision was certainly not sufficient to regulate the role of the police and the public prosecutor in the Syar'iyah Court cases. The Cabinet Secretary explained, however, that if police personnel and public prosecutors in Aceh were in doubt about their tasks in the Syar'iyah Court, legal guidance from the head of the National Police Force and the attorney general, respectively, would be adequate. However, the office of the *kejaksaan tinggi* (provincial prosecutor) seemed ambivalent about this arrangement, arguing that in order to submit a penal case to the Syar'iyah Court a particular legal foundation (a government regulation) would be required.[9] Although Article 17 Qanun 11 of 2002 already provided the public prosecutor with an obligation to investigate criminal offences, this arrangement was regarded by the provincial prosecutor's office as being too weak, as the qanun has a lower legal status than a government regulation, and also because it omitted detailed procedures on how to carry out the investigation into criminal offences.

This manoeuvre by the cabinet secretary was, however, seen by the proponents of the sharia as an attempt to thwart the implementation of the sharia in Aceh. It was suspected that the provincial prosecutor was not acting in good faith and did not want to support the implementation of the sharia in the region but, rather, was withholding the penal rules in particular, despite there being a provision (Article 39) in Law 16 of 2004 on the Prosecution stating that the authority of the public prosecutor includes offences regulated by Aceh's qanun. On 9 June 2004, in response to this suspicion, a meeting between the chief of the Syar'iyah Court, the chairman of the Dinas Syariat Islam (DSI) and the head of the Provincial Prosecutor's Office took place, and it was finally decided that by August 2004, at the latest, the public prosecutor should be ready to submit a penal case to the Syar'iyah Court of Banda Aceh. Up to the time when the tsunami hit Aceh on 26 December 2004, however, no criminal cases had been presented to the Syar'iyah Court.

During that time, other steps were taken by the proponents of the sharia in Aceh to overcome the barriers to the Syar'iyah Court's exercising its penal jurisdiction. Prominent among these were efforts to coordinate various relevant provincial institutions (such as the governor's office, the police force, the prosecutor's office, the general court and the provincial office of the Ministry of Justice and Human Rights) to issue a *Keputusan Bersama* (Joint Decree). This was intended to synchronise their commitment to the implementation of the sharia in Aceh in general, and to the operation of the Syar'iyah Court in particular. The Joint Decree explains the tasks of every provincial institution in relation to their support of the Syar'iyah Court's jurisdiction in examining a criminal offence. This effort was effective and the Joint Decree was eventually signed on 9 August 2004.[10] This called for the Supreme Court to solve the problem of the overlapping jurisdiction between the Syar'iyah Court and the general court, especially with regard to criminal offences, and, on 6 October 2004, the Supreme Court issued a *Surat Keputusan Ketua Mahkamah Agung* (Decree of the chairman of the Supreme Court) that declared the transfer of partial jurisdiction of the general court over muamalat (civil) and jinayat (criminal) cases to the Syar'iyah Court.[11] Apparently, both these legal instruments were provided as shortcuts to expanding the jurisdiction of the Syar'iyah Court in Aceh. However, both instruments have a rather weak standing within the hierarchy of the Indonesian legal system.

The above description of the ambiguity of the Syar'iyah Court's jurisdiction demonstrates that the state has no ultimate goal to generate the shift in Aceh's plural legal orders, in which the Syar'iyah Court would have an ascendant position. The offer of formal implementation of the sharia in Aceh was merely proposed as a governmental means of persuasion to solve the prolonged conflict in Aceh.

TSUNAMI: PUSHING FORWARD THE SHIFT

By the end of 2004, no criminal offences had been examined by the Syar'iyah Court. All cases related to criminal offences, gambling in particular, were dealt with in the Civil Court. However, the tsunami that severely damaged most coastal areas of Aceh on 26 December 2004 unpredictably created a surge of momentum for the further implementation of the sharia in the province, including the actual authority of the Syar'iyah Court.

One may contend that the tsunami is merely a sunnatullah, caused by a geological shift under the earth, that has nothing to do with the implementation of the sharia. Yet there is a belief among Acehnese that, through the tsunami, God told the Acehnese to stop committing sinful deeds, to reconcile with each other and to return to religion as a way of salvation. For some, the tsunami disaster brought the message that the Acehnese people should comply with the rules of the sharia and that the government should enforce its implementation in earnest. The post-tsunami recovery process created a context in which the proponents of the sharia could apply emotional pressure on the central government in order to induce it to be more serious in applying sharia in Aceh.

In the aftermath of the tsunami, the district Syar'iyah Court of Bireuen had, in fact, for the first time convicted more than twenty people for gambling offences, and fifteen of them were publicly caned in the mosque yard in Bireuen on 24 June 2005.[12] The caning in Bireuen could have never taken place without pressure upon the acting governor of Aceh, Azwar Abubakar. In the absence of legal guidance from both the central government and regional legislation as to whether and how the caning punishment should be carried out for sharia offenders in Aceh, Governor Azwar approved the punishment by issuing a decree (*Peraturan Gubernur Provinsi Nanggroe Aceh Darussalam* 10 of 2005) on the Technical Guidance of the Implementation of Caning.

Despite the governor's decree, the provincial and the district public prosecutors had doubts about the required procedures for carrying out the caning punishment, and they waited for the Jakarta attorney general's consent to implement this particular punishment in Aceh. This consent was not forthcoming, but some advocates of sharia persevered and sought a meeting with the attorney general in Jakarta to request his support for the Syar'iyah Court's penal jurisdiction, and for the caning punishment in particular. His support was secured only after persistent efforts were exerted in the context of the highly energised situation following the tsunami. The attorney general gave his approval in an unscheduled meeting on 3 June 2005 at his office in Jakarta.[13] Amongst those who attended the meeting with the attorney general were the chairman of the Provincial Syar'iyah Court, Soufyan Saleh; the chairman of the Ulama Consultative Assembly, Muslim Ibrahim; the chairman of the Aceh Adat Council, Badruzzaman Ismail; the chairman of the Provincial Office of Islamic Sharia, Al Yasa Abubakar; and the chairman of the Religion and Social Welfare section of the Provincial Legislature.[14]

The post-tsunami recovery process not only provided a chance for the Syar'iyah Court to have real jurisdiction on criminal offences, as discussed

Figure 2.1 Female witnesses are sworn in during a guardian appointment session of the mobile sharia court in Lhoknga, Aceh Besar © Arskal Salim

Figure 2.2 An underage orphaned heir and his female guardian are verified by the mobile sharia court to have his land certified in Kajhu village, Aceh Besar © Arskal Salim

above, but it also offered the court other opportunities to exercise a broader civil jurisdiction in land disputes, particularly those involving inheritance matters. In the aftermath of the tsunami, the Syar'iyah Court was immediately encumbered with an immense caseload, due to the rapid increase in legal problems involving inheritance, orphaned children and the status of properties whose owners (and often their legitimate heirs) had died or were missing (Figures 2.1 and 2.2). However, litigation over land issues had actually fallen under the jurisdiction of the Civil Court. As a way out of this situation the Syar'iyah Court looked to the Decree of the chairman of the Supreme Court (discussed earlier) to provide it with the legal authority to adjudicate such land disputes (Saleh 2005). The MPU, whose credibility in Islamic affairs is widely recognised in Aceh, supported the Syar'iyah Court's exercise of authority in these post-tsunami disputes. The MPU released a *fatwa* (legal opinion) (3 of 2005) stating that the post-tsunami Syar'iyah Court is authorised to deal with disputes of ownership and land inheritance.

Conclusion

As Ido Shahar (2008) pointed out, the time has come to understand the relationship between sharia courts and other tribunals in the framework of legal pluralism. Discussions in this chapter have demonstrated this relationship and how the Syar'iyah Court in Aceh has developed from a peripheral legal body, whose jurisdiction was previously limited to family law, to a more significant institution that is gradually securing greater legal authority with regard to financial issues, property disputes and minor penal offences.

The particular case of Aceh, however, demonstrates a new perspective in which the relationship between different state courts was (re)shaped by post-conflict and post-disaster recovery situations. These situations not only drove the contending parties attempting to end the long-standing Aceh conflict, but they also accidentally unlocked Aceh from international isolation. Following the processes of peace and post-disaster recovery, a number of international bodies came to Aceh bringing various legal reform programmes. While the transition to the peace process started the shift in plural legal orders in Aceh, the post-tsunami rehabilitation circumstances hastened and helped the consolidation of this shift.

This kind of dynamic legal pluralism in Indonesia, in Aceh in particular, is not something that is just beginning. As F. and K. von Benda-Beckmann (2006b) suggested, older legal forms are being re-actualised or reinvented to match current interests. In light of this, both the shift in plural legal orders and the contestation between them now taking place in Aceh should be seen as a repetition or continuation of earlier transformations that occurred during

Aceh's colonial legal history, though in different fashion. The current shift in Aceh's plural legal orders, whereby the Syar'iyah Court has been given increased authority, remains, however, an on-going process and has not yet reached the final stage. As the case in Chapter 3 reveals, the extent to which this new-found authority of Aceh's Syar'iyah Court, on land disputes in particular, can actually be exercised is still highly contested.

Notes

1. For a list of Abubakar's publications, please see Bibliography of this book.
2. See 'Potret Buram PN Pasca UU PA' ('The Gloomy Picture of the Civil Court in the Aftermath of Law on the Governance of Aceh'), *Modus Tabloid Hukum dan Politik*, July 31, 2006.
3. In his dissertation on Aceh, Eric E. Morris (1983) made and developed the distinction between the centre, to represent the national government, and the periphery, to indicate the position of the Acehnese.
4. Although further study is necessary to confirm this contention, such developments could be seen as supported by the fact that, in 2004, among more than fifty justices of the Supreme Court, at least fifteen of them have sharia training or Islamic studies backgrounds.
5. 'Lewat Keppres, Syar'iyah Court di Aceh Diresmikan', available at: http://www.detik.com/peristiwa/2003/03/04/20030304-115935.shtml, accessed 4 March 2003.
6. See Presidential Decree 11 of 2003 (Article 3:1) on the Syar'iyah Court.
7. The disapproval was expressed by a senior official of the Cabinet Secretariat (I have been asked to keep the official's name confidential) at a meeting held on 21 April 2004 and attended by representatives from different institutions, such as the Supreme Court, the Ministry of Home Affairs, the Ministry of Justice and Human Rights, the Ministry of Religious Affairs and the National Police Force.
8. See letter No. B.41/Waseskab/05/2004, dated 7 May 2004, and letter No. B.53/Waseskab/06/2004, dated 10 June.
9. 'Belum Ada Dasar untuk Mahkamah Syariah', *Kompas*, 6 November 2003. See also *Pelaksanaan Syar'iyah* Court *di Aceh Masih Terganjal*, available at: http://hukumonline.com/detail.asp?id=9237&cl=Berita, accessed 14 March 2005.
10. This Joint Decree was signed by the governor, the head of the Provincial Police Force, the head of the Provincial Prosecutor's Office, the chairman of the Provincial Syar'iyah Court, the chairman of the Provincial General Court, and the head of the Provincial Office of the Ministry of Justice and Human Rights.
11. See the Decree of the Chairman of the Supreme Court No. KMA/070/SK/X/2004 on the Transfer of Partial Jurisdiction from the General Court to the Syar'iyah Court in the Province of Nanggroe Aceh Darussalam.
12. '15 Penjudi Dicambuk', *Serambi Indonesia*, 25 June 2005.
13. See 'Jaksa Agung Dukung Hukuman Cambuk di NAD', *Republika*, 6 June 2005.
14. The presence of those leading figures in Jakarta was a coincidence. They were returning to Aceh from Semarang, where a conference on the tsunami devastation

had been held by the *Bappenas* (the National Development Planning Agency). The role of Bappenas was crucial here. According to Muslim Ibrahim, who was present in the meeting with the attorney general, the attorney general had initially no time to take the meeting, as he was very busy that week. It was only with the help of Bappenas officials, whose institution is responsible for the post-tsunami rehabilitation and reconstruction of Aceh, that the meeting could take place (interview with Muslim Ibrahim, 17 June 2005).

Chapter 3

Competing Jurisdictions

Dispute settlement of property rights is not a jurisdiction
that belongs to the Mahkamah Syar'iyah.
Such dispute is a part of the jurisdiction of the General Judicature.
Otherwise, the Civil Judiciary would [ironically] turn out to be a
lex specialis court that only examines disputes submitted by non-Muslims.

Chief Judge of Jantho District Civil Court

For many judges in Indonesian Islamic courts, the amendment of Law 7 of 1989 on the Religious Court by Law 3 of 2006 was an impressive step forward. The revised law not only provided the religious judicature with a new jurisdiction on Islamic financial disputes, but it also granted the Islamic court a jurisdiction to examine disputes over *sengketa hak milik* (property ownership), as long as Muslims were parties in those disputes. Earlier, this particular jurisdiction was available only to the civil judiciary.

Soon after the amending Law 3 of 2006 on the Religious Court was passed, judges of the religious judicatures (namely, the Religious Court of Tebing Tinggi, North Sumatra, and the Religious Court of Sidoarjo, East Java) became confident of their right to examine a land ownership dispute that included an inheritance component. Defendants in this particular case had, in fact, raised an objection, in the preliminary hearings, that the religious judicature was illegitimate to examine the case. In addition, they claimed that the civil tribunals, instead, had jurisdiction over this particular case, and therefore they considered the religious judicatures be ineligible to examine the dispute. However, after referring to the amending law above, Article 50, verse (2) in particular, the judges of the Islamic judiciary were convinced that they had full rights to examine the case. When the defendants brought the issue of conflicting jurisdiction before the Religious Higher Courts in Medan and Surabaya, respectively, the appellate judges concurred with the lower judges' decision that the first instance courts had been awarded such jurisdiction and were fully legitimate to decide the case (Firdaus 2009; Sarjono 2011).

All this new legal development, however, does not necessarily mean that the jurisdiction of the religious judicature over property ownership disputes is well consolidated. It was not immediately translated into wide application everywhere in Indonesia, nor was it easily accepted by the other state legal institution, the civil judiciary. Judges of civil tribunals, at least in Aceh, are not acquiescent to this change. In fact, there are a number of cases that demonstrate the resistance of judges of the civil judiciary to relinquishing this particular jurisdiction to be exercised by the religious judicature, or the Mahkamah Syar'iyah.

In examining the state courts that settled inheritance cases in both Central Aceh and West Sumatra, K. von Benda-Beckmann (2009) discovered that the expansion of the jurisdiction of Islamic courts has not actually redirected disputants from civil courts to Islamic courts. My study does not disagree with her findings. Rather, the court cases I examined from tsunami-affected regions in Aceh suggest that both the state courts (civil judiciary and religious judicature) have been competing either to retain or to take over jurisdiction to settle disputes concerning ownership of property. This chapter shows that despite the increasing jurisdiction of the sharia courts of Aceh in recent years, a shift in jurisdiction on property rights disputes has not automatically taken place. Even though Aceh had a stronger basis than other regions in Indonesia for the formal implementation of Islamic law, the Mahkamah Syar'iyah of Aceh must struggle to fully exercise its newly conferred jurisdiction.

This chapter presents multiple case studies to demonstrate that the civil tribunals in Aceh continue to examine property ownership disputes in which the litigants are Muslims, even disputes that involve inheritance estates. It shows that competition for jurisdiction between the two courts is related not only to different understandings of the notion of property ownership as stipulated in the legislation, but also to the historical fact of the relegated position of the religious judicature since Dutch colonial times. The following section therefore briefly traces the jurisdiction of the religious judicature over family and property laws back over the last two centuries. Since Indonesia is a country with a strong civil law tradition, one has to look at the legislation over time to understand the ups and downs of the Islamic courts' jurisdiction in Indonesia's history.

Earlier Jurisdictions in Colonial Times

As early as the nineteenth century, a Royal Decree of the Netherlands (*Staatsblad* 1835 No. 58) was issued to allocate to the Islamic court the right to adjudicate cases concerning marriage, divorce, inheritance and other property issues such as *hibah* (grant) and wakaf. Following this, Staatsblad 1882 No. 152 was issued to officially acknowledge the establishment of a *priesterraad* (Islamic court) in Java and Madura. Staatsblad 1882 stipulated that Islamic courts were to be established in every district in which a *landraad* (civil judicature) was already present. However, it was further arranged that the priesterraad's decisions would not be enforceable unless a landraad's executorial authority was issued to enable each of the priesterraad's decisions come into effect (Cammack 2003: 97; Nurlaelawati 2010: 46).

Fifty-five years later, the new Staatsblad 1937 No. 116 removed the jurisdiction of the Islamic court over inheritance. Based on this Staatsblad, the examination of inheritance disputes was handed over to the landraad, while the Islamic courts' jurisdiction was restricted to include marriage and divorce only (Cammack 2003: 98). This change attracted some fierce reactions from religious judges, which were economically motivated. According to Lev (1972: 19), the revocation of inheritance from the jurisdiction of the Islamic court had implications in reducing income for judges, and this led them to organise a protest against the policy. Despite these protests, the Dutch did not relent.

The exclusion of inheritance from the jurisdiction of the Islamic courts was representative of the general policy of the Dutch colonial administration towards Islam (Hooker 1984). As outlined by Snouck Hurgronje (1857–1936), a Dutch architect of the colonial efforts to manage Islamic developments in the East Indies, the objectives of the Dutch Islamic policy were threefold: (1) to maintain security and order in the colony; (2) to ensure personal liberty concerning religious practice; and (3) to block the growth of Islam as a political movement as well as a predominant culture (Benda 1958; Suminto 1985).

Nonetheless, it was not intended that all three of these objectives were to be manifest in every Islamic policy of the Dutch in the East Indies. The transfer of jurisdiction over inheritance from the Islamic court to the civil judiciary was pertinent only to the last two objectives. Since the first objective was apparently ignored, one would think that the Dutch policy might have had in mind another important goal. As part of their familiar tactics of co-option and 'divide and rule', the Dutch sought to create tensions between proponents of the religious judicatures and the auxiliaries of the civil judiciaries concerning judicial competence over inheritance. In fact, the hostilities between the two camps over this particular point of jurisdiction still remain today.

According to Cammack (2003), the reallocation of jurisdiction over inheritance to the civil tribunals reflected the increasing influence of a group of Dutch scholars and their Indonesian students who favoured the customary rules of numerous ethnic groups of Indonesia over the rules of Islam. The Dutch scholars pointed out that in actual practice many Javanese people followed adat rules rather than Islam in inheritance division. Because it had originated from Arabian contexts, these scholars contended that Islamic inheritance law was irrelevant to Indonesian family life and far removed from the sense of justice prevailing in many communities of the different ethnic groups in Indonesia (Nurlaelawati 2010: 48–9). Seen in a larger framework, the question was not whether Islam or adat customary rules should be applied in dealing with inheritance division in Muslim communities in the East Indies, but rather, which legal values or expressions had precedence and should therefore govern Indonesian plural societies. In Cammack's words (2003: 98): '*adat* and Islam represent more than simply alternative sets of legal rules: they represent competing bases of social authority'. Depriving the Islamic courts of jurisdiction over inheritance was a success for the proponents of adat and a serious setback for the supporters of Islam in Indonesia (Lev 1972; Cammack 2003).

After Indonesia's Independence

The departure of the Dutch from Indonesia by 1945 did not immediately bring a lot of changes. In fact, the position of the Islamic court was vulnerable, given the Indonesian Ministry of Justice's initiative to abolish it by the introduction of Law 19 of 1948 (Lev 1972: 64). This law stipulated that only three domains of courts would exist in the Indonesian judicial system: the Civil Court, the Administrative Court, and the Military Court. Opposing this 'blueprint' of the Indonesian legal system, some Muslim leaders from Aceh, West Sumatra and South Sumatra demanded the re-establishment of the existing Mahkamah Syar'iyah, or religious judicatures, under the Ministry of Religion's auspices. Ultimately, Law 19 was a non-starter and the religious judicatures continued their previous function and developed further under the management of the Ministry of Religion (Nurlaelawati 2010: 52–3).

It was Exigent Law 1 of 1951 that provided the Islamic court with its initial legitimacy after Indonesia's independence. This law not only recognised various forms of Islamic court across Indonesia and their diverse legal bases, but also their different jurisdictional scopes. While the jurisdictions of Islamic courts in Java, Madura and South Kalimantan included marriage, divorce, reconcilement, dowry, custody and maintenance, Islamic courts in Sumatra had a wider jurisdiction. Since they were not affected by Staatsblad 1937 No. 116 as discussed above, Islamic courts in Sumatra were authorised to continue to examine inheritance cases. The law also stipulated that a government regulation would be issued to provide the Islamic courts with further legal arrangements. Last, but not least, the Elucidation of Exigent Law 1 of 1951 stated that an executorial authority from the Civil Court remained necessary to enforce Islamic courts' decisions. Following this law, the Ministry of Religion attempted to unify the Islamic courts, and, where possible, to create an Islamic court institution in numerous areas of Indonesia where official Islamic courts were not already established (Cammack 2003: 99).

In 1957, two government regulations were promulgated as a legal basis for Islamic courts in all parts of Indonesia. While the first regulation (PP 29/1957) addressed the Islamic court (Mahkamah Syar'iyah) in Aceh, the second (PP 45/1957) dealt with the establishment of religious judicatures outside Java and Madura. In fact, the Islamic court in Aceh had been present since 1946, following an instruction from the new Indonesian Republic's governor in Sumatra allowing the Acehnese regional government to restore the independent Mahkamah Syar'iyah. Although this court held jurisdiction over a wider range of issues than did Islamic courts anywhere else in the archipelago, the central government did not recognise its authority and pay its judges until the 1957 government regulation was issued and provided the Mahkamah Syar'iah in Aceh with a clear legal basis (Lev 1972: 81–3).

Thus, twenty years after the promulgation of Staatsblad 1937, the Indonesian legal constellation dramatically altered with the enactment of the 1957 government regulations. These regulations were considered a significant victory for advocates of the Islamic court in Indonesia (Cammack 2003). Together, the regulations not only protected Islamic courts from threats of abolition or absorption into the civil judiciary, but also confirmed the jurisdiction of the Islamic courts over Islamic family laws. Islamic courts outside Java, Madura and South Kalimantan had an even wider jurisdiction, including inheritance, wakaf (land endowment), hibah and *sadaqah* (donations). Despite this, the subordinate position of Islamic courts in relation to the civil judiciary persisted due to a stipulation in both regulations that Islamic court decisions would still have to be enforced through an executorial authority from the Civil Court. In addition, unlike the jurisdiction of the Islamic courts in the rest of the country, that of the Islamic courts in Java, Madura and South Kalimantan did not include inheritance (Cammack 2003: 100). Rather, it was the civil tribunals in these areas, not the Islamic courts, that were authorised to examine inheritance disputes (Nurlaelawati 2010: 52).

It was during the New Order period (1966–98), that the jurisdiction of Islamic courts was strengthened. While the 1974 Marriage Act unified and extended the jurisdiction of Islamic courts in Indonesia over matrimonial issues, the 1989 Religious Court Law not only removed inconsistent titles (such as Pengadilan Agama, Mahkamah Syar'iyah and *Kerapatan Qadi*) for Islamic tribunals all over Indonesia, but also eliminated the disparity of jurisdiction between Islamic courts in Java, Madura and South Kalimantan and those in other provinces. Now all Islamic courts in the country have the same jurisdiction, including Islamic inheritance. Law 7 of 1989 on the Religious Court lists numerous authorities that Islamic courts could exercise in inheritance issues, such as designation of heirs, designation of the estate, designation of individual shares and distribution of the estate. Above all, an executorial authority from the civil judiciary was no longer needed for decisions of the Islamic Courts to take effect. For some, this was an indication of the independence of the Islamic Court and its equal relationship with the Civil Court within Indonesia's legal system (Cammack 2003; Nurlaelawati 2010).

However, there were still two provisions in Law 7 of 1989 that caused a little disappointment among proponents of the Islamic Court. The first was the 'choice of law' that was made available to disputants in inheritance cases. It was stipulated that, before the initiation of proceedings, either or both contending parties could decide to choose to which of two legal forums (the Islamic Court or the Civil Court) they would submit their dispute. (Chapter 4 of this book also discusses this topic in a different context.) According to Cammack (2003: 105), the presence of legal options in this Law (Article 49:1) represented 'the historic debate over the extent to which Islamic rules had supplanted adat in matters of inheritance'. Although the 1989 Religious Court Law was a big success for advocates of state enforcement of Islamic rules in Indonesia, with this particular provision proponents of adat rules could at least hinder the rapid expansion of the jurisdiction of Islamic courts.

The second provision was that the resolution of disputes concerning sengketa hak milik or property ownership case remained under the jurisdiction of the civil tribunals. This provision stipulates that if a dispute over property ownership arises during the Islamic court's examination of an inheritance case (as well as during examination of other Islamic legal issues involving property), the civil tribunals have the right to resolve this dispute in the first instance. Once this dispute is resolved, the case returns to the Islamic court for a final settlement. This procedure, for some, appeared similar to the executorial authority of the Civil Court over Islamic Courts' decisions that was practised prior to the issuance of the 1989 Religious Court Law. It therefore seemed to the Islamic court judges, that the religious tribunal was not independent, because the civil judiciary appeared to have a higher status (Matrais 2008).

Property Ownership Disputes

Law 7 of 1989 on the Religious Court was amended by Law 3 of 2006, and resulted in some progress in widening the jurisdiction of Islamic courts in

Indonesia. The 2006 Law augmented the jurisdiction of the religious judicature in many ways. It not only added new jurisdiction over Islamic financial disputes, but it also stipulated that the religious judicature is the only court for settling property disputes between Muslims. Thus, it eliminated the legal options available in the earlier regulation. Article 49 of this law stipulated the family and property domains of the Islamic court's jurisdictions as follows: marriage, inheritance, *wasiat* (bequests), hibah, wakaf, *zakat* (Islamic alms), *infaq* (gifts), *shadaqah* (donations) and sharia finance.

More importantly, the law conferred on the religious judicature the authority to settle disputes regarding sengketa hak milik. Before 2006, this latter jurisdiction was part of the authority of the general judicature or the civil judiciary. If any dispute of ownership arose, or was put forward by any party, during a court hearing at the religious judicature, the examination of the case had to stop pending resolution by the civil judiciary of the emerging dispute. Now, according to Law 3 of 2006, the authority to settle an ownership dispute does not belong solely to the civil judiciary – such jurisdiction has been conferred also on the religious judicatures, including the Mahkamah Syar'iyah in Aceh, especially in cases where all the disputants are Muslims.

In spite of this newly defined jurisdictional authority, there have been numerous somewhat different understandings among judges of religious judicatures on the mechanism for resolution of disputes regarding ownership of property, as stipulated in Law 3 of 2006 (Article 50). Before looking closely at each interpretation, let me present here two stipulations of Article 50 that have led to debates: (1) in a case where a dispute concerning property rights, or another kind of dispute, occurs in cases that are mentioned in Article 49, objects of that dispute must first be resolved by the civil judiciary; (2) if a dispute regarding ownership of property, as stated in the above verse, takes place between Muslim subjects, the religious judicature examines objects of that dispute along with the cases mentioned in Article 49.

The first interpretation of this particular provision is that a dispute regarding ownership of property is considered under the Islamic court's jurisdiction, as long as any dispute that involves Islamic property rules (that is, concerns joint marital property, inheritance, bequests, grants, land endowments, Islamic alms, gifts, donations and sharia finance) is first submitted, by Muslim parties, to the religious tribunal. This includes disputes involving an intervention by a third party, provided that this intervening party is Muslim. The second proviso is that the dispute is not concurrently registered at the civil judiciary. Both these requirements are prerequisite to allowing the religious judicature to examine a dispute over property rights (Husnaini 2007).[1]

This first understanding is based on the maxim '*lex specialis derogat lex generalis*' ('specific law overrides general law'). This rule is deemed to apply notwithstanding contrary general principles contained in the same legislation. The priority given to *lex specialis* is considered justified by the fact that the *lex specialis* is intended to apply in specific circumstances, regardless of the rules applicable more generally, where those circumstances may be absent. According to this maxim, which is a widely accepted basis for interpretation among jurists and legal scholars in Indonesia, the general principle contained in Amended Law 3 of 2006 (Article 50 Verse 1) is that property ownership disputes belong to the jurisdiction of the civil judiciary. This is exactly the same stipulation mentioned in the previous Law 7 of 1989. The special principle, or the exception to this general stipulation, can be found in the Amended Law 3 of 2006 (Article 50 Verse 2), which states that the religious judicature is authorised to examine the case if Muslims are parties in such a property rights dispute.

The second understanding is similar to the one above. This second interpretation emphasises the exclusion of those disputes (regarding property rights) that have nothing to do with any kind of Islamic property disputes. Thus, property disputes in cases not involving joint marital property, inheritance, bequests, grants, land endowments, Islamic alms, gifts, donations and sharia finance, even those between Muslims, are not part of the Islamic court's jurisdiction. For instance, a case that is focused solely on disputing a claim over land ownership or questioning the truth as well as the validity of a land certificate cannot be adjudicated by the religious judicatures, even if it is submitted by Muslims (Aridi and Asnawi, n.d).[2]

The third understanding is substantially parallel to the views outlined above. Nonetheless, it is a little different from the first view in a case where an intervention is made by a third party. According to this understanding, should a third party join in a dispute being examined at the religious judicature, whether this intervening party is Muslim or not, such dispute must be postponed and forwarded to the civil judiciary for a resolution. Once this intervening dispute is settled by the civil judiciary, judges of the religious tribunal can continue examining the case (Manan 2007: 251–2).[3] Given these interpretations by the Islamic court's auxiliaries of the jurisdiction of the religious tribunals over disputes concerning property rights, one could say that the religious judicature has made another step forward in ensuring its equal status with the civil judiciary. In fact, the expanding jurisdiction of the religious judicature in disputes of property rights reflects, once again, a victory for advocates of the autonomous Islamic court.

In Aceh, as early as October 2004, or two months before the tsunami tragedy, the Mahkamah Syar'iyah claimed that parts of the civil judiciary's jurisdiction had already been transferred to Aceh's sharia tribunals. A former chairman of the Mahkamah Syar'iyah of Aceh, Soufyan Saleh, argued that the Supreme Court of Indonesia had issued a decision, 70 of 2004, on the transfer of several jurisdictions that were initially parts of the general judicature or Civil Court to the jurisdiction of the sharia court in Aceh. According to Saleh (2005), the decision of this highest legal institution in Indonesia could serve as a foundation for the expansion of the jurisdiction of the sharia tribunal in Aceh to include disputes regarding ownership of inheritance property.

Islamic Property Disputes before the Civil Judiciary

The question that has emerged is what happens if Muslims file disputes concerning their rights in cases involving Islamic property issues to the civil judiciary in the first instance? Would these cases be rejected by judges of the civil tribunals, declaring that they are not authorised to hear them?

In the first years after Amended Law 3 of 2006 was passed. Some judges of the civil tribunals got confused. There were two cases where judges of the civil judiciary in Aceh's districts of Bireuen and Jantho refused to adjudicate such disputes, stating that the religious tribunals have jurisdiction over them.[4] Judges of both Civil Courts considered that these cases belonged to the Mahkamah Syar'iyah in their respective districts. They ascertained that the disputes were

Figure 3.1 The judges of the civil judiciary examine a dispute over property rights © Arskal Salim

all about inheritance and that the contending parties were Muslim heirs. Their decisions were not based only on Amended Law 3 of 2006, but also on the Dutch procedural law (*Reglement de Rechtsvordering* Article 132) that remains applicable in contemporary Indonesia. The procedural law, regarding ineligibility of the court, stipulates that 'in the case that judges are not authorised to [examine] because of the type of case [submitted to the court], even though there is no objection being raised [by defendants] to that ineligibility, they are *obliged by their oath* of office to declare themselves unentitled [to hear the case]'.[5]

The case in the Bireuen Civil Court was about an agreement between two persons, ZB and MX. The agreement was made because ZB had to sort out his large debts to avoid having his uncertified land parcel auctioned by a financial institution. MX was willing to help ZB, but on condition that the land parcel would be held as collateral by MX and would be returned to ZB only upon his complete repayment of the loan, in three instalments, to MX. Not long after this agreement, ZB died and was therefore unable to complete all repayments to MX. According to the agreement, MX was then supposed to have control over the land parcel. However, because the sub-district was subsequently split into two areas, the name of the sub-district where the land parcel was located was changed and the land parcel was now under the management of the new sub-district. The children of ZB secretly made an application to the authorities of the new sub-district to have the land parcel certified in their names, as heirs of their deceased father. On becoming aware of a situation that may have disadvantaged him, MX filed a case with the Civil Court of Bireuen. In the preliminary hearings, the children of ZB defended their rights by claiming that the land was inheritance estate from their father and the Civil Court had nothing to do with this legal matter. The judges of Bireuen Civil Court concurred and dismissed the case.

The case in the Jantho Civil Court involved an estate left by a female propositus[6] (NPT). NPT was a grandmother of the female plaintiff (MRM) and the mother of the male defendant (YCB). MRM's deceased mother and YCB were not siblings. Rather, they were stepsister and stepbrother. YCB's deceased father was the second husband of NPT. When NPT's and YCB's father were divorced, all estates that belonged to the propositus (NPT), including her joint marital property with her first husband (the plaintiff's grandfather), were controlled by the defendant. The plaintiff, MRM, wanted to reclaim the land parcels from this joint marital property and claimed that she was a legitimate heir to these properties. The defendant refuted the claim stating that the land parcels were not the joint marital property of the defendant's grandmother and her first husband. Instead, they were all part of his mother's estate, inherited earlier from her parent. The defendant also argued that after his mother's death, a long time previously, her entire estate had been divided among all legitimate heirs, including himself as the surviving son of the propositus. In fact, the land parcels under the defendant's control were now part of that inheritance division. On ascertaining that this case was mostly about an inheritance dispute between heirs of the propositus, judges of the Jantho Civil Court declared that this case was not part of its jurisdiction.

Dissatisfied with these decisions of the lower courts in both Bireuen and Jantho districts, the plaintiffs in the two cases outlined above appealed to the Higher Civil Court in Banda Aceh. The appellate judges found that both Civil Courts had incorrectly applied the law. The cases were not exclusively about Islamic inheritance division or merely about property disputes between Muslims. Rather, both cases were about disputes regarding property rights, which the civil judiciary could legitimately adjudicate. The cases, therefore, were returned to the respective Civil Courts and their judges were instructed to hear and decide the cases.[7]

Commenting on the case from Bireuen, a senior judge at the Higher Civil Court of Banda Aceh, Yasrin Nasution, said, in an interview, that the lower court had not meticulously looked at the way the land right was derived. It was true that the land was part of an inheritance estate, but its status was disputed between heirs and a third party. Because this kind of dispute was involved, Yasrin was convinced that the Civil Court of Bireuen should examine the case and not redirect the litigants to the religious judicature, or the Mahkamah Syar'iyah. With regard to the case from Jantho, the appellate judges established that the case was actually a dispute regarding ownership of inheritance property between a granddaughter of the propositus' first husband (plaintiff) and a son of the propositus' second husband (defendant). According to Yasrin, who chaired the panel of appellate judges, the issue of inheritance was simply introductory to this case, while the main dispute involved was a property rights dispute (sengketa hak milik). Yasrin blamed the lower court's judges for not investigating further by inviting both contending parties to present preliminary evidence to support their respective claims. He stated:

> the plaintiff has no adequate opportunity to argue for the claim . . . where did the land property right come from? Was it a grant, gift or bequest? It may be true that an old person grants a land parcel to an individual because of love and heart attachment between the two, especially when this individual closely looks after the old person until his or her death. Since the plaintiff filed her case to Jantho, it must first be clarified as to what was her legal basis to claim the land parcels belong to the plaintiff; whether it was a grant or bequest, all this was not exposed during the preliminary hearing.[8]

The decisions of the Higher Civil Court of Banda Aceh (above) had assured judges of the civil judiciary that they had legitimacy to examine disputes regarding ownership of property, even between Muslims. From 2008 onwards, many similar cases were submitted to the civil tribunals in Aceh. In fact, it was not only the lower judges of the civil judiciary in Aceh who often rejected defendants' objections to the tribunals' jurisdictional legitimacy to adjudicate cases concerning a property rights dispute between Muslims[9] – the judges of the Supreme Court did likewise.[10]

DAHLAN VERSUS THE VILLAGE TREASURY

The following case from the Jantho Civil Court illustrates how its judges' approach changed after they were informed of the decision of the appellate court regarding their dismissal of the case outlined above. Not long after the Higher Civil Court in Banda Aceh issued its decision, or, more precisely, an instruction, that they should reopen the case that they had previously dismissed, the civil judiciary of Jantho, in hearing a new case, dismissed the defendant's objections to the court's jurisdictional legitimacy to examine it. The case shows how the judges of Jantho Civil Court had learned from their previous incorrect decision and therefore moved to apply the law according to the instruction from the Higher Court.

The case began at the sharia court of Banda Aceh in 1981. Heirs were disputing the division of their inheritance. Dahlan and his siblings contested their eldest brother's taking over the entire estate left by their parents. The judges divided the estate and distributed it proportionally to each heir. However, a land parcel was withheld from the estate due to the lack of proof that the land was owned by the propositus. According to one witness, that particular land parcel originally belonged to someone named Nek Daya who, despite having lived at the same settlement as the heirs' parents, had no kin relationship whatsoever with them or with anyone from the village. The witness, a local *imeum mesjid* (religious leader), told the judges that the *baitul mal gampong* (village treasury) should receive the land on Nek Daya's death, according to the village custom practised in Aceh. The custom holds that if someone dies without a surviving heir, his or her estate will be handed over to the village treasury. The village treasury will then manage and cultivate property of this kind for the benefit of all villagers. This local norm might have influenced the judges and prevented them from allocating the land in question to the heirs. In their final decision, the judges did not include the land as part of the inheritance, nor did they decide who owned the property, but left it open to be claimed or reclaimed at another trial.

As the court was silent on the rightful ownership of the land, the village leader responsible for managing the village treasury filed a lawsuit in 1994 to the Religious Court of Jantho. The case was not brought before the Religious

Court of Banda Aceh that had previously decided an inheritance dispute related to this case. Rather, it was submitted to the religious judicature of Jantho, as the land in question was located in Aceh Besar, which is under the territorial jurisdiction of Jantho's Religious Court. This time the village treasury was acting as the plaintiff, while the defendant was Dahlan, an heir who occupied the land and received any benefit arising from it. The village treasury brought two witnesses before the court to support its claim. Both witnesses explained that the land had belonged to Nek Daya, who used to live with the defendant's parents. The land had passed into the defendant's control when Nek Daya and the defendant's parents died. The witnesses further confirmed that villagers in the vicinity of the land knew that Nek Daya was the original landowner and that he was not survived by any heir. Thus, according to the local custom, the village treasury should have become the legitimate new owner of the land.

The defendant did not attend any of the court sessions and therefore could not provide a rebuttal to the claims made by the plaintiff. He was not even able to make a statement against what was claimed by the witnesses. The Jantho Religious Court eventually decided that the land should fall under the village treasury's control. The nature of this decision is '*verstek*', meaning that adjudication was held in the absence of the defendant. The judges simply considered that Dahlan's absence from the trial was because of his unwillingness to come to the courtroom. Yet in my interview with Dahlan, he said that he did not receive even one notification from the court regarding the case.[11]

The case reappeared in court in 2008. This time, it was not the Mahkamah Syar'iyah, but the Civil Court of Jantho that examined the case, and Dahlan,

Figure 3.2 The Civil Court of Jantho © Arskal Salim

Figure 3.3 The *Mahkamah Syar'iyah* of Jantho © Arskal Salim

who had been the defendant in the 1994 lawsuit, was now the plaintiff. Dahlan claimed that the land in question was an inheritance estate of his parents and that the village treasury had unlawfully occupied the land. It is worth noting that the plaintiff chose the civil judiciary as the forum for settling his dispute. The plaintiff was not aware of the transfer of court jurisdictions as stipulated by Amended Law 3 of 2006 that had been passed two years before he submitted the case to the civil judiciary of Jantho. He preferred to go to the civil judiciary simply because he hoped that through this court's adjudication he would win his case. As K. von Benda-Beckmann (1981) pointed out, a disputant may selectively and interchangeably use a particular forum that she or he thinks will be advantageous for her or his interests. While attending hearings at the Civil Court of Jantho, I had an opportunity to ask the plaintiff why he had gone to the civil judiciary. He explained that the civil judiciary was an impartial institution that had not dealt with this case before. By having the civil judiciary examine his case, Dahlan felt that he would be fairly treated. Above all, as he had lost the case in 1994, he considered the religious judicature to be unfair.

The defendant in this case, the village treasury, was represented by a lawyer who had graduated from the local university of Banda Aceh. In response to the plaintiff's claim, the lawyer contended that the case was about a decision of non-appearance issued by the Religious Court of Jantho back in 1994. For this reason, he considered that the Civil Court of Jantho had no legitimacy, but that Jantho's sharia court should examine the case. Additionally, referring to the 2006 Amending Law on the Religious Judicature, which stipulates that any dispute of property ownership that involves Muslim litigants belongs to the religious judicature's jurisdiction, the lawyer demanded that the Mahkamah Syar'iyah of Jantho should have authority over this particular case.

Learning from its experience of having a previous decision on a similar case cancelled by the Higher Court, the Jantho Civil Court declared that it had full jurisdiction to evaluate the case. In fact, the judges of this court issued a *putusan sela* (interlocutory decision) to justify their position. Although the Indonesian procedural law allows either of the contending parties to challenge an interlocutory decision by appealing to the higher court, the defendant's lawyer did not take this option. Instead, the lawyer preferred to have the case proceed at the civil judiciary. This was because he felt confident about the evidence of property ownership that his client retained. He believed that, regardless of the legal forum in which the case was judged, his client's position would not be disadvantaged. It seems that the lawyer had envisaged the outcome of an appeal, should he challenge the jurisdiction of the Civil Court further in the Higher Civil Court in Banda Aceh. It is most probable that the appellate judges would strengthen the interlocutory decision of the lower court's judges. In fact, in the view of the lawyer, questioning the jurisdiction of the civil judiciary by appealing in the higher courts concerning the problem of contested jurisdiction would only protract the settlement of the case, or, more precisely, the victory of his client.

In connection with the shift towards increased authority for the sharia courts in contemporary Aceh (see Chapter 2), the legal reasoning given to underpin the legitimacy of the civil judiciary of Jantho in examining this case is worth discussing. Despite the 2006 Amending Law, which stipulated that ownership disputes involving Muslims should be transferred to the religious judicature, the judges of Jantho's Civil Court appeared quite reluctant to accept this new legal reconfiguration. In their view, the property rights disputes that belong to the religious judicature were basically related to matters of inheritance, while the dispute regarding ownership of property that they were examining now was different. In my interview with Sugiyanto, the chief judge who led the panel that examined the case, he clarified that this particular case had two contested sources of ownership: the first ownership was through inheritance, while the second ownership was derived by way of a court decision.[12] Because of the nature of this particular ownership dispute, he and his two colleagues were of the opinion that the case should be adjudicated by the civil judiciary, and not by the religious judicature. Sugiyanto further emphasised that if all kinds of ownership dispute where either disputant was a Muslim were transferred to the jurisdiction of the Mahkamah Syar'iyah, the Civil Court of Aceh would be left only with cases that were brought forward by non-Muslims. As the non-Muslim population in Aceh is very small, this would eventually turn the civil judiciary into a special court; something fundamentally paradoxical to the positioning of the civil judiciary as the general judicature in the Indonesian legal system.

The case proceeded with some hearings and evidence presentation. To support his claim, Dahlan called six witnesses, but only two of them offered credible evidence. Nevertheless, the judges did not take their testimony into account, as these witnesses knew the case through the so-called '*testimonium de auditu*', a kind of testimony based on information obtained by listening to others who repeat a story. The judges finally declined Dahlan's claim and granted the village treasury ownership of the land. Nonetheless, the case did not stop at this tribunal. Dahlan made an appeal to the Higher Civil Court of Banda Aceh. This appeal was again fruitless.

Continuing to feel dissatisfied with the decision of the Higher Civil Court that had gone against him, Dahlan submitted the case to Indonesia's Supreme Court in Jakarta. In his memorandum of appeal, Dahlan included two of his sisters as defendants, whereas previously, at the lower courts, they had both been plaintiffs, represented by Dahlan. It had been revealed during the hearings at the lower court that, in compliance with the earlier court's decision, the village treasury had received the transfer of the control of the land in question from Dahlan's two sisters. As the village treasury acknowledged and confirmed this fact, Dahlan thought that his claim of ownership over the land in question as inheritance property was lawful. The Supreme Court's judges, however, not only reinforced all decisions made by the lower courts, but also considered that legal matters introduced by Dahlan were beyond their focus. The examination of a case at this level is restricted merely to cross-checking whether or not all required procedural law, including the court's jurisdiction, has been appropriately upheld. Dahlan's claim was again rejected.

Adopted and Retained Jurisdiction

While the civil judiciary sought to retain its existing jurisdiction on property rights disputes, the religious judicature wanted to extend its jurisdiction to include these disputes. To establish its newly annexed jurisdiction, the religious judicature often emphasised the nature of the cases it examined and maintained that they had involved disputes between Muslims over Islamic property rights (joint marital property, inheritance, bequests, grants, land endowments, Islamic alms, gifts, donations and sharia finance). For this reason, a salient feature of the cases in which the two state courts (civil judiciary and religious judicature) compete for jurisdiction is that the disputes involved are mostly between relatives connected by blood or through marital relationships.

A post-tsunami dispute over certified land, submitted to Banda Aceh's Mahkamah Syar'iyah in 2006, was considered as concerning both inheritance and joint marital property, despite the defendant's claim that the dispute was over property rights and therefore belonged to the jurisdiction of the civil judiciary. The plaintiffs, who were siblings of a deceased wife, claimed that the land in question was a *peunulang* (gift) from the wife's parent. It has been customary in some parts of Aceh for parents to give a parcel of land to their daughter at the time of her marriage (Hoesin 1970). The plaintiffs were therefore shocked to discover that the gifted land belonging to their sister had been certified in the name of the defendant (their sister's ex-husband) without their knowledge. The defendant, whose name appeared on the land certificate, claimed full ownership and refuted the argument of the plaintiffs. He rejected the plaintiffs' claim by referring to Government Regulation 24 of 1997 on Land Registration, which stipulates that the court cannot accept any claim made by a third party against the validity of a land certificate that has been published for more than five years. Additionally, as the land certificate was already in his name, the ex-husband argued that the land had nothing to do with the inheritance estate.

Against the ex-husband's counter-claim, the plaintiffs brought into the courtroom several witnesses who confirmed that the land was a gift, or personal property acquired through the peunulang process, and who regarded this as a common local practice of land transfer from a parent to a daughter. The plaintiffs therefore asked the sharia court not only to cancel the land certificate, but also to declare that the disputed land was peunulang property and that their sister owned it as part of the gift from her parents. The deceased wife's siblings further claimed that, in the absence of surviving children, they would be legitimate heirs and entitled to receive some share of the land left by their deceased sister.

In consideration of these facts, the Mahkamah Syar'iyah of Banda Aceh decided to refute the defendant's objection. The judges of this sharia court not only stated that this case was a matter of inheritance and joint marital property, but also claimed full jurisdiction over cases of this kind, even if they related to the issue of disputed property ownership. On the grounds of Law 3 of 2006, that amended Law 7 of 1989 on the Religious Judicature, the judges of Mahkamah Syar'iyah were bold enough to argue that this case did not involve an expiry date as it did not deal with the issue of land certification. Rather, the sharia court viewed the disputed land as joint marital property that was acquired during the period of marriage of the couple. The land parcel was part of the inheritance estate of the deceased wife and hence must be divided between the ex-husband (defendant) and the wife's siblings (plaintiffs). In the view of judges, the witnesses had not convincingly proved the legal transfer of the peunulang land to the daughter (the deceased wife) from her parent. These witnesses gave a testimony before the court based only on what they had heard from others who had told the story, and had never listened to or watched such a transfer from the parent to the propositus.

On the other hand, the jurisdiction of the civil judiciary over disputes regarding ownership of property continued to survive by way of the particular claim of *perbuatan melawan hukum* or *onrechtmatigedaad* (the commission of a tort). This kind of case is often submitted by Muslim plaintiffs to the civil tribunals to make a claim over land. Article 1365 of the Indonesian Civil Code regulates this concept of unlawful act or 'acts which break the law'. The law states that 'every illegitimate act, which causes damage to third parties, obliges the party at fault to pay for the damage caused'. This means that a person who causes loss to another person, through an act that breaks the law, is held responsible for causing that loss, and is therefore obliged to provide compensation. The civil judiciary is exclusively entitled to examine this kind of tort case, and a number of Islamic property disputes have been registered at the civil judiciary this way. Another case study from the Civil Court of Jantho in 2012, outlined below, demonstrates this jurisdictional dispute.

The case was brought by children of Ibrahim (plaintiffs) versus descendants of Ali (defendants). The plaintiffs claimed that their land had been seized by Ali's mother, who then granted it to Ali. The granting of this land (hibah) was recorded before a land registrar in 1999. When both Ali and his mother died, the property was passed to Ali's heirs (the defendants). The plaintiffs considered that a tort (in this case, a land seizure) had taken place, and so they submitted the case to the civil judiciary.

The defendants responded that the civil judiciary of Jantho did not have jurisdiction to hear this case. They contended that a tort did not apply here because the case was only about hibah and inheritance. Furthermore, they considered that the civil judiciary did not have jurisdiction because both litigants were Muslims. In the view of defendants, this case was only about whether a *hibah tanah* (granting of land) was lawful or not, which comes under the sharia court's jurisdiction. Additionally, the defendants put forward Jantho Religious Court's previous decision, 9 of 1991, on the piece of land now in question, in which it had declared that Ali's mother was the landowner against a claim made by different people (non-heirs of Ibrahim).

The judges of Jantho's Civil Court, however, rejected all the defendants' objections and counter-claims. The judges considered that this was a dispute over property rights between the heirs of different families. As it was not an inheritance dispute within a single family, the judges claimed full jurisdiction to examine the case. In addition, they viewed evidence presented by the defendants as weaker than a land certificate that belonged to the plaintiffs' father, which was dated in 1982. According to the judges, in evaluating two or more records of land ownership, ownership should be determined by looking at which one had a higher status or which had been issued first. The 1982 land ownership certificate belonging to the plaintiffs not only had a higher status, but also preceded the 1999 grant transfer record that purportedly justified ownership by the defendants. Furthermore, the Civil Court did not accept the 1991 Religious Court's decision as grounds for land entitlement. The judges finally decided that the defendants had committed a tort in this case, and they were therefore required to return the land in question to the plaintiffs.

Conclusion

The shift in plural legal orders in Aceh is not as straightforward as might be thought. This chapter has shown that the broadening of the jurisdiction of Islamic courts does not necessarily bring about a major shift towards allowing Islamic dominance in many legal issues, including land disputes between Muslim litigants. In fact, there has been a clear sign of resistance arising out of civil tribunals against the expanding jurisdiction of Aceh's Mahkamah Syar'iyah. This further suggests that the expectation of those who sought to push for the Mahkamah Syar'iyah to play a much greater role for Muslims in Aceh remains on hold for the time being.

Notes

1. Husnaini is a judge of the Religious Court of Banjarmasin, South Kalimantan.
2. Aridi and Natsir Asnawi are both judges of the Religious Court of Yogyakarta.
3. Abdul Manan is a judge of the Indonesia Supreme Court. He is attached to the Religious Court branch of the Supreme Court.
4. See decisions of both the Bireuen Civil Court (08/Pdt.G/2006/PN-Bir) and the Jantho Civil Court (03/Pdt.G/2007/PN-JTH).
5. Added emphasis.
6. The term 'propositus' is derived from medical science to indicate the first person to whom a genealogic lineage is traced, as is done to discover the pattern of inheritable diseases. This term is used here to denote a man or woman who dies and leaves the estate to be inherited by his or her heirs. The use of this term is observable in a number of works that discuss Islamic inheritance law, such as Carroll (1998) and Lukito (2012).
7. For more details, see the two decisions of the Higher Civil Court: No. 60/PDT/2006/PT-BNA and No. 13/PDT/2008/PT-BNA.
8. Interview with Judge Yasrin Nasution, 1 July 2008.
9. See, for instance, court decisions in *Halimah binti Arsyad cs.* v. *Ahmad Yacob cs.*, 08/Pdt.G/2008/PN-BNA; 21/PDT/2009/PT-BNA; 2851 K/Pdt/2009.
10. See a decision of the Supreme Court in *Said Syarief* v. *Said Ilyas cs.*, 3083 K/Pdt/2011.
11. Interview with the plaintiff, Dahlan, 14 April 2008.
12. Interview with Judge Sugiyanto, 1 May 2008.

Part Two

Between Justice and Rights

Chapter 4

Unequal Legal Options

> [Although] the defendant is Buddhist, he has declared that he would voluntarily
> subject himself to the Qanun of Aceh 12 of 2003 on liquor [prohibition].
> The defendant also signed a statement that he would
> be ready to be prosecuted under the Qanun.
> [In fact,] in the first hearing, the defendant stated before the judges that
> he made an option for his offence to be adjudicated based on the Qanun.
>
> Public prosecutor of Meulabouh, West Aceh

Differences in juridical doctrine and practice among Muslims have existed since the early period of Islam. Historically, a unified form of legal structure for different communities was not a popular approach in an Islamic territory. Islamic legal singularity or the centralisation of Islamic law by Muslim dynasties was not common. In fact, most Muslim dynasties at various times and in various places recognised and accepted intra- and extra-legal pluralism among Muslims themselves and among other religious communities.

The millet system of the Ottoman Empire is perhaps a good example of how legal pluralism was present at some previous times in Islamic history. The millet system of the Ottoman Empire lasted for more than 400 years. It was founded during the reign of Sultan Mohammed II (1451–81 CE), but by the mid-nineteenth century it had gradually been abolished. The millet system was introduced to enable the Ottoman Empire to cope with socio-political problems resulting from diverse and complex ethnic and religious identities. Through the establishment of the millet system, the Ottoman government granted virtual sovereignty to each religious community, in perpetuity, without its being subject to renewal, abolition or limitation. Each of the religious communities (for example, Jewish and Christian) had the right to preserve its own courts, to appoint judges and to apply legal principles for the use of co-religionists (Shaw 1976: 151; Braude 1982: 69–81; Karpat 1982: 141–6).

As pointed out by Timur Kuran (2004: 476), Islam has a distinct version of legal pluralism. Islamic legal pluralism gave Muslims fewer options than it gave to Christians or Jews. Comparing Muslim majorities and non-Muslim minorities who were subjects of the Ottoman Empire during the eighteenth and nineteenth centuries, Kuran (2004: 476–7) discovered that non-Muslims were free to choose and move between the different jurisdictions of the Islamic court system and their own autonomous denominational courts. Meanwhile, however, in business disputes, this choice of court was not available to Muslim subjects. Thus, in commercial disputes in particular, the Ottoman millet system provided unequal legal options (that is, in the choice of legal forum) for Muslim and non-Muslim subjects. However, in criminal matters all were subject, regardless of their religious backgrounds, to the exclusive jurisdiction of the Islamic court (Kuran 2004: 484). The fact that Muslim litigants must submit their financial disputes only to the Islamic court, whereas non-Muslims were allowed to go to any of the different jurisdictions, has been regarded as asymmetric legal pluralism in which broader legal options are available for some particular groups, but not for others (Kuran 2004: 507).

Drawing on Kuran's study, as cited above, this chapter investigates similar situations found in the millet system in contemporary Indonesia. Elsewhere (Salim 2008) I have pointed out that the Ministry of Religious Affairs sought to transform the Ottoman millet system into its own new Indonesian version. Since its inception, the ministry has initiated and shaped most of the legislation in terms of religious categories by infusing religious identity as the key criterion for classification, thus building walls between citizens of different religions. The official establishment of Islamic courts in 1989 strengthened this particular kind of religious configuration in Indonesia, where a variety of legal sub-systems has been acknowledged in the realm of a unified Indonesian legal system.

As will be discussed in the following sections, a system similar to the Ottoman millet system has appeared in contemporary Aceh, albeit with differences. Unlike the Ottoman millet system, which gave neither Muslims nor non-Muslims the option of moving between different legal regimes in criminal jurisdictions, the special autonomy of Aceh does allow non-Muslims plural legal options in the implementation of sharia penal laws. This choice of law, however, is not available to Muslims. Muslim offenders in Aceh have no right to opt out of being adjudicated and sentenced by the Syar'iyah Court. This chapter thus argues that although pluralism is very central in Islamic legal thought and practice, in the context of the current implementation of sharia criminal laws in Aceh it is ignored, thereby making legal options unequal.

Plural Legal Options: Colonial Legacy

Plural legal options in dispute and crime settlements are twofold: choice of law and choice of forum. In choosing a forum in which to settle a dispute, litigants look for the applicable law that they prefer. Similarly, in choosing a particular applicable law, disputants or offenders favour a specific forum.

Plural legal options are available in the legal system of a country largely due to the same legal configuration having been in the system that preceded it. Plural orders in Indonesia's legal system are the legacy of the Dutch colonial legal structure, which was based mostly on racial or ethnic groups. The Dutch colonial administration treated diverse groups of the Netherlands East Indies population differently, based on their racial classification (Fasseur 1994).

When ruling the East Indies (the former name of Indonesia), the Dutch colonial system classified its subjects into three legal classes: Europeans, Indigenous Islanders and foreign Easterners. Each group had its own legal system: separate regulations administered by different government officials and enforced in separate courts of law (Burns 2004; Mills 2006; Lukito 2012). For Europeans (and also for Japanese and Indonesian aristocrats), the laws that applied were the European laws applicable in the Netherlands; for Indigenous Islanders (that is, ordinary Indonesians), the applicable laws were the customary laws of their own communities; and for Foreign Easterners (Chinese, Arabs and Indians), each of these ethnic communities was free to have its own laws.

In addition, in 1917, a regulation, entitled *Vrijwillige Onderwerping aan het Europeesch Privaatrecht* (Voluntary Subjection to the European Private Law), was introduced to allow both Indigenous Islanders and foreign Easterners to voluntarily make themselves subject to European laws (Mills 2006). This voluntary legal subjection to European laws was observed in various ways, by: (1) total subjection, (2) partial subjection, (3) ad hoc subjection and (4) presumptive subjection (Lukito 2012: 237). As this regulation was not applicable to Europeans, and only provided Indigenous Islanders and Foreign Easterners with the right to opt for laws other than their own, it engendered a sense of inequality before the law. Different laws were applied to different groups of the East Indies' population. Under this scheme, Europeans were considered to have higher legal status than the other groups.

All these systems continued even after Indonesia's independence in 1945. For the new state of Indonesia, this colonial legal classification and these plural legal options were actually at odds with the principle of the independent state that treats all nationals as equal before the law. Nevertheless, despite all the efforts that have been made to include all its citizens under the same laws, the Indonesian state has been unable to develop the unification of law within its legal system. Although some Indonesian national legislation (such as Basic Agrarian Law 5 of 1960 and Marriage Law 1 of 1974) have sought to appeal to legal centralism, all these laws have eventually resulted in legal pluralism (Donovan 1998). The unification of law largely exists only on paper, while, in practice, the independent state of Indonesia continues with the Dutch legacy of a plural legal system.

The Dutch provision for voluntary legal subjection, as mentioned above, has, in fact, become a reference for re-establishing plural legal options in the current legal system of Indonesia. This regulation inspired Indonesian legal scholars and lawyers to adopt and apply it in other legal contexts. Perhaps, the first evidence of this was Law 7 of 1989 on the Islamic Religious Judicature. Article 49 of this law stipulated jurisdictions of the Religious Courts in Indonesia that included mainly Islamic personal and family laws. However, the law provided choices of law for Muslims in property disputes.

Legal Options in Islamic Inheritance

Despite inheritance being allocated to the jurisdiction of the Religious Court, which would apply Islamic inheritance law, each Muslim disputant may consider choosing which law to apply to in inheritance division. The Indonesian government was aware that some sections of Muslim communities in Indonesia were unwilling to apply Islamic inheritance law in dividing the inheritance estate and, instead, preferred the customary law. For this reason, legal options were made available for Muslims in settling inheritance disputes. Those who wanted a settlement based on Islamic law should go to the Religious Court, while those who preferred to use the principles of customary law, or even the Dutch heritage civil law, in solving their inheritance disputes, should file the case at the General Court (Lukito 2012: 100).

A year after the enactment of the 1989 Law on the Religious Judicature, the Supreme Court circulated a letter, 2 of 1990, to all state courts under its supervision clarifying how to deal practically with plural legal options in inheritance disputes. According to this letter, choices of law take place before a case is brought before the judge. Once a Muslim disputant has chosen and registered the case at the Religious Court, another disputant loses the right to bring the inheritance case to another legal forum. If, however, both disputants simultaneously register the case in different courts, the Supreme Court must be invited to resolve a jurisdictional dispute between the two lower courts. The case is then considered pending until the Supreme Court has decided which of two courts has legitimacy to adjudicate the case.

In the view of some Muslim leaders and Islamic judges, plural legal options, as such, were unnecessary, partly because having such options would incline one to think that the Religious Court does not have all-inclusive legitimacy, which is contradictory to the fact that it is one of the official state courts in Indonesia. Indonesia's Islamic judicature therefore sought to eliminate this right to choices of law, and eventually succeeded when Law 3 of 2006 cancelled plural legal options in inheritance disputes. To establish a complete jurisdiction over all Islamic legal family issues, this law provides that the Religious Court is the only venue in which Muslims may settle a dispute on inheritance. Thus, the faith of the disputants became a determinant factor in ruling to which court an inheritance case should be brought. Should any of the immediate family members of the deceased have a faith other than Islam, the Religious Court would consider him or her ineligible to a portion of the inheritance.

Although this law cancelled plural legal options in inheritance disputes, plural legal options remain in practice, especially when there is a dispute over the ownership of the property in question. The discussion of various cases of competing jurisdictions between the religious judicature and the civil judiciary in Chapter 3 confirms this contention. As shown in the previous chapter, Muslims in Indonesia apparently still enjoy plural legal options. They remain free to bring a case, on property disputes in particular, to be examined by the Civil Court.

LEGAL OPTIONS IN ISLAMIC BANKING AND FINANCE

In non-penal issues, plural legal options for Muslims remain. Although Law 3 of 2006 stipulates that the new jurisdictions of the Religious Court include commercial cases, including disputes on sharia finance, it could not force Muslims to discard their rights to choices of law and choices of forum. This is because other relevant legislation, such as Law 21 of 2008 on sharia banking, provides Islamic banks (including non-Islamic banks that operate based on the sharia system) and their customers with a right to settle disputes at a legal forum other than the Religious Court, such as the Civil Court.

Basically, according to Law 21 of 2008 on sharia banking (Article 55: 1–2), the Religious Court has authority to deal with any kind of sharia banking dispute. Nevertheless, apart from submitting a case to the Religious Court, parties involved (for example, an Islamic bank and its customers) may also make an agreement in their written contract that, should a dispute arise, they are free to settle such dispute based on selected legal means to which they have both agreed and have written into the contract, including bringing the dispute to the Civil Court. The elucidation of this Article clarifies that such means of dispute settlements as are written into the contract could take the form of one of the following options: (1) *musyawarah* (mutual consultation); (2) banking mediation; (3) mediation through the National Sharia Arbitration Board; and (4) adjudication by the Civil Court. Given this arrangement, one can surely argue that plural legal options remain possible in sharia banking disputes, especially by way of written agreement. This means that in the absence of a written agreement on dispute settlement, all disputes related to sharia banking and finance would be examined by the Religious Court.

What about non-Muslims? Do they have plural legal options in financial or commercial disputes? What would happen if they had a dispute with an Islamic financial institution? As a general rule, non-Muslim disputants have to go to the Civil Court to settle disputes that relate to ownership and contracts. However, when it comes to disputes in Islamic finance where no prior written agreement has been made regarding legal settlement, non-Muslim parties have no option other than to submit their case to the Religious Court.

Although some have argued that the Elucidation of Law 3 of 2006 has provided non-Muslims with a right to choices of law in Islamic financial disputes,[1] this provision is not precisely about plural legal options for non-Muslim disputants. The tone of this provision suggests that non-Muslims must be presumed to have automatically submitted themselves (*veronderstelde onderwerping*) to the jurisdiction of the Religious Court that will apply Islamic law. Since they have no freedom to move across legal orders, plural legal options for non-Muslims in Islamic financial disputes do not exist. As pointed out by Supreme Court Justice Rifyal Ka'bah, all involved parties, even if they are non-Muslims, are considered to have become voluntarily subject to Islamic commercial laws once they sign a contract on sharia banking services and products.[2] From this description, not only are plural legal options observable, but also voluntary legal subjection is implied for non-Muslims in Islamic commercial disputes. As this legal arrangement is already in place for non-Muslims in financial cases nationally, its local application in criminal offences for non-Muslims in Aceh is not a novel invention.

Choice of Laws for non-Muslims in Aceh

As part of Indonesia, Aceh has experienced legal pluralism in many ways. Plural legal orders (as discussed in the previous chapter) are not the only legal reality. Since 2006, plural legal options have been introduced in Aceh by two national laws. The first was Law 11 of 2006 on the Governance of Aceh,[3] which added a new jurisdiction on Islamic criminal offences to the Syar'iyah Court of Aceh. The second was Law 3 of 2006, which amended the law on Religious Judiciary issued previously in 1989. This amending law extended the jurisdiction of all religious courts in Indonesia, including the Syar'iyah Court in Aceh, to cover a wide variety of commercial issues and property disputes whose litigants are Muslim. Beginning from 2006, as a means of viable legal settlement, the Syar'iyah Court could adjudicate ownership disputes that involved Muslim litigants.

With these two laws, plural legal options were established for both Muslims and non-Muslims to choose between two different state courts: the Syar'iyah and General Civil Judicatures. Nevertheless, different conditions govern the legal options available to Muslims and to non-Muslims. In some commercial disputes, non-Muslim litigants in Aceh must stay with the General Judicature, while Muslim parties in particular situations have the option to go to either of the state courts. Yet in certain penal trials, non-Muslims who commit an offence have a right to opt for being adjudicated by the Syar'iyah Court or otherwise, while Muslim offenders are not allowed to move between jurisdictions, but must stay with the Syar'iyah Court of Aceh.

Initially, during the discussion at the national legislature of Law 11 of 2006 of the Governance of Aceh, some Islamic parties proposed that sharia law should be applied not only to Muslims who live in Aceh, but also to all residents of Aceh regardless of their religious beliefs. The Syar'iyah Court would then be the only state court to examine penal cases in Aceh, including adjudicating offences committed by Aceh's non-Muslim residents.

A number of Christian politicians were against the proposal. They refused to agree that Islamic sharia should be applied to non-Muslims residents of Aceh, and contended that the Islamic Court of Aceh had no authority to judge cases involving non-Muslim citizens. Instead, it was suggested by a Christian-based party (PDS) and a big nationalist party (PDIP) that non-Muslims be given the freedom to choose the law under which they would be tried.

Responding to this suggestion of plural legal options for those involved in penal offences, the State Secretary, Yusril Ihza Mahendra (who was also a leader of an Islamic party), disagreed, and insisted that Muslims and non-Muslims should be tried by the same Islamic court. Expressing his disagreement, he was quoted as saying: 'In the case of adultery, non-Muslims who committed adultery with Muslims would undoubtedly opt for trial by the Criminal Code because it was more lenient than the stoning or other forms of corporal punishment stipulated under Islamic Law.'[4] Mahendra was probably right, as a person's choice is often motivated by cost–benefit calculations. Non-Muslim offenders in Aceh would thus be likely go to a court that gives a lighter sentence.

Looking for a compromise, Golkar, the former ruling party during the New Order period, offered a solution that sought to accommodate the two contending positions outlined above. It was recommended that sharia penal law should be applied to non-Muslims in Aceh on two conditions: (1) that they had committed crimes against Muslim residents; and (2) that they had engaged in criminal offences jointly with Muslims.[5] After continued discussion, the final draft provision on criminal jurisdiction maintained that the Syar'iyah Court had conditional authority to adjudicate non-Muslim offenders.

Article 129 of Law 11 of 2006 stipulates two conditions. The first concerns plural legal options for non-Muslims: 'In the event of an Islamic criminal act [jinayat] committed jointly by two or more persons, among whom are one or more non-Muslims, the alleged non-Muslim perpetrator(s) may choose to submit themselves to jinayat [Islamic penal] law [instead of the National Criminal Code].' However, the second condition states that there is no choice of law for non-Muslims: 'Any non-Muslim who commits jinayat which is not covered by the National Criminal Code or by other criminal provisions outside the Criminal Code shall have jinayat law applied to his/her case.' Thus, there is ambiguity concerning the arrangement with regard to plural legal options for non-Muslims in Aceh. While the former provision clearly upholds the choice of laws, the latter seems to restrict plural legal options in the absence of similar penal rules at the national level. This may lead one to think that national legislations are overruled by regional regulations, while in fact, according to Indonesia's legal system, national legislations have higher status than regional regulations.

Islamic Crimes in Aceh: Three Implementing Principles

The rules concerning the criminal jurisdiction of the Syar'iyah Court (as provided in Article 129 of Law 11 of 2006 on the Governance of Aceh) have ushered in the discussion of three principles in the implementation of Islamic penal laws in Aceh.

The first is the territorial principle. This means that all residents of Aceh, whether they are Acehnese who live permanently in Aceh or visitors coming to and staying in Aceh for certain periods, are subject to the jurisdiction of Islamic criminal justice. If an offence is committed within the boundaries of the Aceh region, this territorial principle covers perpetrators who are Muslim or non-Muslim, Acehnese or non-Acehnese, and Indonesian citizens or foreign citizens. This principle was reinforced by the provision of Article 129(2) of Law 11 of 2006. This provision maintains that any non-Muslim who commits an offence that is not regulated in the national penal law or other laws would have Islamic criminal law imposed on him or her. There is no doubt that certain sharia laws would be applied to non-Muslims, especially those that are not included in any national laws, such as *khalwat* (close proximity or intimacy) between people of different sexes who have no marriage relationship. In connection with this, a local Aceh newspaper, *Serambi*, reported on 24 July 2006 that an Italian working for an international NGO in Aceh was caught committing khalwat with an

Acehnese girl. It was also discovered that the man had used an illegal drug. The couple was taken to the police office. Yet it was unknown whether they were eventually prosecuted because of the khalwat or not. Commenting on this incident, a local elder in Banda Aceh was quoted as saying that he hoped anyone who violated sharia law (in Aceh) would be punished in accordance with the applicable qanun regardless of whether they were non-Indonesians.

The second principle is the personal principle. This infers that the basis for the implementation of sharia in Aceh is religious adherence to Islam. Any Muslims (whether or not they are Acehnese or permanently domiciled in Aceh) who commit an offence regulated in jinayat law are liable to be adjudicated by the Syar'iyah Court. Under this principle, non-Muslims are theoretically excluded. This principle, in fact, is the very basis of the implementation of sharia in Aceh. An earlier legislation on the Special Autonomy of Aceh (Article 25 of Law 18 of 2001) maintained that the authority of Aceh's Religious Court extends only to judging disputes between, or offences committed by, Muslims.

The former head of the Sharia Provincial Office, Al Yasa Abubakar, explained that non-Muslims in Aceh are not subject to the implementation of sharia, principally for two reasons (Abubakar 2006). The first is that their freedom must be respected and protected. As compliance with sharia law is required only for Muslim individuals, it is very unwise to make non-Muslim persons bound by sharia. The second reason is that because of the small size (less than 2 per cent) of the population of non-Muslims in Aceh (see Appendix I), it would be difficult for non-Muslims if they were required to comply with regulations imposed for the Muslim majority.

The third principle is that of voluntary legal subjection. This principle is the exception rather than the rule in the implementation of sharia in Aceh. It has been regulated that it is the personal principle, incorporating the jinayat rule, which is to be applied in all cases. However, if non-Muslims, for one reason or another, are happy to voluntarily choose to comply with a particular sharia law in the qanun, their choice is considered valid and acceptable.[6] As discussed earlier, this voluntary legal subjection principle already existed in Indonesia prior to the introduction of Law 11 of 2006.

To further support this principle, Abubakar (2006: 146) offered a particular legal reasoning to justify the voluntarily submission by non-Muslims (especially by Protestants, of whom, according to the 2010 census, there were about 40,000, constituting the second largest religious community after Muslims in Aceh) to the jurisdiction of sharia law in Aceh. Referring to the Protestants' standpoint when Indonesian marriage law was discussed and ratified in the early 1970s, Abubakar (2006: 147) explained that the Protestant churches refused to agree to the point that stipulates that marriage becomes valid only if it is undertaken by way of religious law, because, unlike Islam, their religion does not have its own divine law. The Protestants argued that imposing marriage laws in Indonesia for believers in different faiths, based on their respective religious laws, would have compelled Protestants to invent new religious (legal) norms in marriage – something that would be considered religious innovation or heresy according to the Protestant faith. Thus, the marriage law for Protestants is not religious law, but the national state law, Law 1 of 1974 on Marriage. With this mode of reasoning, Abubakar (2006: 147) argued that any part of sharia law that was adopted by the official state law would very likely be accepted by Protestants in Aceh. This is because, according to Abubakar (2006), what would bind them are actually the state laws (that is, Qanuns of Aceh), and not certain particular religious laws. After all, as he pointed out, none of the Protestants' religious teachings would be violated if, instead of going to the Civil Court, they decide to be examined by the Syar'iyah Court.

LIQUOR CONSUMPTION: BETWEEN QANUN AND THE NATIONAL CODE

The choice of courts or the choice of laws has been possible in Aceh for non-Muslim perpetrators of offences against Islamic criminal law (jinayat) because of two parallel laws (with different contents) that regulate the same offences. One is derived from the national law, which is widely applicable in Indonesia, and the other stems from Aceh's regional regulation, which applies locally within the province of Aceh. Although they contain rules on the same criminal offences, these regulations are not always similar, especially concerning the underlying norms, the sanctioned acts and the forms of punishment.

Let us take as an example liquor consumption and everything related to it that is considered an offence. The big difference between the two laws has been what kind of acts are considered criminal. No one denies that the qanun has a wider scope than the national regulations. While all liquor-related issues have been codified in Aceh's Qanun 12 of 2003, reference to the same issue stipulated in the National Criminal Code is limited (Articles 300, 492, 536, 537, 538 and 539). Table 4.1 summarises the differences between local and national regulations.

According to the National Criminal Code, a person is not punishable just for the consumption of liquor. As long as the person drinks and gets drunk at home, no single criminal offence is violated. He or she is liable to punishment only when there are damaging consequences from the drinking of alcoholic beverages. Likewise, selling liquor with an alcohol content of less than 55 per cent in authorised places to persons who are not drunk is not considered an infringement of Indonesian penal laws. All these actions, however, are totally banned and penalised in Aceh. While national regulations were intended to restrict the

Table 4.1 Regulations on liquor in Aceh and Indonesia

No.	Issues related to liquor	Aceh's Qanun 12 of 2003: Provisions (Articles 5–8)	Aceh's Qanun 12 of 2003: Penalties (Article 26)	National regulations*: Provisions	National regulations*: Penalties
01	Self-consuming	Prohibited for anyone and penalised in all situations within Aceh's territory	40 lashes (for Muslims only)	Penalised if one gets drunk on the street and endangers others or public order	Jail: 6 days–3 months (Arts 492 and 536 of Criminal Code)
				Penalised if drunken person causes severe injuries or another's death	Jail: 7–9 years (Art. 300 of Criminal Code)
02	Selling and trading	Prohibited and penalised anywhere in Aceh's territory for anyone and any business enterprises or corporates, including international ones owned by, or employing, foreigners	Jail: 3 months–1 year and/or Fines: 25–75 million rupiah	Penalised if sold to drunken person, sold to lower rank soldiers outside military canteen, or sold to underage children	Jail: 3 weeks–max 1 year (Arts 300, 537, 538 of Criminal Code)
				If granted Ministry's permission, liquor at less than 55% alcohol is allowed to be sold in hotels, bars, restaurants or authorised venues that are not close to places of worship, schools or hospitals	
03	Producing	Prohibited and penalised for anyone and business enterprises or corporates, including international ones owned by, or employing, foreigners	Jail: 3 months–1 year and/or Fines: 25–75 million rupiah	Liquor less than 55% alcohol allowed if granted Ministry's permission	Licence temporarily suspended or revoked if exceeding granted permission
04	Providing and serving	Prohibited and penalised for anyone and business enterprises or corporates, including international ones owned by, or employing, foreigners	Jail: 3 months–1 year and/or Fines: 25–75 million rupiah	Penalised if forcing person or underage children to get drunk	Jail up to 1 year (Art. 300 of Criminal Code)
				Penalised if providing free liquor in a public party or promising it as a prize	Jail for 12 days (Art. 539 of Criminal Code)
05	Keeping and stocking	Prohibited and penalised for anyone and business enterprises or corporates, including international ones owned by, or employing, foreigners	Jail: 3 months–1 year and/or Fines: 25–75 million rupiah	Liquor less than 55% alcohol allowed if granted Ministry's permission	Licence temporarily suspended or revoked if exceeding granted permission

Table 4.1 (continued)

		Aceh's Qanun 12 of 2003		*National regulations**	
No.	*Issues related to liquor*	*Provisions (Articles 5–8)*	*Penalties (Article 26)*	*Provisions*	*Penalties*
06	Distributing and supplying	Prohibited and penalised for anyone and business enterprises or corporates, including international ones owned by, or employing, foreigners	Jail: 3 months–1 year and/or Fines: 25–75 million rupiah	Allowed if distributed and supplied to hotels, bars, restaurants or authorised venues not close to places of worship, schools or hospitals	
07	Promoting	Prohibited and penalised for anyone and business enterprises or corporates, including international ones owned by, or employing, foreigners	Jail: 3 months–1 year and/or Fines: 25–75 million rupiah	Not allowed for importers, distributors or sellers	Penalised with relevant criminal legislation
08	Importing and transporting	Prohibited and penalised for anyone and business enterprises or corporates, including international ones owned by, or employing, foreigners	Jail: 3 months–1 year and/or Fines: 25–75 million rupiah	Liquor less than 55% alcohol allowed if granted Ministry's permission	Licence temporarily suspended or revoked if exceeding granted permission
09	Assisting or jointly doing 2–8 above	Prohibited and penalised for anyone and business enterprises or corporates, including international ones owned by, or employing, foreigners	Jail: 3 months–1 year and/or Fines: 25–75 million rupiah	Allowed if granted Ministry's permission	Licence temporarily suspended or revoked if exceeding granted permission
10	Issuing permission for supply of liquor for hotel, restaurants, etc.	Prohibited and penalised for all government institutions	Jail: 3 months–1 year and/or Fines: 25–75 million rupiah	Allowed for mayors/regents and governor of Jakarta	

* National regulations include the National Criminal Code, Presidential Decision 3 of 1997 and regulations issued by the Minister of Trades (359 of 1997, 15 of 2006, 43 of 2009, 53 of 2010 and 11 of 2012). There are fines mentioned as penalties in the National Criminal Code. As it was a colonial legacy, the Code refers to the equivalent currency during Dutch colonial times. The amounts of money stipulated therein are nothing; less than US$1!

distribution and availability of liquor in a very limited range of places, Aceh's qanun sought to eliminate the consumption of liquor and prevent it and all other similar products from being accessible in Aceh.

The question of which one of the three implementing principles is applied by Qanun 12 of 2003 on the prohibition of liquor is worth discussing. There is no doubt that the qanun has applied all implementing principles. Two implementing principles (personal and territorial) are explicitly stated in the Elucidation of the Qanun, and the other principle (voluntary legal subjection) is derived from Article 129 of Law 11 of 2006 as discussed above. The Elucidation of the Qanun clarifies that the punishment of forty lashes is applied based on the personal principle, while imprisonment of three months to one year and/or fines of 25–75 million rupiah for all other liquor-related offences is upheld on the grounds of the territorial principle. This means that while Muslim offenders are restricted to adjudication only by the Syar'iyah Court and are liable for all kinds of punishments (caning, imprisonment or fines), non-Muslim offenders in certain situations are free to go to another court where they will only be fined or sentenced to imprisonment, but not caned. In fact, non-Muslim drinkers who choose to go before the Civil Court and examined based on the Criminal Code may receive a lighter sentence or even be allowed to go free.

Legal Options of non-Muslims in Penal Offences

Although a choice of criminal jurisdictions is available, on paper, to non-Muslims, a couple of cases indicate that such a choice remains vague in practice. This section will discuss two cases where non-Muslims were examined by the Syar'iyah Court. Although they were given the option to move across legal orders, their choices were not entirely independent.

Case 1

Lisa, who is forty-seven years old, is a Buddhist of Chinese descent. She was born, and has lived her entire life, in the district of Pidie. As a housewife, she has no regular income. To support herself and her family, she sold liquor covertly to a limited number of customers in Sigli city. She was supplied with liquor (whiskey with 16.37 per cent ethanol) from the neighbouring province, North Sumatra. She placed small orders (two dozen bottles) for the liquor. Every time these sold out, Lisa would ask again for the same number. For this, she casually employed a van driver to transport her order of liquor from Medan to her home in Sigli. The driver is also a resident of Aceh. He is from Takengon, the district of Central Aceh. Although this driver was liable for assisting Lisa in this offence and, hence, could be summoned to the courtroom as a defendant, no information was available as to why he was not brought before the Syar'iyah Court for a hearing also.

Based on information received from people living nearby, one Thursday night in August 2008, a group of policemen executed a raid on Lisa's home. They discovered fifteen bottles of whisky. All this was confiscated as evidence of a crime. Originally, there had been twenty-four bottles at Lisa's house, but nine of them had already been sold to her customers. Lisa did not deny that these bottles of whisky belonged to her and were for sale.

The case reached the Syar'iyah Court of Sigli in November 2008. The public prosecutor accused Lisa of having violated Article 6(1) of Qanun 12 of 2003 on liquor. It was alleged that she had kept and sold prohibited beverages in Aceh's territory. The public prosecutor asked the Syar'iyah Court to declare the defendant guilty and to sentence her to four months' imprisonment. The policemen who raided Lisa's house were witnesses before the court for this case. The result of a test by the Provincial Office of Medicine and Food Monitoring was presented to confirm that the liquor found in Lisa's house was intoxicating.

After evaluating all this evidence, the judges found that an offence had taken place and that the crimes of keeping and selling liquor had been committed, the intoxication level of the confiscated liquor was verified, and Lisa was judged an offender. With regard to the defendant, whose religion is not Islam, the judges drew on two implementing principles of Aceh's Qanun in order to establish that the court had legitimate jurisdiction over this case. In the view of the judges, the defendant qualified for the term 'anyone' in Article 6(1) of Qanun 12 of 2003, where 'anyone' meant all individuals who are resident in the territory of Aceh. Additionally, the judges learned that the defendant had declared before the court that she had voluntarily submitted herself to the criminal jurisdiction of the Syar'iyah Court as governed by Article 129 of Law 11 of 2006. The judges were convinced that they were correctly applying the law and that no mistake (error in persona) was being made by penalising a non-Muslim offender in Aceh. Because she had committed acts prohibited in Aceh, the judges penalised the defendant with four months' imprisonment, as the pubic prosecutor had demanded. The judges maintained that sharia laws are now officially implemented in Aceh and applicable to all residents, regardless of whether or not they are non-Muslim. For this reason, the judges continued, the defendant was not free to act against the sharia law in Aceh.

Case 2

Rakim, who is forty-four years old, is a resident of Meulaboh city. A Buddhist, he is one of the few non-Muslims living in the district of West Aceh. Rakim has no formal occupation. Yet his neighbours know that he is running a small home business. In September 2009, legal auxiliaries, including the sharia police unit, the municipal civil force and the national police, undertook a joint raid on Rakim's house. They discovered 346 bottles of liquor in a deep bunker, which Rakim acknowledged belonged to him. He had purchased this liquor, which had an alcohol content of more than 5 per cent, from someone whom Rakim had known for quite some time and who he often met in Medan, North Sumatra. Rakim did not, however, know the home address of his business counterpart in Medan.

The public prosecutor accused the Rakim of illegally possessing, supplying and selling liquor. For his commission of acts prohibited in Aceh, the public prosecutor asked the Syar'iyah Court of Meulaboh to sentence the defendant to ten months' imprisonment. The defendant replied that such a punishment would be too harsh and untenable, since he still had a family to support. The defendant requested a jail sentence of three months as a fair penalty. The judges of the Syar'iyah Court refused this request after learning that the defendant had previously been sentenced by the General Court of Meulaboh for the same offence. After his first conviction Rakim was punished with a one-year suspended sentence. This meant that he was not required to go to jail unless he committed a similar crime during the period of his sentence. As the defendant had now repeated the crime, even though a long time afterwards, the Syar'iyah Court this time imposed a heavier penalty than that proposed by the public prosecutor. The defendant received a maximum penalty of one year's imprisonment for his offence. Rakim was punished more severely than the public prosecutor had requested, because he showed no regret before the judges.

The defendant did not accept the Syar'iyah Court's decision. With legal assistance from a Meulaboh-based barrister, Rakim challenged the court's jurisdiction, as well as its decision, in the Syar'iyah Higher Court in Banda Aceh. In his *memori banding* (memorandum of appeal) presented at the level of the Court of Appeal, the defendant claimed that, for four reasons, the district Syar'iyah Court in Meulaboh had no authority to examine his case. First, the defendant was a non-Muslim subject. Second, it was argued that, since he was non-Muslim, it was the National Criminal Code that governed his offence. Third, he did not voluntarily subject himself to Aceh's Qanun 12 of 2003 on liquor. And, finally, criminal acts and penalties included in this qanun are valid only where Muslim subjects are involved.

In the contra memorandum of appeal, the public prosecutor rejected all the defendant's arguments. The contra appeal declared that the defendant had stated and confirmed his willingness to be voluntarily subject to the Syar'iyah Court, and to Aceh's qanun on liquor in particular. His confirmation, the contra appeal continued, was, in fact, presented three times. The first, when the defendant signed a declaration while being questioned or investigated at the police office. The second, when the defendant signed a declaration form prepared by the public prosecutor during the process of submitting his case to the court. And the third, was his verbal declaration before the judges during the first hearing at the courtroom.

The public prosecutor's contra memorandum, above, may suggest the time-frame for when a non-Muslim is considered to have voluntarily agreed to be bound by the Islamic criminal jurisdiction in Aceh. This would clarify what is not stipulated or remains unclear in the qanun. Thus, a non-Muslim is not regarded as having given his or her tacit consent to being voluntarily bound by the qanun simply by his or her action of living in or travelling to Aceh. This consent is something to be determined once the prosecution for an offence has started. Nonetheless, as this case shows, once a non-Muslim officially and legally declares his or her willingness to be bound by the qanun in relation to an offence, he or she is not permitted at any later point to retract this statement. Given this state of affairs, the principle of voluntary legal submission, as applied for non-Muslim offenders, seems to be an oxymoron. Since it is voluntary, a non-Muslim offender should also have the choice to revoke his or her declaration of submission at any time.

Assessing all the arguments and evidence presented in this case, the Appellate Syar'iyah Court in Banda Aceh decided that the lower court had correctly applied the law and had not exceeded its jurisdiction. The punishment handed down by the first instant court to the defendant, which was one year's imprisonment, was thus reinforced. The Appellate Court clarified why the decision of the lower court was already appropriate. In the view of the judges who reviewed the case, the application of Article 26(2) of Qanun 12 of 2003 does not require religious adherence. This provision applies widely to all people who happen to stay in Aceh. In fact, the clarification went further, citing Article 129 of Law 11 of 2006, and stated that this provision strengthens the choice of laws for non-Muslim offenders.

Apparently, the appellate judges argued, inconsistently, that neither the Criminal Code nor other national regulations cover the offence when committed by a non-Muslim defendant, and, hence, the qanun should come into force. As seen in Table 4.1, this kind of offence has indeed been regulated. Both the national penal law and local regulation of Aceh stipulate a similar penalty for this kind of offence, but with intricate conditions and requirements. It is very likely that the Civil Court would have sentenced Rakim to the same penalty as the Religious Court had imposed on him. Given this probability, the choice of criminal jurisdictions does not bring any advantage. The choice of criminal jurisdictions has not made any difference at all in terms of the punishment handed down by either of the state courts, especially for this particular offence of selling liquor in Aceh. The fact that the defendant received a harsher punishment than was demanded by the public prosecutor was very much related to the judicial consideration of the judges, and not to jurisdictional choice.

Conclusion

Kuran (2004) argued that legal pluralism for Muslim and non-Muslim subjects under the Ottoman legal system was asymmetric. The preceding discussion on the implementation of Islamic law in Aceh also shows such asymmetric legal pluralism. Nevertheless, while asymmetric legal pluralism under the Ottomans took place in commercial disputes, it exists in Aceh mainly in connection with criminal offences. In both cases, only non-Muslim subjects have options to choose between different courts. Non-Muslim offenders in Aceh are able to navigate between the Civil Court and the Religious Court. However, once their choice is made, it cannot be revoked.

Legal pluralism in family law is not similar to legal pluralism in criminal law. The former may have strengthened the recognition of identity and the sustainability of particular religious communities (Welchman 2000; Rabo 2005). Yet the latter would not necessarily bring the same result. As argued by Cribb (2010: 66), legal pluralism in criminal law has created an impression that the state denies 'common experience to its subjects by keeping them on a tangle of different legal and social footings'. Muslim offenders in Aceh may have feel this way especially, because they may wonder why non-Muslim offenders can evade harsh punishments (for example, caning, hand amputation or stoning to death) as regulated in the qanun now or in the future, when all this should apply to all the residents in Aceh without exception. As in family law, legal pluralism in criminal law may have created boundaries between different religious communities. Yet these boundaries can result in inequality in the legal options available to these different religious communities.

Notes

1. The Elucidation of Article 49 Law 3 of 2006 states: 'Yang dimaksud dengan "antara orang-orang yang beragama Islam" adalah termasuk orang atau badan hukum yang dengan sendirinya menundukkan diri dengan sukarela kepada hukum Islam mengenai hal-hal yang menjadi kewenangan Peradilan Agama sesuai dengan ketentuan Pasal ini.' ('What is meant by "between Muslim people" includes those individuals or corporations that voluntarily subject themselves to (be adjudicated by) Islamic law that becomes under the jurisdictions of the Religious Court in accordance with the provision of this Article.')
2. See http://www.hukumonline.com/berita/baca/hol16720/perbankan-syariah-masih-mencari-peradilan-yang-kompeten, accessed 25 May 2013.
3. Articulating further the special status of Aceh as an autonomous province within

the state of Indonesia, this law intended to signify the end of almost three decades of armed conflict in the province between the Indonesian government and the Free Aceh movement. The law provides some legal and political concessions by granting various exceptional authorities to Aceh. On judicial issues, among others, the law spells out that Islamic sharia law is to be applied in Aceh and that the Syar'iyah Court is the state court that will deal with disputes or offences related to all legal sharia matters stipulated in Aceh's bylaws.

4. 'Govt wants non-Muslims tried by Islamic Court in Aceh', *The Jakarta Post*, 26 April 2006.
5. 'Christian politicians against sharia for non-Muslims', *Asia News*, 27 April 2006.
6. In the view of some Islamic judges, there was no legislation in Indonesia that prohibited non-Muslims from opting to be examined by Aceh's Religious Courts. Additionally, no valid legal reason exists for judges to prevent this from taking place.

Chapter 5

Contested Lawmaking

If Aceh wants to apply sharia entirely [*secara kaffah*], the legislature should not conceal any single particular punishment in Islam including *rajam* [stoning].

Bachrom M. Rasyid, an Islamic party (PPP) legislator (2004–9)

The government keeps opposing the *rajam* punishment as it contradicts national and international laws. [Furthermore,] the law should conform to the conditions of local people.

Irwandi Yusuf, Governor of Aceh (2007–12)

It was after midnight on a Saturday in June 2008. People of a small village in North Aceh were watching live coverage of the European Championship football match on their televisions. On that early morning, Sardan, fifty years old, walked soundlessly into the goat stall belonging to one of his neighbours. In his hand was a sharp knife. He intended to use it to slaughter a goat inside the stall. He might have done it, had the goat not groaned and bleated. The goat owner, who lives nearby, was immediately alerted by the terrible noise he heard from the goat stall. Aware that a thief had intruded into the stall, he shouted loudly for help. His outcry quickly attracted the attention of the surrounding neighbours, who were still awake viewing the TV sports programme. The villagers hurriedly ran to the stall and discovered Sardan trying to butcher a goat. They were outraged and lost control of their tempers. Sardan, who was alleged to have previously committed this kind of crime repeatedly, was punched many times in the face. Disastrously, the villagers almost cut off his left arm. This vigilante action was perhaps the harshest communal chastisement ever imposed since Aceh was formally granted permission to apply Islamic sharia law in the post-Suharto period.

Aceh officially began the implementation of sharia in 2001. Yet the punishment of cutting off a thief's hand is not (yet) applicable in Aceh. As of 2003, crimes violating Islamic norms were introduced into the local legislation in Aceh, but in a very limited scope. The Aceh provincial regulations, known in Aceh as qanuns, had listed certain minor Islamic crimes, such as gambling, liquor consumption and the khalwat of an unmarried couple. Passed in 2003, those qanuns stipulated a variety of punishments for offenders. Apart from fines and imprisonment, one particular penalty was regarded as *ta'zir* (discretionary punishment). The ta'zir penalty specified in those regulations was caning only. The other two primary categories of Islamic punishments, namely *hudud* (that is, fixed punishments for certain crimes, such as stoning to death for adultery and hand amputation for theft) and *qisas* (just retaliation, mostly applied as the punishment in the case of homicide), despite being prescribed in the Qur'an and hadiths, were not ratified in any of Aceh's regulations.

New Islamic Crimes and Punishments

Only later, in September 2009, did the outgoing provincial legislature pass two qanuns on Islamic crimes.[1] Despite fierce opposition from within Acehnese communities, one of these qanuns included a stipulation on rajam for married perpetrators of adultery. Replacing the 2003 qanuns, these two newly enacted qanuns introduced some new offences, including *ikhtilat* (intimacy between an unmarried couple), *zina* (adultery or fornication), *qadzaf* (false accusation), sexual harassment, homosexuality, lesbianism and rape.

Ikhtilat, or intimacy, was defined as intimate behaviour by an unmarried couple in outdoor as well as indoor locations. The ikhtilat provision would then prosecute any intimate actions of an unmarried couple either in private or at public venues. This provision thus created a broader offence than that recognised in the previous qanuns as khalwat between unmarried people, which takes place mostly out of sight.

The offence of zina was also redefined in the amended qanun. Different to the offence of zina as stipulated in the current Indonesian penal code, the formulation of zina in this qanun was quite extensive. In the Indonesian penal code, adultery, or zina, becomes an offence only if a spouse of the adulterer reports it to the police. The qanun, however, outlines zina as acts of adultery or fornication undertaken by the mutual consent of a couple, and it constitutes a crime even if the offended spouse does not report it to the police.

Figure 5.1 A billboard banning *khalwat* as the devil's way to fornication, located not far from Lhoknga beach, Aceh Besar © Arskal Salim

The definition of zina also distinguishes it from rape, another offence newly included under Islamic penal law in Aceh. Rape mainly refers to sexual acts carried out by force or threat. The enacted qanun defines 'by force' as forcing someone to do something she or he does not want to do, where the forced person is not capable of refusing or resisting. Yet, contrary to the National Law 23 of 2004 on domestic violence, the qanun states that it cannot be used to punish a husband who forces his wife to have sexual intercourse.

One obvious difference in the way offences are dealt with in the enacted qanuns, as opposed to current Indonesian penal law at the national level, is the type of punishment that would be imposed. Under these two amended qanuns of Islamic crimes, some penalties from the previous qanuns were expanded and a new way of determining punishments was introduced. Depending on the sort of offence and how many times it had been committed, the caning punishments imposed on offenders ranged from a minimum of ten lashes to a maximum of 400 lashes. Meanwhile, the duration of imprisonment was calculated based on the amount of caning, on a formula by which every lash was equal to one month in prison. Furthermore, these qanuns took the unique approach (for Aceh, at least) of adopting gold as the currency for charging the payment of fines. The drafters of these qanuns stated that a lash or a month's imprisonment is equivalent to a fine of 20 grams of gold. The maximum fine is 4,000 grams of gold for raping a child.

The formulation of fines and other kinds of punishments based on gold invited wide criticism. Several professors of Islamic law at the *Institut Agama Islam Negeri* (State Islamic Institute, or Ar-Raniry IAIN) in Banda Aceh, the provincial capital, have questioned the idea of making gold the reference for calculating the amount of fines. In their view, this method of setting fines is irrational, because gold is very costly and few Acehnese could afford it. In addition, there is no precedence or jurisprudence in the Indonesian criminal legal system for gold to be used for the payment of fines.

Of all these punishments, stoning to death for married adulterers stands out. Nevertheless, the wording of this provision in the qanun remains ambiguous at best. Article 24:1 of the qanun states: 'Any person who deliberately commits adultery is to be punished with 100 lashes if the offender has not yet married, and to be penalised by 100 lashes as well as rajam if the offender has ever married.' Despite its brevity, there is no clarification in this provision about what is meant by rajam, and also no procedures on how to carry it out in any other section of two qanuns on Islamic crimes. Even an Acehnese law professor was unable to explain whether or not the punishment should make use of stones; whether an adulterer must actually be killed or may be allowed to run away during the (attempted) execution process; whether this kind of capital punishment is to be forcefully upheld by the state or whether it is to take place only when an offender voluntarily makes an open confession before the court; and what happens if someone voluntarily seeks to be stoned to death for his or her own salvation in the afterlife.

THE ORIGIN OF THE STONING PUNISHMENT

Where did this severe penalty come from? Historically, stoning of adulterers can be traced back to the era of Sultan Iskandar Muda in seventeenth-century Aceh. Advocates of the penalty often say they are only trying to restore some of Aceh's past Islamic principles. Nevertheless, the inclusion of this particular punishment in the draft qanun startled and dismayed many people not only in Aceh and Indonesia, but also in the international arena.

The stoning penalty was completely absent from the initial bill presented by the provincial government to parliament. In fact, the earlier draft prepared by the Provincial Office of Dinas Syariat Islam did not even mention anything related to it. Professor Al Yasa Abubakar, who was formerly the chairman of the Provincial Office of Islamic Sharia, and thus the leading figure in earlier efforts to implement Islamic law in Aceh, said that the initial draft qanun he prepared did not contain rajam as a punishment for married adulterers. Instead, his version only included 100 lashes for adulterers and did not distinguish between married and unmarried offenders (Abubakar 2008).

How and in what ways could the stoning penalty appear in the qanun? The stoning provision first arose out of a discussion at a meeting of the *panitia khusus* (usually abbreviated to '*pansus*' – special drafting committee). The pansus was set up to intensively discuss the bill at the legislature. The Islamic parties led this legislative committee. Bachrom M Rasyid, a legislator from the United Development Party (PPP) (an Islamic party), took the position of chairman of the committee, while Bustanul Arifin, a legislator from another Islamic party, the Prosperous Justice Party (PKS), served as secretary. To support the tasks of the committee, a number of legal experts, including specialists on sharia law, were recruited. These experts not only helped the legislators with the technicalities of legal drafting, but they also engaged in drafting the stoning provision and endorsed such punishment as part of the committee's revised and proposed qanun.

One of the experts who assisted the legislative committee was Muhammad Rum. He was the principal of an Islamic boarding dayah in Seulawah, Aceh Besar, and was actively involved in the Sharia Board of the PKS in Aceh. At a public hearing with the Supreme Court judges of Jakarta, who visited the legislature office on 10 August 2009, Rum made a remark advocating the stoning to death penalty for adulterers. In his view, this punishment not only has a strong foundation in Islamic legal tradition, but it also has historical roots in Aceh. In his opinion, there is no dispute among the classical Islamic madhhab (schools of law) about the implementation of punishment by stoning; all of them view it as valid.

For the leaders of Islamic parties in the provincial parliament, this was all about applying sharia law comprehensively. The chairman of the committee, Bachrom M Rasyid, said:

> If Aceh wants to apply sharia in its entirety [secara kaffah], the legislature should not hide any single Islamic punishment, including rajam. As this specific punishment existed in the early days of Islam and has been practiced in a few Muslim countries, the Special Committee thus proposed to include it in the qanun on jinayat.[2]

In the view of supporters of the stoning provision, punishing married adulterers with something that falls short of stoning (for instance, by caning them) would suggest that Aceh lacks the will to implement sharia rigorously. This attitude reveals that the intention of the legislative committee to incorporate the stoning punishment into the revised qanuns on Islamic crimes had merely an emblematic or symbolic purpose. Whether or not those qanuns would be enforceable does not seem to have been their main concern. They were satisfied because the provision of the stoning punishment was now part of the revised qanuns on Islamic crimes.

The actual enforcement of the punishment was no longer the legislature's responsibility. Instead, responsibility went to the government of Aceh and Aceh's sharia courts. Following this, a day after the legislature enacted the qanuns, Jufri Ghalib, a former judge of the Higher Sharia Court of Aceh, commented that the stoning punishment had been included due to political interests, rather than because the penalty as such was written in the classical fiqh textbooks. Members of the outgoing legislature still wanted to pass the qanuns, despite being aware of the impracticality of the punishment of stoning. As this severe penalty was now included in the qanuns, Judge Jufri expressed his deep concern that the court would face difficulties in imposing the penalty of stoning to death should judicial procedures to carry it out be unclear. If this situation were to occur, he added, very often Aceh communities, and also those legislators, would have the sharia court to blame for not being able to produce a verdict as stipulated in the enacted qanuns. Drawing an analogy between the qanun and a car, Judge Jufri illustrated, 'if the car is non-starter or breaks down on the road, they would point the finger at us without pondering that it is actually their deficient product'.[3]

Criticisms of the Stoning Punishment

The introduction of the punishment of death by stoning for married adulterers has been controversial. The final revised qanuns of the legislative committee not only caused heated debates, but also received strong criticism from the executive branch of the Acehnese provincial government, who initially prepared the bill but without including the stoning penalty. The disapproval even emanated from people who have been leading figures in the implementation of Islamic law in Aceh, such as Al Yasa Abubakar. While he was still the chairman of the provincial sharia office, the draft qanuns he had prepared did not contain stoning to death as a punishment for married adulterers. This does not mean that he considers this punishment to be incorrect in principle, but in his view the implementation of Islamic penal law in Aceh should take place gradually. He clarified that only after other aspects of society had changed – for instance, if the justice system, legal infrastructure and social welfare were truly established – would it be time to introduce all elements of Islamic penal law.

Meanwhile, on behalf of the Governor of Aceh, the head of legal and social relations affairs of the provincial office, Hamid Zein, reacted to the revised bill saying:

> We don't intend to disagree with the application of rajam in Aceh, but [for the time being] we want its application to be deferred . . . We think at this time the caning penalty is still more than sufficient, rather than applying rajam immediately.[4]

In addition, Zein sent an alert to the legislature, stating that the *Komisi Nasional Hak Asasi Manusia* (KOMNASHAM – Indonesian National Human Rights Commission) had invited the United Nations to review the existing qanuns in Aceh, especially those providing for severe punishments. His doing so makes it look very much as if the executive was seeking support and legitimacy for their objections to the bill.

For the legislators, especially those from the Islamic parties, the proposal to include the stoning punishment into the qanuns on Islamic crimes was a part of their efforts to formally implement sharia law in Aceh. This has been a central goal of Islamic parties in Aceh, and in other parts of Indonesia as well. The Islamisation of laws is thus a living political agenda for Islamic parties. In spite of their failure at national level to incorporate the Jakarta Charter (a provision that would oblige the state to apply sharia for Muslims) into the constitution during debates in the People's Consultative Assembly in 2002 (Salim 2008), the fact that Islamic parties in Aceh were able to lead the legislative committee in introducing more Islamic penal law suggests that they have successfully established a de facto Islamic state in a particular territory of Indonesia.

After the Enactment: Tensions and Protests

Despite fierce opposition from the government of Aceh and from numerous social circles, the outgoing Aceh legislature (2004–9) enacted the two qanuns on Islamic crimes prescribing that married adulterers should be stoned to death. This fact demonstrated that the legislative process was based on politics and not on the sort of socio-cultural consensus needed if regulation is to be effective. The decision was very much determined by the fact that the outgoing legislature was less interested in whether the qanun would be implemented and more interested in being able to claim that they were the legislators who should be remembered by future generations for making tougher Islamic penal laws in Aceh.

The outgoing legislature may be seen to have successfully passed the stoning punishment, but this appears to have a fragile standing for two reasons. First, the provincial legislature passed the bill only two weeks before their term ended and the newly elected legislature replaced them. The outgoing legislature is therefore seen to have passed the qanuns during 'injury time'. Secondly, Governor Irwandi and the new legislative members, who were sworn in only in early October 2009, rejected the qanuns on Islamic crimes passed by the outgoing legislature. In fact, the governor sought to resist these qanuns by not signing them and sending them back to the new legislature, considering that both were still drafts that were in need of revision or amendment. Referring to national and international laws, Governor Irwandi fiercely opposed the punishment:

> The government of Aceh refuses the jinayat law because it is not consistent with our proposed draft. We don't know what will happen to that law. The government keeps opposing the rajam penalty as it contradicts national and international laws. [Furthermore,] the law should conform to the conditions of the local people.[5]

The resistance of the government of Aceh is well justified by a provision in the Helsinki Agreement (1.2.4). It was stated that, until 2009, the legislature of Aceh would have no right to enact any laws without the consent of the head of the Aceh administration. This means that once the governor rejects a qanun, even if it has been passed by the legislature, such a qanun lacks the required legitimacy. This legal framework is surely applicable to de-legitimise the stoning penalty in the enacted qanuns.

In the meantime, the new legislative body, which was dominated by the Partai Aceh (a party without Islamist orientation and belonging to the ex-combatants of the Free Aceh Movement), had set aside the controversial qanuns. The new legislature of Aceh agreed not to include these qanuns on Islamic crimes in a short list of the *program legislasi Aceh* (Aceh legislation programme) during their period of tenure (2009–14). According to Abdullah Saleh, the spokesperson of the legislative bureau of the new legislature of Aceh, neither of the qanuns on Islamic crimes have high priority because 'the Acehnese people are not yet ready. They first need to have understood [the contents of Qanun]. Otherwise, that Qanun will create injustice.'[6]

However, political developments in 2013, especially with the 2014 legislative election approaching, have brought some optimism for those who wanted the qanuns on Islamic criminal laws to be passed in Aceh. The Party of Aceh, the dominant faction in the provincial legislature, has led an effort to revise both qanuns, but this time without the stoning to death penalty prescribed for offenders of zina. It seems that, by shifting its position from being against to advocating for the qanuns of Islamic crimes, the Party of Aceh has sought to demonstrate its full commitment to enforcing sharia in Aceh. Abdullah Saleh was quoted to have said that the legislature had agreed to prioritise twenty-one bills, including the one on Islamic crimes, in a short list of the Aceh legislation programme in 2013.[7] Despite this, it is possible that this commitment is merely virtual rather than real. It remains to be seen, in the aftermath of the 2014 election, whether or not the Party of Aceh has been wholeheartedly supporting the actual application of sharia.

Three Responses

One might ask why has the introduction, in the newly amended qanuns on Islamic crimes, of the punishment of stoning to death been strongly opposed, while the application of caning in Aceh has been subject to less criticism? To offer an inclusive answer to this question, it is worth considering three kinds of response to the stoning punishment: (1) academic, (2) political and (3) critical.

Academic Response

The academic response is based on the view that the existing qanuns on jinayat are incomplete. There are two obvious weaknesses: (1) there are often various interpretations when defining what is an offence; and (2) it is always uncertain whether an offender should be arrested and put in a prison during the adjudication process. According to this kind of response, to let this situation continue would only demoralise the legal apparatus of sharia in Aceh. In fact, it could become doubtful, hesitant and apathetic in implementing the rules of the qanuns. Also, this situation could possibly result in the destruction of what has been achieved so far in terms of the application of sharia in Aceh. With this vision in mind, the academic response does not welcome the introduction of the stoning punishment for the time being. Professors and lecturers of IAIN Ar-Raniry were among those who leaned towards this response. They were of the opinion that the formulation of the qanuns on Islamic crimes, and of the stoning punishment in particular, was deficient. In the view of the proponents of this response, to allow this punishment, without a clear manual on how to carry it out in the current circumstances of Aceh, would only exacerbate the existing problems of vague procedures in applying all qanuns related to sharia law.

The academic response has its own distinct framework for the implementation of sharia in Aceh. Both Professor Al Yasa Abubakar and Professor Syahrizal, who has been recently appointed as head of the Provincial Office of Islamic Sharia, have repeatedly stated that the enforcement of sharia in Aceh should be in parallel with the national legal system (Abubakar 2008; Syahrizal 2007). They both hold this view, and make every endeavour to demonstrate that Islamic sharia in Aceh remains relevant and applicable in modern times. Al Yasa has gone further, arguing that the stoning penalty is not a valid punishment for married adulterers because it is not mentioned in the Qur'an, the most authoritative source of law in Islam. In fact, according to him, the practice of this penalty was suspended after the revelation of Sura al-Nur (24: 1–3), during the Prophet's lifetime.[8]

Another important academic figure who rejects the stoning punishment is Professor Rusjdi Ali Muhammad. His objection is mainly that such a penalty remains in dispute and no consensus among various Islamic schools of law has been reached to acknowledge it. In his view, since classical Muslim jurists had never reached a unanimous view on this kind of death penalty, it is not religiously obligatory to implement the stoning punishment in Aceh, where pluralism in the understanding of Islam is observable. This is because choosing just one among the variety of legal interpretations available in Islam, by making the stoning punishment mandatory, would eliminate the civil right of every Muslim to subscribe to whatever Islamic legal school he or she prefers.[9]

The academic response can also be identified as a gradual approach. This means that its proponents do not necessarily oppose the application of sharia in general, or the stoning punishment in particular. Instead, what they seek is to implement sharia in Aceh in a rational way. For them, being rational means enforcing sharia gradually and realistically. As far as the gradual implementation of the definitions of, and penalties for, Islamic crimes in the legislation in Aceh is concerned, there are at least three areas that require careful attention by academics.[10]

The first concerns the steps to be taken in introducing sharia punishment for offenders. According to Al Yasa, caning must be introduced into law first, then amputation, and finally the death penalty. As caning has been in force since 2005, the next step should have been the introduction of the penalty of amputation. But, Al Yasa quickly emphasised, this step should be carefully prepared, by taking all local contexts of Aceh comprehensively into account. Al Yasa regrets that these three gradual steps are not consistently undertaken. In fact, the stoning to death punishment was abruptly introduced in the qanuns enacted by the previous legislature.

The second concern is about the types of offence. In Al Yasa's view, as the first step, zina should not be considered an offence separate from ikhtilat. He criticised the enacted qanuns on Islamic crimes that, respectively, regarded zina and ikhtilat as individual offences. For Al Yasa, zina has to be part of another offence, ikhtilat. This implies that if a couple is accused of having committed adultery (zina), both are presumed to have had intimate contact, and if there is not enough evidence to prove this offence the accused couple could still be punished for committing an offence of ikhtilat or intimacy. In this case, the zina offence would be deemed to have taken place only if one person, or a couple, voluntarily confess that they have committed adultery. This was the actual practice in the Prophet's lifetime. In a nutshell, as far as the offence of zina and its punishment by stoning are concerned, the gradual approach would, preferably, start with voluntary submission rather than legal coercion, which usually involves and necessitates intricate evidence.

The third concern is the role of adat leaders, or village elders. The gradual approach requires that village elders play active roles in settling disputes or adjudicating on penal offences. Unfortunately, the enacted qanuns are unclear about the active role of village leaders in dealing with offences of Islamic crimes. Instead, one of those qanuns vaguely stipulates that disputes or offences may be settled through the adat mechanism. This brief provision is not enough to clarify what 'adat mechanism' means, how it is practised and through what means, or which actor is responsible for settling an Islamic penal case like zina or ikhtilat. Some people might think that they need to refer to the relevant local regulations on adat or village justice to deal with the case. However, this could send the wrong message to the villagers, who may react unexpectedly by taking the law into their own hands.

Political Response

The political response is grounded on the notion that the introduction of the stoning punishment will be detrimental to the position of Aceh in the world, economically and politically; that it will not only discourage international investment in Aceh, but also result in Aceh's being labelled, by the world in general, as one of the fundamentalist Islamic states, like certain countries in the Middle East region. Local politicians and the former combatants of the Free Aceh Movement (GAM) can be seen to echo this kind of response, since, from the beginning, their main concern was not the implementation of sharia rules, but economic and political objectives. In any case, they have often said that much would have to be done before the stoning punishment could be applied, including improving knowledge of Islam among various Muslim individuals and communities in Aceh.

However, these people do not want to be seen as antagonistic to the application of sharia. Therefore, they cannot openly oppose the enacted qanuns on Islamic crimes, since such a manoeuvre would lead to their being portrayed as being 'anti-sharia'. As pointed out by Bowen (2013: 164), 'actors engaging in public debate about new laws in Aceh have to frame their positions in terms of sharia'. As they fear they could lose political support in the next election if they blatantly refuse sharia, politicians have sought to show their commitment to sharia in a very distinctive way. In an interview with a local tabloid, Governor Irwandi persuasively showed his position of adopting sharia values, on the one hand, while, on the other hand, he expressed his firm stance against the harsh penalties of sharia:

> Islamic sharia does not simply involve punishment or labelling. Islamic sharia must be upheld in accordance with sharia, and does not need to be focused only on a single aspect alone. Economic empowerment must be considered part of sharia, making people honest, improving welfare and increasing healthy life are all core values of sharia. The punishments are only a means to achieve the main objectives of sharia. It is [therefore] not plausible to have [a qanun stipulating that] hands of the thieves [be] cut off if a society still has many economic problems; the government remains unjust; welfare is not yet achieved; and unemployment is still unresolved. I totally disagree with that, and I have stated that I will revoke such a bill.[11]

Thus, the political response appears to wish to defer (though it does not actually say it wishes to eliminate) the severe punishments in the qanuns. This, however, has raised allegations from some Muslim circles that politicians were not wholeheartedly supportive of the implementation of sharia in Aceh. In fact, it is felt that, from the very beginning of Governor Irwandi's term in power (2007–12), he showed reluctance to uphold the sort of sharia stipulated in the qanun. The grounds of this allegation were threefold, as described below (Salim 2009).

First, when the formal implementation of sharia was initiated, between 2002 and 2005, checkpoints were frequently established to stop women going past without wearing headscarves. However, since 2006, the Wilayatul Hisbah has rarely done this. The reason often given is that the government provided inadequate support, and the Wilayatul Hisbah frequently complained that they did not have enough funds, even to buy petrol for their vehicles. Moreover, when the Wilayatul Hisbah was restructured in early 2008, as part of the civil police unit, or *Satuan Polisi Pamong Praja*, many considered this restructuring to be part of a systematic effort by the government to weaken the implementation of sharia in Aceh.

Secondly, people in Aceh felt that, as of 2006, khalwat had become a more common phenomenon. Not only did it take place behind closed doors, but was also frequently observed in open spaces. In the view of these people, this demonstrated the failure of the Wilayatul Hisbah to undertake regular inspections of places where unmarried couples were supposedly committing khalwat. They blamed the Irwandi government for not taking any serious steps to uphold the sanctions of the qanun. In fact, they were surprised to discover that the number of offences that were submitted to the sharia courts in various districts and cities has decreased dramatically over time, while at the same time information or news of people caught committing khalwat appears almost every day in the local newspaper, *Harian Serambi*.

Thirdly, after the first caning took place in mid-2005 in Bireun, other districts began imitating this and punishing the offenders of qanun. However, from early 2007, the overall number of offenders being lashed in Aceh decreased, despite continued sentencing by the sharia courts in various districts. For example, in February 2009, twenty-two offenders in Bireun were awaiting caning. The explanation often given for this was that the budget did not suffice to cover the costs of caning. More importantly, as pointed out in Afriko's study (2010), Governor Irwandi was not happy with caning being implemented in Aceh because such a punishment tends to lead international observers to discount Aceh as a candidate or destination for foreign investment.

Critical Response

The critical response is founded on the idea that international conventions and Indonesia's legal system must serve as a fundamental reference for any qanun enacted in Aceh, including the qanuns on Islamic crimes. The subscribers to this response were those who had been actively engaged in post-tsunami recovery activities organised by local, as well as international, NGOs in Aceh. Many young intellectuals from the University of Syiah Kuala and a few scholars from the IAIN Ar-Raniry also supported this response.

The exponents of the critical response not only drew on human rights issues and conventions to criticise the qanuns, but also invoked the existing Indonesian legal system to support their view. On the one hand, the introduction of harsh penalties in the qanuns was seen to potentially discriminate among people and create injustices. On the other hand, it was conceived that the inclusion in the qanuns of punishment by stoning had contravened higher laws applicable in Indonesia. Such a death penalty would not only challenge the civil rights and freedoms enshrined in Indonesia's constitution, but also contravene international covenants on human rights (for example, the Convention against Torture and Other Cruel Inhuman or Degrading Treatment or Punishment), which had already been ratified by the national legislation (Law 5 of 1998).

The supporters of this response perceived that the preliminary process of lawmaking was unfair. An activist from the University of Syiah Kuala wrote:

> A petition sent by NGO activists to the DPRA in order to suspend the passing of the qanun must be seen not as opposing Islamic sharia or representing a foreign interest that is anti-sharia. Yet, their voices have to be regarded as a part of people's aspiration that sought to participate in the collective lawmaking process, so that direction and objectives of the qanun can be effectively achieved once it is enforced. To listen to one camp and abandon the other does not reflect the principle of democracy. Discussing Islamic sharia is not a monopoly of those who are considered the most knowledgeable about the sharia rules. Other groups who may be perceived as secular people and

have limited knowledge about sharia, their ideas must also be paid adequate attention.[12]

Although the legislature had invited them, on a number of occasions, to engage in discussing the draft qanuns, these NGO activists did not feel satisfied with this limited involvement. The community participation that is necessary in every law-making process was considered insufficient in this case not only because the views of the critical groups were not seriously taken into account, but also because the public hearings that they attended to voice their opinions to the legislature often ended in disarray. When the legislature organised a public hearing, some Muslim organisations and leaders of traditional dayah, who have been advocates of the introduction of punishment by stoning, were also invited to join the meeting, along with the NGO activists who were critical of its introduction. Needless to say, such public hearings very often became an occasion of dispute between two competing camps, rather than a forum where the legislature listened to and learned of the aspirations of particular groups within the society.

For the critical response proponents, the qanuns that accommodate punishment by stoning must be postponed for two reasons. First, because many provisions in these qanuns are flawed. A meticulous revisory study of the stoning punishment is therefore needed to check its religious and historical accuracy and its consistency with higher laws. Secondly, is the fact that the Acehnese people are not yet ready to accept the implementation of this severe penalty in the current situation in which many ordinary people remain ignorant and uneducated. According to the critical response, people first need to be prepared and to be well informed about what the punishment actually is, and what are its legal intricacies. Otherwise, it may cause vigilante reactions and chaotic situations. In this respect, the critical response pays particular attention to the arbitrary sanction imposed by adat leaders, who expel those who have committed adultery from one village and force them to live in another village far away.

Counter-responses

To all three of the responses outlined above, the advocates of the punishment by stoning offered a rejoinder. This rejoinder was made by a number of figures, including the legal expert of the legislative committee of the outgoing legislature, Muhammad Rum, as mentioned above. Rum wrote a short article and published it in the Aceh daily newspaper, *Serambi Indonesia*. This article was also posted on the website of the Aceh Institute on 18 November 2009. As a specialist in sharia law, Rum has a strong background and training in Islamic studies. His higher degrees are from a university in Saudi Arabia. At the time that he was providing assistance to the previous legislature, Rum was also completing a doctoral degree at the IAIN Ar-Raniry Banda Aceh. He has been politically active in the Sharia Board of the PKS. Although he lives in Aceh, Rum is not an Acehnese. He originally comes from South Sulawesi, another region in Indonesia where some local Muslim groups wanted to imitate Aceh's way of enforcing sharia.

Rum's arguments against these responses rejecting the stoning punishment were underpinned by Aceh's historical facts and his own legal reasoning. He did not draw on national laws at all, although there is quite enough support from this source of law especially to emphasise Aceh's special autonomy. He did make a reference to international contexts, although for some this sounds very naive and merely rhetorical.

The greater part of his rejoinder was directed at the political response. Basing his argument on local evidence, Rum sought to counter the point made by Governor Irwandi, who considered punishment by stoning to be foreign and imported. Rum contended that this kind of punishment could be traced back to seventeenth-century Aceh, under the rule of Sultan Iskandar Muda. In addition, he referred to the struggle of Teungku Muhammad Daud Bereueu-eh, the leader of the Darul Islam rebellion in the 1950s, who sought to revive the dignity and success of the Aceh sultanate. It appears to Rum that the stoning punishment has been part of local knowledge for hundreds of years, and therefore it is correct to regard this particular punishment as home-grown.

In terms of prospective international investment in Aceh, which politicians often offered as an argument against the implementation of stoning, Rum responded that the introduction of this punishment has nothing to do with incoming investment. To support this claim, he presented evidence from Saudi Arabia and a few other countries in the Middle East that enforce Islamic penal laws. He argued that despite the fact that these Muslim countries apply corporal punishments for adulterers, financial investments from western countries have continued. Additionally, Rum explained that the emergence of Islamic parties in Turkey in the last decade has not prevented a number of European investors from doing business in this country. Nevertheless, the extent of the truth of Rum's claim certainly needs further corroboration, especially because he puts Aceh and those Arabic-speaking countries in equivalent positions.

Rum's rejoinder was also addressed to the academics. He considered that the argument of Al Yasa, who stated that stoning to death was not a Qur'anic punishment, was weak. According to Rum, not every legal rule in Islam must be found in the Qur'an. Some are to be located in the Prophetic *Sunna* or hadiths. As an example, he referred to procedures for practising daily prayers. Since the Qur'an is silent on how to perform a prayer, would the quintuple daily prayers be rejected or classified as a disputed matter? Rum was correct to say that rules in Islam could be also discovered by looking at Prophetic tradition or hadith. Nonetheless, Rum's analogy, comparing the stoning punishment and the five prayers as if they had equal status, remains contested. For some Muslims, the stoning punishment and the five prayers are not similar. They have different degrees of importance, scope and position in Islamic teachings.

Apparently, Al Yasa and Rum have different frameworks to their legal thinking. Unlike Rum, who is a literalist Muslim, Al Yasa is a contextualist thinker, if not a rationalist. In Al Yasa's view, it is unclear whether the stoning punishment is *ijtihadiya* (based on legal reasoning) or *tawqifiyya* (based on a legal template). It seems that Al Yasa does not consider the stoning punishment to be tawqifiyya because, according to him, the practice during the Prophet's lifetime is not monolithic. At one time, the punishment ended with the death of adulterers, but at another, an adulterer was allowed to run away while the stoning was taking place. Given this plural practice, Al Yasa suggested that the adulterers should not necessarily be punished by stoning to death. In fact, the stoning punishment may be replaced with any other kind of penalty, including 100 lashes as he had proposed in earlier draft qanuns.

As international human rights law was a prevalent conceptual framework in this law-making debate, the proponents of the stoning punishment sought to engage with this particular discourse as well. The language and the argument they developed on this controversial issue were quite striking. They articulated legal reasoning, by pointing to the offender's human rights. The chairman of the legislative committee, Bahrom Rasyid, argued:

> If the human rights aspect must be taken into account when discussing the stoning punishment, one should not forget the right of an offender to have forgiveness from God. This right to look for repentance must be considered as a part of freedom of belief. Because, in the eyes of the offender, being stoned to death is actually a way of seeking repentance. The offender believes that the stoning punishment imposed on him or her in this world will redeem his or her sins, and thus prevent him or her from receiving more tortures in the afterlife.[13]

This kind of legal reasoning has hard evidence. It is known that in Aceh several individuals who had committed adultery came to see Al Yasa when he was still in charge of the Provincial Office of Islamic sharia. They not only made a confession, but also requested punishment by being stoned to death. They believed that such a punishment would allow them to repent in the world and gain salvation in the afterlife.

CONCLUSION

The foregoing discussion shows the controversy surrounding the introduction of the stoning punishment in Aceh. Its proponents and opponents all present justifications to support their own views and to refute their challengers' arguments. Each camp draws on and invokes elements of the quadrangle of law (local, spiritual, national and international) in their legal reasoning. Following Menski's (2010) idea that plurality of pluralities characterises legal pluralism, all this demonstrates how each of the legal quadrangle components has been variously understood and utilised in divergent ways to maintain different positions. We have seen in the legal reasoning of both proponents and opponents of the stoning punishment that none of the legal quadrangle elements takes only one form. Local knowledge, religious injunctions, national laws and even international human rights are plural.

The case of legal pluralism in Aceh, in fact, confirms that one should ponder the plurality of pluralities carefully, especially when it comes to the way the 'international norm' is pluralistically understood. In Aceh, the human rights norm is not necessarily singular as it is commonly understood. Regardless of its usage for specific conditions and meanings, the notion of human rights has been reinterpreted by the advocates of the stoning punishment in a way that takes it out of its original and appropriate context. This not only reveals the condition of plurality of pluralities, but also shows that none of the competing modes of legal reasoning is completely voiceless.

NOTES

1. These two *qanuns* were: (1) on *Hukum Jinayat* (Islamic penal rules); and (2) on *Hukum Acara Jinayat* (Islamic penal procedures). The former identifies what are considered to be actions that violate norms of the Islamic *jarimah* (criminal law) and the penalties that should be imposed on the *uqubat* (offenders). The latter deals with the institutions responsible for applying the rules, how to establish evidence, the procedures for litigation and the methods for the examination of judges. Initially, both were drafts prepared and drafted by the Provincial Dinas Syariat Islam under the leadership of Al Yasa Abubakar. Both qanuns were drafted without including the stoning punishment
2. Interview with Bahrom Rasyid, 14 August 2009
3. Interview with Jufri Ghalib, 15 September 2009.
4. *The Globe Journal*, 23 June 2009.
5. *Serambi Indonesia*, 24 October 2009.
6. *Gatra*, 11 November 2009.
7. *Serambi Indonesia*, 26 February 2013.
8. Interview with Al Yasa Abubakar, 14 August 2009.
9. Interview with Rusjdi Ali Muhammad, 22 July 2009.

10. This is based on interviews with Al Yasa Abubakar, 14 August 2009, and Rusjdi Ali Muhammad, 22 July 2009.
11. Irwandi Yusuf's interview is available at: http://beujroh.org/id/bungong.php?mn=d-Bgng&idnews=3&id=14, accessed 24 July 2009.
12. Aceh Institute, 6 October 2009.
13. Interview with Bahrom Rasyid, 14 August 2009

Chapter 6

Disputed Land Ownership

Meunyoe buet ka mupakat, lampôh jirat jeut ta peugala.
(If a consensus is to be achieved,
even the cemetery land can be pawned.)

Aceh proverb

As landowners, both Ihsan Gani and Teuku Taufik (these are not their real names) were supposed to receive a compensation payment on 20 June 2007. The compensation was due to the acquisition of their respective land parcels by the government. The money would have been transferred to their respective bank accounts. However, the payment was withheld. Some village leaders, who live nearby the expropriated lands, had made a claim that both individuals were not the valid landowners. The village leaders submitted their claim to the Civil Court of Jantho district. Given this lawsuit, the payment to Gani and Taufik was not fulfilled, pending the court decision. Thus, a court dispute over land ownership started between Gani and Taufik on the one side, and the villagers on the other.

According to Fitzpatrick (2008), land acquisition has been a main cause of land disputes, especially when it comes to who are the legitimate recipients of the compensation. Disputes in Aceh over the payment of compensation involve allegations that certain landholders are not eligible parties to the compensation, or that payments have been delayed by disputes or are not forthcoming at all.

The 2004 disaster in Aceh not only led to a massive loss of human lives, but also resulted in the devastation of huge parcels of land in the coastal areas.

Boundary lines and land parcel markers were largely obscured. Because of this, certain surviving individuals, neighbours and communities sought to establish a claim to land or to reclaim it. In a few cases, they even blatantly grabbed land parcels whose original owner or heirs were no longer known. This, in turn, ushered in a number of disputes concerning issues such as land boundaries between neighbourhoods, land reallocation and exchanges, inheritance rights to a land parcel and compensation payments. The situation became worse as the National Land Agency (BPN) office in Banda Aceh, which keeps land records, was substantially destroyed. In tsunami-affected areas many personal identity documents were badly damaged or lost (Fitzpatrick 2005). For this reason, restoring and confirming land rights has never been an easy task in post-tsunami Aceh.

Islam and Land Disputes

Despite the palpable relationship between Islam and land issues, especially in relation to the moral foundation that Islam provides, there is no discipline that could be called 'Islamic land law'. Therefore, Islamic land law, if it exists at all, is best understood with reference to other Islamic rules, especially those concerning marriage, gifts, inheritance and wakaf (Sait and Lim 2006: 33, 43). With this in mind, the question is, how has Islam been involved in land dispute settlements? In what ways it has played a role?

One way to identify how Islam is employed in dispute processes is through the extent to which it is applied in legal reasoning. According to Bowen (2003: 9–10), Islamic legal reasoning is the human effort, which is imbricated with social and cultural life, to resolve disputes by drawing on Qur'anic and hadith texts, *qiyas* (logic), *ijma'* (the consensus of the community), *maslaha* (public interest) and *al-'urf* (local customary practice). From an Islamic legal perspective, these sources are arranged hierarchically. But in the practice of reasoning about cases and justifying decisions reached, Muslim authorities and ordinary Muslims have always found themselves having to tack among competing values, norms and commands.

In post-tsunami Aceh, Islam was generally invoked to address land disputes by means of a fatwa issued by the council of ulama. The fatwa dealt with land issues by engaging local religious institutions, such as the sharia court and the *Baitul Mal* (Islamic Treasury), in five ways, as set out below.

First, the fatwa supported the increasing jurisdiction of the Sharia Court of Aceh to examine land rights confirmation, particularly those involving inheritance matters (see discussion in Chapters 2 and 3).

Secondly, the fatwa stated that land and property belonging to tsunami victims who no longer had legitimate heirs would be transferred to the Muslim community through the Baitul Mal through an order made by the Sharia Court of Aceh.

Thirdly, the fatwa declared that wakaf land that was abandoned or left uncultivated due to the disaster could be sold and exchanged in accordance with Islamic teachings and for the benefit of the Muslim community.

Fourthly, the fatwa asked the government to prevent the public notary from legalising land transactions in the tsunami-affected areas until land boundaries and evidence of land ownership had been lawfully settled.

Lastly, the fatwa held that claims for inheritance rights to land parcels in the tsunami-affected areas would be no longer valid after the end of 2009. An exception would be made for surviving orphaned children, who would be allowed to file for their rights until they reach nineteen years of age.

Despite this fatwa being issued early in the aftermath of the tsunami, it was arguably ineffective. This is not only because it has little, if any, influence on the land law system, but also due to the very nature of fatwas, which are not legally binding. As a result, many cases of land disputes, even if they involve Muslim parties, cannot be resolved by religious courts as the fatwa above suggested. In fact, the manual of land acquisition published by the government requires each of the parties involved to bring a case to the Civil Court, rather than to the Sharia Court, should a dispute arise that cannot be settled informally.

For that reason, one wonders whether religion plays a role concerning various guidelines for land dispute settlement. As Sait and Lim (2006: 8) pointed out, Islam provides a conceptual framework, such as *shura* or *musyawarah* (consultation) and *'adl* (justice), which can be used as important devices to resolve conflicts over land rights. Categorically, there is no doubt about the influential quality of both concepts, which are embedded in Islamic consciousness and administrative practice (Rosen 2000). Yet the way these concepts are put into practice is diverse, and might be different from time to time and from one place to another. After all, the extent to which the utilisation of such Islamic concepts of consultation and justice is effectively functioning in managing land disputes in Muslim societies remains in question.

The question of when and how religion matters in land dispute settlements is worth investigating. It becomes more pertinent because, in Aceh, Muslims constitute the majority population and the formal implementation of Islamic sharia has taken place. Thus, for some, it is always taken for granted that religion, in one way or another, should play a substantial role, including in land dispute settlement. The extent to which religion in its various manifestations plays a role in bringing a land dispute to an end is interesting. As will be discussed below, a land dispute case is useful for comprehending clearly how and why religion is (or is not) invoked by each of the contending parties to support their claims.

THE STATE OF DISPUTES

The land parcels in question are located in one of the areas in Aceh badly affected by the tsunami, namely, Lhoknga. Lhoknga is a sub-district of Aceh Besar. It is less than 20 km southwest of Banda Aceh, the capital of the province. The sub-district of Lhoknga has four *mukim* (a community consisting of several villages).[1] These mukim are Lhoknga, Keuh, Lamlhom and Lampuuk. The case took place in the mukim of Lhoknga, which has four *gampong* (villages): Mon Ikeun, Weuraya, Lamkruet and Lampaya. In Mon Ikeun, capital of the mukim of Lhoknga, a number of public buildings and places were badly or totally destroyed by the tsunami. These included a couple of military base camps, a police station, a hospital, several schools, government offices, a complex for sea tourism, a no longer used airfield, a golf course, the cement company of Semen Andalas Indonesia, and its housing compound for its workers.

Most importantly, there is national highway that crosses the sub-district of Lhoknga, connecting the capital city of Banda Aceh with Meulaboh on the west coast of the province. As the road lies along the coastline and in flat areas, it was greatly affected by the tsunami and suffered extensive damage. Many sections of the road deteriorated, and also several spots were flooded by seawater. The reconstruction process of this important highway required its relocation to areas further inland onto land belonging to various landowners. Therefore, the acquisition of the land for the purpose of road reconstruction was inevitable. While the budget for the road reconstruction came from USAID, an aid agency of the United States, the Indonesian government was responsible for providing funds to pay compensation to landowners whose lands were expropriated.

In connection with this land acquisition and the compensation payments, two major land disputes took place in this area, which involved individuals versus the Lhoknga community.

The first dispute was between Ihsan Gani and the Lhoknga community. What was at stake was 6,102 square metres of land parcels located on the right-hand side of the former road. They were valued at no less than US$110,800 (Rp. 1,220,400,000). Gani was supposed to receive this payment since he had kept a land document originating from colonial times, or before Indonesia's independence in 1945.

The second case was between Teuku Taufik and the Lhoknga community. Taufik possessed land parcels of around 7,204 square metres, which were subject to land expropriation. Taufik's land was located near to the coastline. He held a land certificate issued by the BPN in 1991 and was therefore entitled to receive compensation amounting to at least US$130,800 (Rp. 1,440,800,000).

IHSAN GANI VERSUS THE LHOKNGA COMMUNITY

The ancestry of the Gani family was not Acehnese in origin. This family is considered to be Malay, from North Sumatra. It is not clearly known when Gani's ancestor came to Aceh for the first time, but the family has lived in Banda Aceh for many years. Ihsan Gani himself, who is seventy years old, was born in Aceh. Because their homes in Banda Aceh were destroyed by the tsunami, the family moved to Ketapang, Aceh Besar. They have never lived in Lhoknga, the site of the land dispute. The available information about the background of the family is that they were politicians, and several members of the family had occupied positions in the legislatures at national and provincial levels during the first five decades of Indonesia's independence. Until 2009, Ihsan Gani remained actively involved in a political party.[2]

The land rights of this family were originally documented under the name of Ihsan Gani's oldest brother, who died in the 1990s. Ihsan Gani then represented his brother's surviving heirs. His claim of entitlement to the compensation payment was based on a rather complicated land document stating his rights of *erfpacht*. Erfpacht was one of the land rights acknowledged by the Dutch Civil Code. According to Article 720 of the Civil Code, which is now the *Kitab Undang-Undang Hukum Perdata* Indonesia, erfpacht is 'the right to fully enjoy the property belonging to others with the obligation to pay an annual tribute in the form of money, results or outcome to the landowners as a recognition of their ownership . . .' The Dutch Agrarian Act stated that the rights of erfpacht could be held for up to seventy-five years. In the colonial period, the leased lands could be the property of individuals, or the adat community (*hak ulayat*) or government land (Biezeveld 2004).

Figure 6.1 A land document belonging to the defendant Gani © Arskal Salim

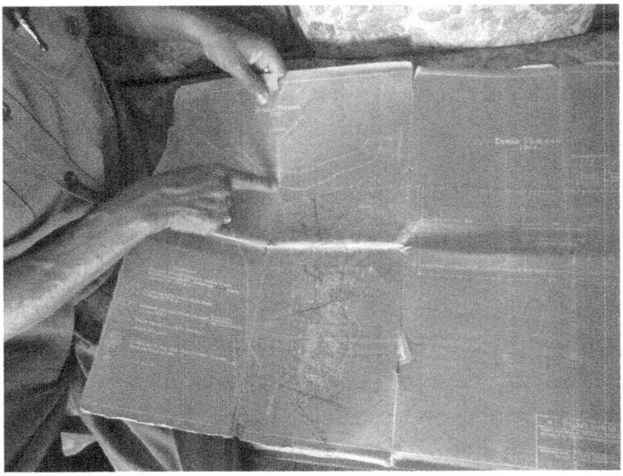

Figure 6.2 The defendant Gani pointing to a blueprint map showing where his land was located © Arskal Salim

Gani's right of erfpacht arose out of a purchase transaction that he made with a Dutch company, N. V. Cultuur Maatschappij Lho'Nga. The director of this Dutch company was F. F. Rell. He controlled the piece of land (33,829 *bouw*) and had cultivated it as a plantation in Lhoknga since June 1908, four years after the formal conquest of the Aceh kingdom. This right of cultivation was derived from the Dutch government. It was not clear, however, how this piece of land initially came under the control of the Dutch.

The transfer of the right of erpacht from the Dutch company to Gani took place in Kutaradja (now Banda Aceh) in August 1953, four years after the Dutch officially acknowledged the independence of Indonesia. In 1955, Gani's land rights, in the form of erfpacht, were then authorised by the Minister for Justice of Indonesia. Soon afterwards, the rights were transferred to the name of N. V. Perkebunan dan Perdagangan Meutia (Meutia Plantation and Trade Company Limited).

In 1960, the government of Indonesia introduced the Basic Agrarian Law (BAL). This land law was intended to bring some changes in land rights and ownership. As argued by Fitzpatrick (1997), although this land reform has the clear objective of unifying various applicable land regulations in Indonesia, the BAL is not a syncretistic amalgam of western and adat land principles. Instead, it operates contrary to the adat land law. This is due to the fact that although the BAL states that its basis is custom, the adat land law has a weakened position. While the BAL has quite easily adopted almost all the Dutch legal legacy, this national law has difficulties in converting a number of aspects of the adat land law. Adat land law remains valid only to the extent that it is consistent with the provisions of the BAL itself, the interests of national unity and the state.

The situation became worse as subsequent land policies regarded all uncultivated communal lands, widely known as hak ulayat land, as 'the state hak ulayat', on the grounds of Article 33:3 of the Indonesian Constitution and the provision of BAL itself (Article 3), which declare all land in Indonesia to be under the 'control' of the state (Wignyosoebroto 1996). According to Fitzpatrick (1997), this notion of state hak ulayat has enabled the state to grant rights to uncultivated hak ulayat land without obtaining the consent of the relevant local community and without triggering the legal obligation to pay adequate compensation to holders of expropriated titles.

With regard to the right of erfpacht and hak ulayat land, the BAL generally stipulates that individuals who have the erfpacht rights to hak ulayat land could register with, and receive from, the state a full statutory right over particular parcels of such land. However, the BAL has changed the nature of the rights of erfpacht and given it a new name, *hak guna usaha* (HGU, 'rights to cultivate'). The BAL (Article 3 of Conversion Rules) states:

> The right of erfpacht for a large-scale plantation company, which already exists at the time this Act comes into effect, shall become a hak guna usaha as meant in Article 28(1) [of the BAL] for the remaining term of the rights of erfpacht in question, which shall not exceed 20 years.

The BAL, however, does not clarify what happens to the right of erfpacht after twenty years of cultivation. It may be understood from other provisions in the BAL (Article 28:1) that such rights should be returned to the state in 1980 or to the initial holders (for example, hak ulayat land would be given back to the adat community). From a legal point of view, the right of erfpacht only lasts for twenty years, namely from 1960 to 1980. After 1980, all lands, the rights to which are based on erfpacht, should become the state's property. If this interpretation is correct, it is obvious that the BAL has sought to transform the status of numerous areas of land, including hak ulayat land, into state land (Fitzpatrick 1997).

How do all these rules apply to the right of erfpacht that Gani once held? Gani considered that his right of erfpacht remained valid. His registered land did not automatically become the state's land in 1980. From a legal perspective, Gani's right of erfpacht should have expired in 1980, and the land should have been returned to the state, unless his right was renewed under the scheme of hak guna usaha. This scheme would have extended his right for one more term (twenty-five years), or until 2005 at the latest.

However, Gani was unable to renew or make a reconfirmation of his land rights in 1980. He had an excuse for this. He explained that since the late 1950s

– it was in this period that the rebellion of Teungku Daud Buereueu-eh took place – almost the whole area of the land was occupied by the army and used for its military base camps and facilities. Gani rationalised that, for this reason, he had no chance to make a claim over his lands as it would have endangered his life. In spite of this, Gani was able to retrieve his right in 1980, by having a letter issued by the former army commander in chief, Colonel Syamaun Gaharu, who was responsible for the security of Aceh from 1956 to 1960. This letter confirmed the truth of Gani's statement, that the military had occupied most areas of his lands in Lhoknga during the period when he was due to renew his right of erfpacht.

Judging from a legal administrative perspective, the fact that Gani was unable to renew his land rights in due time, whatever excuse he had, implies the loss of his entitlement, and this should prevent him from being an eligible recipient of compensation. For this reason, in June 2007, the government, which was in this case represented by the Board of Rehabilitation and Reconstruction (BRR) of Aceh, issued a statement confirming that the land in question was state land. However, Gani refused to accept this judgment and sought support in getting his rights back. Basing his request on Syamaun Gaharu's letter, Gani approached the army commander's office in Aceh, asking it to provide him with a supporting letter declaring that the land, which had been used by the military before the tsunami, had now been formally returned to him. This letter worked effectively. The BRR relented and then asked the land acquisition committee to provide compensation to Gani. One may wonder if a financial arrangement played a significant role behind this drama – some are sure that, in Indonesia, money has a powerful influence in almost every social and political situation.

The Lhoknga village leaders could not accept either Gani's claim over the land or the decision of the BRR to pay compensation to him. These leaders sought to challenge the decision and aimed to have the payment cancelled. In the view of the Lhoknga people, the land in question originally belonged to the people and was hak ulayat land. Therefore, according to Teungku Basri (this is not his real name), who is sixty-three years old and one of the community elders, the land could not be easily owned by outsiders.[3] According to Aceh's custom, this kind of land was known as '*tanah mukim*' or '*tanah kullah*' (Abdurrahman 2006a), and the transfer of rights over it is subject to strict community control. At most, outsiders can obtain only limited rights of use to this land, with the consent of the community and on the payment of 'recognition money', known as '*hak tamong*' in Aceh (Sufi 2002: 31).

Teungku Basri further explained that when the Dutch completely defeated Aceh in 1904, there were only limited scenarios available for them to hold the hak ulayat land: borrowing it, leasing it or capturing it from the people. It was unclear to him how the Dutch obtained control over the land and then provided a Dutch company with the right of erfpacht to that land. As the Dutch left Aceh in 1942, Basri considered that the lease of the land should have expired and the erfpacht rights should have been returned to the original landowner. Basri emphasised that 'because the [real] owner is [now] unknown, [the land] must go to the [local] government, which is the mukim [structure]'.[4] For Basri, who also chaired the Lhoknga committee for land disputes, the past powerful position of the mukim, which controlled the lands and natural resources of the area, must be taken into account in the current situation. This historical argument of hak ulayat land was then reasserted in the statement of claim sent out to the court.

Despite the fact that the legal basis for the Lhoknga community's claim seems to be weak when seen from the perspective of Indonesian land law, what is obvious from this case is that adat land and state land cannot be easily identified in a precise way. Did the lands in question belong to the state? Which level of the state structure has full control of those lands, the local village government or the national government?

Teuku Taufik versus the Lhoknga Community

Teuku Taufik (who is sixty-four years old) is an Acehnese who has lived in Lhoknga since childhood. His mother's origin was in Lhoknga, while his father came from another sub-district in Aceh Besar. Taufik acknowledges himself as the fourth generation descendant of Teuku Umar, a renowned hero of Aceh, who cleverly but determinedly fought the Dutch. Taufik has 'Teuku' as part of his first name as an indication that he has a linkage with the Acehnese aristocratic family in the past. It is no wonder, then, that he maintains that some areas of land in the district belonged to his ancestors. Taufik held a number of leadership positions in Lhoknga for almost a decade. His last position was as chief of the mukim Lhoknga. In fact, this position remained formally his for the duration of the land dispute. He was then replaced through an election in mid-2008.

The location of Taufik's land was less than 100 metres from the coastline and not very far from the site of the cement company. Unlike Gani, who had held his land documentation prior to the introduction of the BAL in 1960, Taufik had held his land rights only since the early 1990s, or about thirty years after the BAL was enacted. Seen from a legal administrative point of view, Taufik's right to the land was much stronger than Gani's, because Taufik acquired his land title by a formal procedure, in accordance with the current Indonesian land system. His right to the land is known as a *hak milik* (statutory title), which is the strongest and fullest right to land under the BAL.

The origin of Taufik's land rights is connected with the opening of the cement company in 1980.[5] When the company commenced its operation, by constructing buildings and facilities in the area, Taufik opened a stall there selling food and drinks. He was not alone. Other people, either from Lhoknga itself or from outside it, came and operated similar businesses there. As none of these stalls had a valid licence, they were considered illegal, and the government razed them to the ground in 1981. Although frustrated, Taufik remained resilient and sought a way to re-establish his business there. He went to meet several leading figures of Lhoknga, including the *camat* (head) of the sub-district, the head of the sub-district police station and the head of the mukim and other elders to get their advice and assistance in gaining legitimate use of the land. None of these figures whom Taufik asked could do anything, since the land belonged to the state (*tanah negara*).

However, a suggestion was offered which made Taufik optimistic that he could restore his business. This suggestion came from people who knew the complicated procedure of getting a land title and how to change the status of a piece of land from state to private. He was informed that the occupants of abandoned, or vacant, land could obtain a licence from the BPN to cultivate the land and, after long-term occupation, this licence could be transformed into a statutory right by providing a payment to the government. Taufik put this suggestion into practice by cultivating the land in the area for almost ten years, and made the required payment with the money he received from selling his parent's lands located in another sub-district. In 1991, Taufik eventually received a statutory title certifying his rights to land parcels of almost two hectares, including the piece of land in question.

Why and how did the Lhoknga community come to challenge the evidence presented by Taufik? The argument they put forward was not very different to that used against Gani. The Lhoknga community made a land claim based on hak ulayat land. They objected to Taufik's entitlement to compensation by sending a protest note to the various institutions concerned. They argued that the land in question belongs to the adat community. Indeed, they quoted the Acehnese customary rule that asserts that land located near to the coastline cannot be privately owned since it is hak ulayat land.[6]

One could say that by presenting the argument of hak ulayat land, the Lhoknga people sought to revive the sovereignty of adat, especially in the sense of the authority of the mukim over lands. As pointed out by Bowen (2003), adat revivalism includes the struggle for more local authority in the control of territory and its resources, more emphasis on local norms for dispute settlements and natural resources management, and more attention to the triumph of past sovereignty. This is particularly true in Aceh, given the recent formal acknowledgement that adat may play a greater role in various social aspects of the law.

Taufik made a counter-claim, saying, among other things, that before he formally took up his position as head of the mukim in 2002, none of his predecessors or any other elders in Lhoknga had confirmed whether the mukim of Lhoknga owns hak ulayat land. Additionally, he argued that hak ulayat land is available only in the village, or desa, and not in the *kelurahan*.[7] Since the 1990s, Mon Ikeun, the village where the land in question is located, had been redefined as a kelurahan. Because of this, Taufik contended that hak ulayat land is no longer available in the kelurahan of Mon Ikeun at all. Implicit in Taufik's counter-argument is that once a village becomes a kelurahan, all hak ulayat land in the area becomes state land. Nevertheless, this logic seems to be problematic, especially in the context of Aceh, given that the government of Aceh, based on Law 11 of 2006, attempted to transform all kelurahan in the province back to gampong, whose structures are similar to desa in other provinces. In this eventuality, will those particular areas of state land that were originally hak ulayat land revert to their previous status (as hak ulayat land)?

Furthermore, in an effort to argue against the Lhoknga community's claim, Taufik asked his son, Teuku Hidayat, to represent him in registering a lawsuit at the Civil Court of Jantho. Filed on 19 July 2007, while this same case was being examined by the judges, Taufik's counter-statement contended that the land in question belonged to him and accused the Lhoknga community, as represented by four gampong leaders and a secretary of the mukim, of seeking to impede the payment of compensation to the legitimate beneficiary. This counter-statement further stated that the claim of the community leaders was groundless, and had much to do with their grudge against Taufik himself. To make this allegation convincing, the counter-statement mentioned three issues.

First, it asked why it was only now that those leaders claimed the land in question as hak ulayat land when, in fact, they knew that Taufik had occupied it for sixteen years (from 1980 to 2006), and that there were five permanent buildings belonging to Taufik on that land before the tsunami.

Secondly, it inquired why those leaders claimed only Taufik's land as belonging to hak ulayat land, and did not include other certificated neighbouring lands. In fact, owners of these neighbouring lands had received the compensation payment from the BRR.

Thirdly, it questioned why the Lhoknga leaders made the claim of hak ulayat land only on those expropriated lands (7,204 square metres) and not on the whole area (19,680 square metres) that belonged to Taufik. For all these reasons, Taufik asked the court to punish the Lhoknga leaders who sought to thwart the compensation payment by decreeing that they should pay him a large amount of money, 2 billion rupiah. This money was requested not only because the community leaders were accused of having committed an *onrechtmatigedaad* (tort act), but also to recompense Taufik for the loss of his social integrity as a respected figure in Lhoknga.

Consultation and Negotiation

As each of the contending parties remained adamant in their claims, the case was then brought to the Civil Court of Jantho. The first hearing took place on Thursday, 28 June 2007. A council of three judges was assigned to examine the case – two male and one female. As the two male judges have since been posted to other courts in different cities, one to Sigli and one to Langsa, only the female judge remains working at the Jantho Civil Court. Her name is Christina Simanullang and I met her one afternoon at the court of Jantho. Although she is Christian, Simanullang was wearing a headscarf during office hours. She explained that there were only three brief hearings before this case was then peacefully resolved by the parties themselves. During the first hearings, the judging council did almost nothing, except to persuade the parties to make the compromise.[8] This advice, that disputes should be solved by way of compromise, is in fact a required legal proceeding, as stipulated in the circular of the Supreme Court. Should the judging council neglect to advise parties to try come to a peaceful settlement, the final decision of the court would not be lawfully acknowledged.

A barrister for the Lhoknga community, Fauzan (this is not his real name), had been actively pushing each of the disputants towards a settlement during the recess period. Fauzan (who is forty-four years old) had legal training from the University of Syiah Kuala, Banda Aceh. He is Acehnese and lives in Darussalam, another sub-district of Aceh Besar. Fauzan has no kin relationship at all with the Lhoknga community. He did not even know why the community decided to approach his legal firm to represent the cases before the court. In his capacity as their barrister, Fauzan received a mandate from the heads of four villages (Mon Ikeun, Weuraya, Lamkruet and Lampaya) and a secretary of the mukim of Lhoknga. This mandate included the task of conducting a peaceful settlement.[9]

As I learned from the barrister, the Lhoknga community contacted him only two days before the compensation was to be paid to Gani and Taufik. Therefore, he did not have much time to study both cases carefully before preparing a statement of claim on behalf of the Lhoknga community. What was crucial for him was to submit the statement of claim to the court in due time, thus preventing the compensation money from being transferred to Gani and Taufik.

Having studied the two cases more deeply, the barrister found that, from a legal perspective, none of the contending parties had strong evidence to claim land rights, and, hence, they were most likely not in the position of beneficiaries. In his legal view, Gani's right of erfpacht had expired as it had not been renewed. Gani has, indeed, lost his entitlement. The only support he held for his claim to land rights was the letter provided by the army commander of Aceh, which has no legal standing before the law. However, in Fauzan's opinion, the statutory title that Taufik had obtained from the government remained viable from a legal point of view. This was so, given that Taufik's term of occupation of those land parcels was less than twenty years, as required by Indonesian land regulations.

At the same time, the barrister viewed the Lhoknga community's argument of hak ulayat land as weak also. In his view, the Lhoknga community's right to hak ulayat land had expired when they were unable to gain the rights to these 'waste' lands in the 1980s, as the right of erfpacht had elapsed earlier. According to this lawyer, the failure to transfer the wastelands officially to the ownership of individuals or the community would lead to such land parcels being classified as state land. If the court adjudication were to go through, it was most likely that the judges would issue a decision allowing the government, with the aim of acquiring public utilities, to confiscate the land in question without making compensation to any of the disputants.

Having been informed of the possible outcome of the judicial adjudication, the Lhoknga people responded that they would be happy to accept such a decision if that implied that none of the parties would receive the compensation. This is very typical of the approach of many people in Aceh, and has been widespread in practice among them for a long time. It is expressed in local language as 'sihet bek roubah abeh' ('instead of having something curved, it is better to have it broken'). Despite knowing this aphorism very well, the barrister did not want to see this outcome become a reality, not only because the adjudication process would take years to complete, but because the road construction could not commence while the case remained unresolved. After all, as a lawyer, Fauzan was thinking about how the community would get the money to pay him. Certainly, he would not provide a pro bono legal service.

Given that the possible, or probable, outcome was as outlined above, the barrister took into full account the judges' advice to compromise, and tended to actively direct the negotiation process. At first, the disputing parties were reluctant to negotiate, and were disposed to threaten one another. While the Lhoknga community mobilised a massive number of people to attend the hearings at the Jantho court, Gani's son, who has been a chief of the Aceh Transition Committee (KPA, the body established to accommodate former GAM combatants) of the sub-district Aceh Besar, invited his members to support his father's case. Meanwhile, Taufik had an army group behind him that backed up his stance. As this fierce situation escalated, the barrister made every endeavour to bring all parties to the negotiation table to look for a win–win solution.

Between June and early September 2007, the barrister attended a number of community meetings in Lhoknga to discuss the disputes and to find a formula for an agreed compromise. At these meetings, the barrister informed the community about the current situation on the land in question and the possible outcomes of the disputes. He advised the meetings that there was no point going on with the court adjudication. Instead, he suggested that a peaceful settlement would be the best resolution. On the other side, he approached Gani and Taufik, persuading them to be open to negotiation.

The consultation and negotiation process between the contending parties mostly took place in a courtroom of the Jantho Civil Court. It was Gani who first gave way to the compromise. He offered to contribute a part of his compensation payment towards rebuilding the mosque. The Lhoknga residents initially asked that two-thirds of the whole payment (that is, 800 million rupiah, or more than US$72,000) should go to the mosque. Gani refused this demand and sought to retain a larger portion, but the community was adamant. The barrister then took the initiative, bargaining from 500 million rupiah down to 300 million rupiah of the whole payment. After continuous persuasive negotiation, both Gani and Taufik finally agreed to offer 300 million rupiah each, meaning that the Lhoknga community would receive 600 million rupiah (or around US$54,500) in total for their mosque.

However, there was still discontent among the Lhoknga community over the final result of this negotiation. Teungku Basri did not like the way the barrister undertook his tasks, and was unhappy with the amount of money that the community would receive. In his opinion, the barrister took legal initiatives beyond the expectations of the villagers, but, although Basri was the chairman of the Lhoknga committee for land disputes, he did not have enough power to argue against the agreement reached by all the authorities of the mukim of Lhoknga who had given the barrister full mandate. These village leaders supported the result of the negotiation and signed the agreement.[10]

On the surface, the peaceful agreement was a win–win solution. Yet it was more than that. It ratified the land rights of both Gani and Taufik. The agreement stated that, as the plaintiff, the Lhoknga people should withdraw their registered statement of claim from the court. Moreover, as a negotiated agreement had eventually been reached, the Lhoknga community should make no more claims in the future over any land parcels belonging to Gani or Taufik in the same area that had not been expropriated.

Role of Religion: Persuasive or Decisive?

Was religion a factor in motivating the Lhoknga community to claim back land rights such as these? As I found in a statement of claim sent out to the Civil Court, and also as revealed in my interviews, aspects of religion were invoked. I learned that the mosque of Lhoknga was put up as a 'stake'. In almost every mukim in Aceh there is only one 'official' mosque where Muslim residents perform Friday prayers. As a place of worship, the mosque strongly reflects the religious fervour of the Acehnese. This explains why this mosque has a central position in the lives of the people of Lhoknga. Since this mosque was affected by the destructive earthquake and tsunami in 2004, reconstructive work was certainly needed. Given this circumstance, one could say that the goal of having the compensation money from the government to defray the expenses necessary for the restoration of the mosque is religiously motivated.

It is plausible to contend that non-religious reasons actually underlie most of the claims made by the Lhoknga community. On the surface, it would appear that the plaintiffs to this dispute were motivated by financial considerations in making their claims over land rights, but the extent to which the Lhoknga community was driven by this particular motivation remains an enigma.

Arguably, in these two disputes religion took a persuasive rather than a decisive role. Religion becomes a contributing factor in the settlement of land disputes in the way that it is employed as a persuasive means of bringing the disputing parties to a compromise. In the Lhoknga case, the objective of reconstruction of the mosque was relatively successfully used to persuade both Gani and Taufik to allocate a part of the compensation they received towards it. But this ploy could work only because of the religious beliefs that Gani and Taufik hold. Gani, for instance, acknowledged that in making this allocation he not only sought to end the conflict, but also to make a contribution for religious purposes, even if, at the end of the day, the money he donated was used for other expenses:

> They asked me to provide a help to the mosque. I [then] offer support as much, or as less, as I want to . . . and it does not take me a long time to think to help because the mosque is located in Lhoknga . . . My intention was to help [the reconstruction of] mosque. So, if there is a kind [of manipulation], that's [not my business, but] their own affairs with God. It's up to them if they wanted to tell me untruths . . . All I give is for the mosque reconstruction and not even a single cent is dedicated to the people. This is a donation, not a project fund . . . And if I don't see any result of the reconstructed work on the mosque in the next three or five years, I will not make a correction at all![11]

In Gani's view, the way that the Lhoknga community put the mosque up as a stake was a religious masquerade to appropriate the land rights of others. He suspected that the mosque was not the real motive behind their claim to land rights. Gani believed that in the afterlife they would be asked to take responsibility for having 'sold' the mosque. When I was in Lhoknga doing fieldwork in 2008, the mosque had been partially renovated, but the budget for this renovation came from the BRR. In an interview with Teungku Basri, he told me that the money from Gani and Taufik was to be spent on extending the rear area of the mosque and for building a parking area.[12] However, when I made a short visit to Aceh late in 2008, the mosque still remained in the same state.

In terms of the legal reasoning in this dispute, religion appears only vaguely. Both Gani and Taufik underpin their claims largely with documents that derived from the applicable national land laws. The argument of hak ulayat land put forward by the Lhoknga community is customary in nature rather than religious. The Lhoknga community neither cited the scripture nor stated that the land is God's wealth left to human beings for their use.

In fact, the Acehnese customary ideas on land issues have a close relationship with religion, which holds that the earth and what it has on it are God's creatures. According to Sufi (2002: 28–9), there were two kinds of land in Aceh before the twentieth century. The first was the uncultivated land, known as '*tanoh kullah*' ('land that belongs to Allah'). This was under the control of the mukim, and hence it was also often called '*tanoh mukim*' (Abdurrahman 2006b). The second was the cultivated land, which was called '*tanoh milek gob*', meaning that the land belongs to the person who has used it.

Although the land in question was claimed to be tanoh mukim or tanoh kullah, the argument presented by the Lhoknga community hardly made any reference to this concept of divine ownership. In addition, al'urf (local customary practice) that might reflect the influence of Islamic legal theory in the Lhoknga community's reasoning failed to materialise in these land disputes. The argument of hak ulayat land as part of al'urf in Aceh is no longer systematically tenable. The colonial land regulations and the Indonesian national land laws have disrupted it. According to Fitzpatrick (1997), although both these legal systems acknowledge the status of hak ulayat land, in reality they have sought to subvert it and even to expropriate, in particular, the uncultivated land.

Religion may be seen to be expressed in the practice of musyawarah, as a means by which land disputes are resolved. From an emic point of view, the Acehnese consider that the practice of musyawarah is both religious and customary in nature. It is intended to achieve *suloh* (amicable settlement) of disputes. The term 'suloh' is derived from the Arabic '*sulh*', which means 'peace' Another similar local term, '*duek pakat*', also implies the notion of musyawarah.

Village musyawarah in Aceh are mostly conducted in a mosque or in a *meunasah*.[13] Aswar (2007) described musyawarah as:

> . . . like a banyan tree for justice seekers. Its leaves can protect from sunlight and rain, its trunk can be a place to lean on, its branches can be a place to depend on, and its roots can be a place to sit on.

As Aswar (2007) explained, usually, before starting a musyawarah, the participants first perform *berwudu'* (ablution) as if they are preparing to observe a prayer. In the musyawarah, elders of the village (*imeum mukim*, *keuchik* and *teungku meunasah*) direct the meeting to discuss the problem, to hear different opinions, to consult and negotiate with the parties involved, who are present, and to suggest a resolution. At the end of the musyawarah, the disputants ask each other for forgiveness. In closing the musyawarah, a *teungku* (religious leader) reads a prayer (*istighfar* and *syukur*). To celebrate a peaceful agreement after conflicts, tensions or enmities, which is reached through musyawarah, a number of social rituals are conducted. These rituals may include *peusijuk* (joint prayers), *kenduri* (having a traditional meal together), *sayam* (fines in the form of slaughtering of stock) or *diet* (fines in the form of cash payment), depending on the case being settled (Hoesin 1970: 170–1).

Given the above description, which shows that musyawarah is naturally a religious as well as a traditional custom in the Acehnese community, one could argue that it has a key role in achieving a peaceful settlement for every dispute that takes place among villagers. This deliberate consultation through the village meeting is believed to bring back social equilibrium and harmony, and, to achieve this ultimate goal, even a religious rule could be put aside, provided that the final decision is achieved through unanimous agreement among the participants of the musyawarah. A very popular hadih maja justifies this: 'meunyoe buet ka mupakat, lampôh jirat jeut ta peugala', meaning that if a consensus is to be achieved, even the cemetery land can be pawned. This aphorism underlines the belief that consensus is so important that even a graveyard, which is considered a sanctified element in the life of many Acehnese, can be compromised to achieve it.

Interpreted in the light of another maxim widely shared among Acehnese, '*agama ngon adat han jeut cre, lagee zat ngon sifeut*' ('religion and adat cannot be separated, both are like the substance of a thing and its attributes'), one may contend that the unity of adat norms and religious values within Acehnese society lies in the process of deliberate consultation for peaceful settlement. In other words, the musyawarah is the key means by which the Acehnese seek to make sense of their social world, in which religion and adat are united. For this reason, it seems sufficient to argue that, since the contending parties in the two cases discussed above finally avoided court adjudication and were inclined to end their disputes through the musyawarah, religion can be said to play a critical role in managing land disputes in Aceh.

However, seen in the light of an etic account, the assertion that the musyawarah reflects the indispensable role of religious practice in settling the two land disputes being discussed in this chapter warrants at least four criticisms.

First, the musyawarah that led to a peaceful settlement of the land disputes examined above was not merely a religious one. Musyawarah is common to many ethnic groups in Indonesia, and has also been traditionally practised among other religious communities whose religion is not Islam (Bräuchler 2009). Indeed, the institution of musyawarah in many societies in the archipelago is not necessarily religious in nature. It existed, in fact, long before the introduction of Islam.

Secondly, the musyawarah that finally led to agreement in the two cases above was largely driven by the court procedure, in which the nature of this kind of musyawarah is supposedly secular. Instead of being conducted in a mosque or in a meunasah, as is the general practice in Aceh, this musyawarah took place in a room at the Civil Court of Jantho.

Thirdly, it was the barrister who actively directed the musyawarah that brought all disputing parties to a compromise, and not religious traditional figures such as the imeum mukim, keuchik or teungku meunasah, who are usually closely involved in the 'religious' musyawarah.

Fourthly, the peaceful agreement resulting from this musyawarah was not concluded by a social ritual such as a peusijuk or kenduri. The resolution of this dispute was instead marked by the withdrawal of claim statements from the court by the respective parties. Above all, as far as Islamic legal reasoning is concerned, the consensus produced by this musyawarah was not completely equal to ijma' as there was a dissenting opinion. Teungku Basri, chairman of the committee of land acquisition disputes, continued to oppose the final outcome of the settlement.

Because of these criticisms, I maintain that the musyawarah, which helped to resolve the land disputes discussed above, cannot be seen solely as reflecting the crucial role of religion. Despite the fact that the musyawarah is both religious in nature and customary in character within the Acehnese community, the musyawarah that ended these two land disputes is not a necessarily religious mode of conflict management. This is because the musyawarah is found in different settings and is advocated by various institutions and agencies.

The Limited Role of Religion in 'Irreligious' Disputes

The description of the two land disputes above demonstrates how different interpretations of facts, norms, rules, institutions, actors, motivation and interests have been interwoven in transforming claims into disputes and then converting disputes into settlements. Religious, economic, financial and socio-political factors were all actively mixed up in these cases. Specifically, each of the disputing parties invoked, or dismissed, religion, albeit symbolically, in several aspects of their cases. First, religion appears to provide part of the motivation for making the claims for compensation arising from the land acquisition project. Secondly, it constitutes a line of reasoning that underpins the claimants' argument for land rights. Thirdly, it serves as a means to bring the disputes to an end. Religion, epitomised by the mosque as a place of worship for Muslims, has been invoked to play a persuasive role in bringing the contending parties to a compromise. Yet religion – in terms of actor, institution, mechanism and legal reasoning – has not been fully represented so as to play a decisive role in resolving those disputes.

These disputes not only provide a space for one particular norm to defend its position, but they also become an arena in which to choose a 'justification' for the claimed interests of each party. The way the disputants employ various forms of reasoning, including religious, in such 'irreligious' disputes reveals a practice of 'justification shopping' among the Acehnese. Although land issues are not directly part of the Islamic rules that are being formally applied in Aceh, religion was mobilised, albeit symbolically, to justify a claim for land rights. This position allows each of the disputants to choose to use a particular argument in one case, but then to try to avoid using this same argument in another situation, in an attempt to have their claim accepted (K. Benda-Beckmann 1981).

Finally, since there is an increasing number of works that tell readers, from an Islamic perspective, about the employment of religious devices in effectively settling disputes (Rashid 2004; Hassan 2006; Lukito 2006), it is well worthwhile balancing these with an account of the musyawarah that has brought land disputes in Aceh to an end, in which the 'mechanism' was not necessarily traditionally religious. Such an account does not simply aim to show the (un)reliability of the religious element in any given dispute settlement, but, importantly, to disclose an example of practices, in land issues in particular, where religion, even it were given official status to play a greater role, has some limitations.

NOTES

1. This configuration is different from that in other parts of Indonesia where the territorial structure is hierarchical, from the province down to the village. Aceh has a quite distinct hierarchical division: the province at the uppermost level, then the *kabupaten* or *kota* (district), the *kecamatan* (sub-district), which is further broken down to *mukim* (a community consisting of several villages), and then to *gampong* or *desa* (village) and *lorong* (sub-village) at the lowest level. According to Abdurrahman (2006b), mukim and gampong in Aceh have a dual function. They are not only parts of government structures, but they both also serve as entities of distinct indigenous communities.
2. All descriptions about Ihsan Gani and his land are based on interview with him on 5 May 2008.
3. Interview with Teungku Basri, 2 May 2008.
4. Interview with Teungku Basri, 2 May 2008.
5. All descriptions on the origin of Taufik's land is based on interview with Taufik's son, Teuku Hidayat, 18 April 2008.
6. Interview with Teungku Basri, 2 May 2008.
7. Though desa and kelurahan are part of a sub-district and both are translated into

English as 'village', a kelurahan has less power than a desa. A kelurahan is part of the regency/city government bureaucracy and is led by a *lurah*. The lurah is therefore a civil servant, and directly responsible to the head of the sub-district. It was because all administrative offices of the sub-district of Lhoknga were concentrated in this village, Mon Ikeun, that its status was changed in the 1990s from desa to kelurahan.

8. Interview with Judge Christina Simanullang, 7 April 2008.
9. All descriptions on the role of barrister Fauzan in this case are based on interview with him on 22 April 2008.
10. Interview with Teungku Basri, 2 May 2008.
11. Interview with Ihsan Gani, 5 May 2008.
12. Interview with Teungku Basri, 2 May 2008.
13. Meunasah is a multipurpose building set up in almost every village in Aceh, which serves not only as a centre of worship, but also as a meeting place for the local community.

Part Three

Between Villages and Courtrooms

Chapter 7

Orphaned Grandchildren

Learn the laws of inheritance and teach them to the people;
for they are one-half of useful knowledge.

Prophet Muhammad

For more than three years after the 2004 Boxing Day tsunami that hit coastal areas of Aceh, twenty-five-year-old Rosdiana and her three surviving younger brothers had been wondering whether they were entitled to the estate left by their grandfather and grandmother, who died in the tsunami. Rosdiana and her brothers had also lost their father and all of their uncles. One aunt survived. As the only surviving child of Rosdiana's grandparents, the aunt was given control of the inherited property. Acting on her consultation with village elders, the aunt took over all the estate. According to the elders, it was the aunt who became the legitimate heir, while Rosdiana and her brothers had no right to the property, because a so-called '*patah titi*' had taken place.

The Village Customary Law

The term *patah titi* means, literally, 'broken linkage' or 'missing link'. It refers to a situation where a parent, usually the father, dies earlier than, or at the same time as, his parents, while his siblings survive. This leaves his children orphaned, but with aunts and/or uncles. The customary legal principle stipulates that to become an heir, one must be alive when the propositus dies. So if several people, who are linked by a line of inheritance, die concurrently, or one earlier than another but depending on the order in which their deaths occur, the configuration of heirs may be changed so that one or more heirs are foreclosed. Under this condition, the orphaned grandchildren are foreclosed by their uncles or aunts and they will not receive a share of the estate of the deceased grandparent.

In the village, an orphaned grandchild who does not receive an entitlement is often described as '*sudah patah titi*' ('suffering from a broken linkage'). The law professor of the Syiah Kuala University at Banda Aceh, Teuku Djuned, stated that the patah titi originated in the Shafi'i Islamic jurisprudence that has, for centuries, influenced local inheritance practices in Aceh (Salim 2006: 37). For instance, a Shafi'i legal textbook, *Nihaya al-Muhtaj* by al-Ramli,[1] explains that a son of a predeceased son is still considered a son, but his right to inheritance can be foreclosed by the presence of his uncle. Likewise, a daughter of a predeceased son is considered a daughter, but she can be excluded if she has a surviving uncle.

In some parts of Aceh, the patah titi is considered customary law. It has been a major reference for the division of inheritance, even in the post-tsunami age. What is more, in several Aceh villages, the patah titi is a stigmatic statement that impedes one's right to inherit. The patah titi is not only used as a justifiable reason to refuse orphaned grandchildren who ask for their share, but is also used to negate the inheritance rights of children whose parent is not predeceased at the grandparent's death. This is especially the case when the inheritance estate is not immediately divided following the death of the grandparent.[2] In this case, even when a son or daughter of the grandparent dies after the grandparent's death, the orphaned grandchildren are no longer considered heirs. The grandparent's wealth is divided among only his or her surviving children, and the orphaned grandchildren receive no share.

THE LAW OF THE COURT

In the view of judges of the Sharia Court of Aceh, the practice of patah titi in many of the country's villages is unlawful. The judges' disapproval of the practice stems from the introduction of the 1991 Compilation of Islamic Law (KHI). Article 185 of this Compilation states that:

> an heir who dies before the propositus may be replaced by his/her children . . . [and] the share received by the substitute heir may not exceed the share of an heir of the same degree as the person who is replaced.

Given this regulation, from the early 1990s, almost all judges in Aceh began to make decisions that invalidated the village practice of the patah titi. In other words, it is very likely that the claims of orphaned grandchildren to the estates of their deceased grandparents would be accepted by the court.

In the Indonesian courts, the replacement of predeceased heirs is not a new phenomenon. Some judges had accepted the possibility of this particular situation even before the introduction of the 1991 KHI. This is partly to do with the Dutch legal legacy, namely, the rule of *plaatsvervulling* (representation), as found in the existing Indonesian Civil Code. Articles 841–848 of the Code regulate how the replacement of predeceased heirs is implemented. The plaatsvervulling rule provides the right to descendants, but not to ascendants, to act as successor in the same capacity and to receive every right that would otherwise have been received by his or her predecessor.

More than thirty years before the introduction of the KHI in 1991, the Supreme Court issued a decision on the replacement of heirs based on plaatsvervulling. Ismuha (1978) described a case examined by the Supreme Court in 1959, and argued that the principle of plaatsvervulling was employed to eliminate injustice in that particular inheritance estate division. As plaatsvervulling in inheritance cases is a long-standing principle that has resulted in a number of jurisprudences of the Supreme Court, the provision of the substitute heirs, in Article 185 of the KHI, is seen as underpinning and corroborating this principle.

However, as the following two cases of the replacement of heirs show, the Supreme Court has not applied this rule consistently. In both cases, the propositus died in the 1980s, or prior to the introduction of the KHI in 1991. Yet the cases were treated differently when lower courts, and later the Supreme Court, examined them in the 1990s.

Case 1

Initially examined by the Religious Court of South Jakarta, this dispute involved the descendants of three brothers: ZAS (the propositus) and his two full brothers, MRS and YS (predeceased). While YS had died earlier, in 1975, ZAS died in 1985 and was survived by his daughter and widow. Acting as the plaintiffs, the children of YS filed a suit in 1992 claiming that they were entitled to property that had belonged to ZAS, on the grounds that they were substitute heirs of their predeceased father. The defendants of this case were: (1) a widow; (2) a daughter of the propositus; and (3) MRS, another surviving brother of the propositus. In their counterclaim, the defendants argued that the propositus died in 1985, before the introduction of the KHI, and, hence, the provision of the substitute heirs could not be applied. In addition, an inheritance statement from the Civil Court in May 1985 confirmed that they (the defendants) were legitimate heirs, while the predeceased brother (YS) was not considered an heir. The Religious Court did not accept the defendants' counter-claim. Instead, it made a decision in favour of the plaintiffs' position as the substitute heirs, and allocated a share that was similar to what would have been received by their father had he lived. The case was then appealed, and the Higher Religious Court annulled the lower court's decision. The case was taken to the Supreme Court in 1994, which confirmed the decision of the High Court (Effendi 2004: 258–63). As a result, the plaintiffs did not qualify as substitute heirs.

Instead of explaining its legal reasoning for overriding the rule of the substitute heirs in this case, the Supreme Court declared the outcome by supporting the decision of the High Court. The High Court argued that Article 185 of the KHI did not apply to this case because the death of the propositus took place before the introduction of KHI in 1991. In the High Court's view: 'Should all inheritance division that took place before 1991 be disputable based on Article 185, then there will be no legal certainty, which is contradictory to Article 229 of the same regulation.'[3] In the view of judges of the Higher Court who examined this case, the KHI has no retroactive effect (Effendi 2004: 266).

Why did the Supreme Court consider that, since the dispute was brought before the court only after 1991, the KHI provision of the substitute heirs could not be applied? This decision, that Article 185 did not apply for a death prior to 1991, however, was not in evidence in another, quite similar case (see below).

Case 2

This case involves a dispute between the descendants of Amaq Adam (who died in 1988) who had two wives. With his first wife, Adam had two sons, Sabri and Azharuddin, and a daughter, Mujenah, who died in 1964. Mujenah was survived by her two children, Misniarti and Sunardi. From his second marriage, Adam had two orphaned grandchildren, Sahman and Sodah. Seen in their relationship with the propositus (Adam), the disputants in this case were the surviving sons (Sabri and Azharuddin) and an orphaned grandson (Sahman), who had access to the deceased's property, versus three orphaned grandchildren (Misniarti, Sunardi and Sodah), who were excluded as heirs. It is unclear why Sahman and Sodah, who had similar positions as orphaned grandchildren from the second wife, were contending with each other. This is probably due to gender difference. As grandson, Sahman received a share, but as granddaughter, Sodah did not.

In 1997, the three orphaned grandchildren filed a lawsuit in the Religious Court of Selong, West Lombok. They claimed that, according to Article 185 concerning the substitute heir, they could replace their predeceased mother's position as daughters of the propositus, and were hence entitled to a share of the inheritance. To refute the plaintiffs' claim, the defendants argued that Article 185 could not be applied in this case, because the propositus had died three years before the introduction of the KHI in 1991. The judges of the first instance court were not convinced by the defendants' argument. In their view, since the inheritance estate had not been divided, it was appropriate to apply the KHI, even though the propositus had died before its introduction. The judges therefore accepted the claim of the plaintiffs as the substitute heirs and gave the orphaned grandchildren on each side a share that was similar to what would have been received by their respective predeceased mothers.[4]

When the case came to the Appellate Court in 1998, the decision of the lower court was annulled. The judges at the Higher Court of Mataram, who examined this case, explained that the KHI began to be applied only after 1991. As the propositus died before 1991, the orphaned grandchildren were not yet considered the substitute heirs as stipulated by Article 185 of the KHI. In the judges' view, at the time of Adam's (the propositus') death in 1988, the applicable law was the Islamic inheritance rule, which stipulates that all properties of the deceased go only to surviving heirs. As the surviving heirs at that time were two sons (Sabri and Azharuddin), they were the legitimate heirs not the others (the plaintiffs) as children of the predeceased daughters.[5]

The plaintiffs were not satisfied. They appealed to the Supreme Court, which cancelled the decision of the Higher Court of Mataram and adjudicated the case in its own right. In their decision, the Supreme Court judges reinforced the decision made by the first instance court of Selong, as they saw it as correct and appropriate.[6] According to Boediarto (2000), even though it took place in 1988, this inheritance case could be settled by referring to the KHI provision on the substitute heir, because the dispute arose and was brought before the court in 1997 – after the introduction of the KHI.

The Law of the Muslim Jurists

The other grounds for accepting the idea of heir replacement was a reinterpretation of the term '*mawali*' as found in the Qur'an 4.33.[7] This reinterpretation was proposed by Hazairin (1906–75), a renowned Indonesian professor who launched a radical reconstruction of the framework of the Islamic inheritance law (Sugiono 1999; Feener 2007). Much of Hazairin's effort to interpret Qur'anic verses on inheritance was devoted to the notion of replacing predeceased heirs, but with a slightly different approach.

With regard to the issue in question, Hazairin translated 'mawali' to mean 'representative of heirs'. According to Cammack (2008), Hazairin arrived at this reinterpretation because he considered the verse to mean that the inheritance share from either the parents or the relatives should be given to the mawali, and not to the person or persons implied by 'each' at the beginning of the verse. In Hazairin's view, the verse then reads: 'Unto [Fulan] We have appointed [representative] heirs (mawali) to that which parents and near kindred leave.'

According to Hazairin, the term 'mawali' is not a principle of replacement or substitution (Cammack 2008: 332). Rather, it is a representation of inheritance. The inheritance right that the mawali holds is not based on a derivative right from the predeceased heir. The mawali, therefore, does not replace the original predeceased heir in order to inherit, but she or he inherits in her or his own right. Through the reinterpretation of mawali, Hazairin's theory of the representation of heirs is nothing more nor less than the Qur'an's provision (Sugiono 1999: 83).

Hazairin's classification of heirs is worth discussing here. He held that the Qur'an allocates to the descendants of predeceased heirs the right to inherit a property that was to be given to the dead parent had she or he survived. Unlike the Sunni inheritance law, the Shafi'i school, in particular, recognises three categories of heirs: Qur'anic heirs (*dzawu al-furud*); agnatic or residuary heirs (*ashaba*); and distant relatives (*dzawu al-arham*). Hazairin (1964) proposed a new classification of heirs, which also has three categories:

1. dzawu al-furud: heirs entitled to a fixed Qur'anic share;
2. *dzawu al-qaraba*: heirs who share a blood relationship with the descendent, but fall outside the first category;
3. mawali: heirs who fulfil the criteria of both categories above and will emerge as representative heirs should the original heirs die.

Hazairin's classification is quite complex. He suggested a new class of heirs, whereby twofold hierarchies of priorities can be observed. The first category of heirs has a higher hierarchy than the second category, while within each of the first and the second categories, the original heirs secure the first place and the representatives, or mawali, are in second place, should the original heirs die earlier than the propositus. With this reformed classification in mind, Hazairin sought to reinforce his claim that mawali is a *wakil ahli waris* (representative of an heir) and not an *ahli waris pengganti* (someone who replaces an heir,, or 'substitute heir').

One can find some commonalities between Hazairin's theory of mawali and the rule of plaatsvervulling: both allow the heir replacement and share the view that a substitute heir fully takes the place of, and receives an inheritance share on behalf of, the predeceased heir. Thus, it is no wonder that Hazairin's reinterpretation of the term mawali was suspected of 'Islamising' the Dutch legal legacy of plaatsvervulling through justifying it by citing the Qur'an.

The idea of heir replacement had been known in Aceh probably through the rule of plaatsvervulling, as well as through Hazairin's reinterpretation of the term mawali. Law students at Aceh universities, who later became judges at the religious courts, were most likely familiar with the concept of heir replacement, because they studied the Civil Code and Hazairin's books on the Islamic inheritance law.[8] So, before the introduction of the KHI, the norm of the replacement of predeceased heirs was already known in Aceh, mainly by those with a background of legal training. Yet the custom of patah titi in the division of inheritance had been widely practised in the villages.[9]

Soon after the introduction of the KHI in 1991, the judges of the Sharia Court of Aceh formally introduced the principle of the substitute heir. Through adjudication on inheritance disputes, judges grant orphaned grandchildren an entitlement to the grandparent's estate. The court's decision that allows heir replacement, however, has met with the stern resistance from local teungku, who have traditional Islamic school backgrounds. In the view of many teungku, the norm of the replacement of predeceased heir does not exist either in the Qur'an or in the hadith. Moreover, the KHI provision on the substitute heir is not acceptable, for it contravenes Shafi'i inheritance law, which has largely influenced customary practices in Aceh. Therefore, even after the introduction of the KHI, orphaned grandchildren in some parts of Aceh still did not receive a share of a grandparent's estate. The situation is different in other parts of Indonesia, such as West Java, where customary norms recognise the replacement of a predeceased heir (Suparman 2005), and, hence, the decisions by religious courts to grant orphaned grandchildren inheritance, based on the KHI, face no challenge.[10]

Disseminating the Norm to the Villagers

To avoid injustices arising from the post-tsunami village practices of inheritance division, the Sharia Court of Aceh worked with the IDLO, an international agency based in Italy that provided legal assistance to tsunami survivors. Together, they organised two legal assistance programmes with content derived mostly from the applicable national laws, including the KHI. The two programmes involve: (1) developing a film programme intended to increase women's legal awareness of inheritance issues in particular – women became the programme's main audience because they were considered to have limited knowledge of, and a lack of access to, property rights; and (2) preparing professional trainers to educate village elders and local religious leaders on how to mediate and resolve cases between disputants effectively.

This collaborative project was partly a means of disseminating norms and laws on inheritance division. The film programme, for instance, focused on how the division of an estate should be carried out in accordance with national laws, with special reference to gender equality. Usually, the film was shown at a meunasah in each village, and was followed by a question-and-answer session. When the programme came to Rosdiana's village, she had an opportunity to inquire about her case. She learned from the programme that the sharia court did not recognise the practice of patah titi; hence, she and her brothers could take the position of their deceased father to receive a share of their grandparent's estate. With this knowledge in hand, Rosdiana informed her aunt about what the Sharia Court of Aceh would do in the case of inheritance for orphaned grandchildren. However, Rosdiana's aunt was unwavering in her conviction that she was the only lawful heir, and Rosdiana and her brothers were not legitimate heirs because of the patah titi.

Rosdiana did not give up. She sought to meet the recently elected keuchik (head of the village) to tell him what she had learned. In addition, she asked the keuchik to help her settle the case. This village leader was ready to help, but first he asked Rosdiana to provide him with details of properties left by the grandparent. Rosdiana could not meet this requirement of the keuchik as none of the villagers would supply her with information on the lands belonging to her grandparent. Instead, the villagers helped the aunt to collect all the information relating to the land, because, in their eyes, the aunt was the sole legitimate heir.[11] This action illustrates how strongly the villagers adhered to the customary law of patah titi. Although the keuchik disagreed with the patah titi, his promise to help Rosdiana was vague, if not ambivalent. Given that the keuchik was an authority in that village, he was certainly more than able to influence his people to help Rosdiana. The keuchik appears to have been in a dilemma between two contending legal visions: the customary rule and the KHI provision.

The second programme of dissemination was the recruitment of a number of judges, lawyers and law faculty staff as trainers. After receiving legal training on mediation, these trainers were sent to the tsunami-affected villages to educate heads of villages, local religious leaders and other village elders, and to teach them the laws applicable in Indonesia – on land and inheritance, and on child guardianship in particular.

During some training sessions, fierce debates arose between trainers and participants over whether orphaned grandchildren should receive an inheritance share. With their knowledge of the KHI, the trainers introduced the principle of the substitute heirs. They explained that the KHI is a national law with legal standing in Indonesia, and had been applied by the sharia courts in Aceh.[12] Yet these explanations failed to persuade all participants.

At least three arguments were put forward to oppose Article 185 of the KHI, as well as to maintain the practice of patah titi. First, the idea of heir replacement was rejected simply because the parent of the grandchildren predeceased the propositus and there were surviving children of the propositus who foreclosed the orphaned grandchildren. The second argument was that the principle of the substitute heirs, as stipulated in the KHI, has no foundation in the Qur'an. Some participants went further, contending that the KHI is a man-made law, while Islamic legal jurisprudence that has been practised in Aceh is

Figure 7.1 Mediation and legal skills training for village leaders
© Arskal Salim

purportedly derived from a divine source. Therefore, these participants refused to accept such a religious innovation. A third argument had it that the provision of heir replacement completely contradicted the customary law of patah titi. The KHI was therefore considered an alien norm that would contravene their traditional local values. In fact, in the light of the prolonged armed conflict in Aceh, some considered the KHI to be a product of the Javanese who oppressed the Acehnese.

To justify the principle of the substitute heir and to convince those participants who remained adamant, the trainers presented some Qur'anic verses on justice, as well as on orphans. The trainers argued that the relationship between surviving children and the propositus is not much different from that between orphaned grandchildren and the propositus. As far as justice in Islam is concerned, the trainers explained, they are equal members of one extended family. So it is unjust if the surviving children obtain all the estate and the orphaned grandchildren receive nothing.[13] Additionally, citing the Qur'an 4:8[14] and 4:10,[15] the trainers asserted that both these verses actually underpinned a command that surviving children should share the property left by the propositus with orphaned grandchildren.

According to Marluddin, a judge at the Higher Court of Aceh and a trainer in the programme, the Qur'an 4:10 actually works against the practice of patah titi in Aceh. For this reason, Judge Marluddin did not accept the rule of patah titi and did not view the death of a grandchild's parent as a 'missing link' that would prevent this grandchild from qualifying as an heir. In his view, what would prevent a grandchild from inheriting a grandparent's estate was not the presence of an uncle, but the presence of a father. When the father dies, the wall between grandparent and grandchild collapses, and this discloses the grandchild's access to the inheritance.[16]

Extending the Substitute Heir to Collateral Relatives

The exclusion of orphaned grandchildren from their grandparents' estates has been a customary rule in Aceh for centuries. Given the resistance to the principle of the substitute heir, the judges of the sharia court dealt with this issue carefully and gradually. Although the Supreme Court decided, from the mid-1990s, to enlarge the scope of the substitute heirs to include children of collateral relatives (orphaned nephews or nieces), this jurisprudence of the Supreme Court was not applied in Aceh until at least 2007. It seems that the Sharia Court of Aceh was ready to extend the application of the principle of the substitute heirs from orphaned grandchildren to collateral relatives only after having been assured that the norm of heir replacement was familiar in Aceh.

However, not every judge at the Sharia Court of Aceh welcomed the extension of the substitute heir principle to descendants of collateral relatives. One case, from the 2007 dossier of the Jantho Sharia Court of Aceh Besar district, involved a dispute on the inheritance of property that belonged to a victim of the 2004 tsunami. The propositus, Zainal bin Machmud bin Ahmad, was not survived by a widow, a child, a parent or a sibling. His closest relatives were, on the one side, sons of his predeceased sister and daughters of his predeceased brother, and, on the other side, a child of his predeceased consanguine uncle. So the contending parties in this case were the propositus' nephews and nieces (the plaintiffs) versus the propositus' cousin (the defendant).

The council of judges of the Sharia Court of Jantho, who examined this case, accepted the principle of the substitute heirs, but they preferred to apply the three categories of heirs of the Shafi'i inheritance law: (1) dzawu al-furud; (2) ashaba; and (3) dzawu al-arham. Under this categorisation, there are fifteen male and female Qur'anic heirs and ten male residuary heirs who have priority to inherit, based on their respective hierarchical position in the family lineage. Meanwhile, a member of the distant kindred will qualify as an heir only when those twenty-five heirs are no longer available.[17]

In the view of the judges of the Jantho Sharia Court, the nephews were regarded merely as distant kindred, because they were sons of the predeceased sister of the propositus, and, hence, would not be able to inherit if one or more of the twenty-five heirs were alive. Similarly, the nieces were regarded as distant kindred. The judges did not want to apply Article 185 of the KHI to this case,

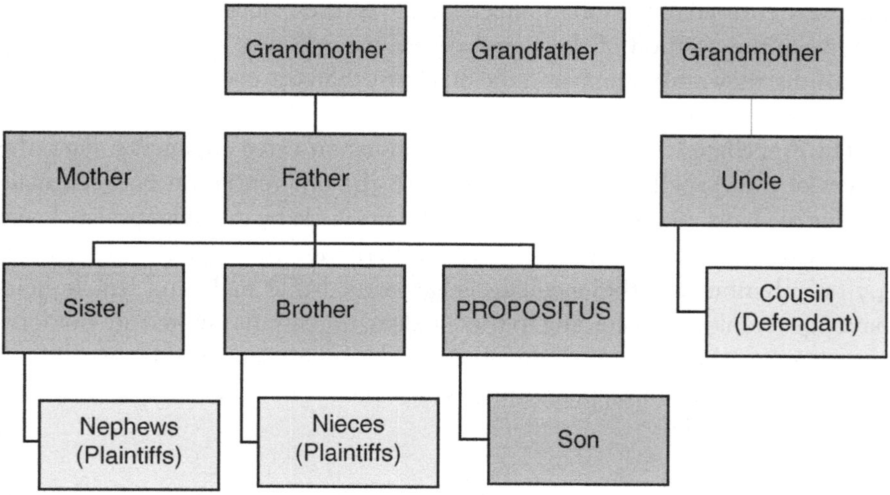

Diagram 7.1 Extending the principle of the substitute heir to collateral relatives

because they understood that the principle of the substitute heir has to do with ascendants or descendants of vertical lineage only. As nephews and nieces were descendants of collaterals, said the judges, Article 185 did not apply. They further emphasised: 'If Article 185 of the KHI is forcibly applied to the case under examination, it will damage or obscure the real Islamic inheritance system.' Nevertheless, it is unclear what the judges meant by the phrase 'the real Islamic inheritance system'. Does it refer to the Qur'an, the Shafi'i Islamic jurisprudence or to the KHI?

Given that the judges refused the claims of both plaintiffs, it is apparent that they decided that the cousin was the only surviving relative who could take a position as a residuary heir. To justify this decision, the judges argued that the cousin was among the twenty-five heirs under the categorisation of Shafi'i inheritance law. It was the cousin who would inherit the estate of the propositus in the absence of main heirs, such as a spouse, child, father or mother.[18] By considering that the cousin replaced his predeceased father, the judges were able to apply to this case the principle of the substitute heir as stated in Article 185 of the KHI. Nevertheless, they chose to underpin their decision not on this principle, but on that of Shafi'i jurisprudence. It could be that the judges considered the latter much closer to 'the real Islamic inheritance system'.

When this case reached the Appellate Court in January 2008, the Higher Sharia Court of Aceh found that the decision made by the first instance court was flawed. The judges of the Higher Court declared that the plaintiffs (the nephews and nieces of the propositus) were the substitute heirs, and, hence, they were entitled to the inheritance estate.[19] As these nephews and nieces were to replace the position of their predeceased parents, who were siblings to the propositus, they ranked higher in the hierarchy than the cousin, thus preventing him from receiving a share.

The Appellate Court's decision was founded on three arguments. First, the judges of the Appellate Court refused both the differentiation between male and female heirs and the categorisation of heirs made by the judges of the lower court with particular reference to Shafi'i inheritance law. By citing the Qur'an 4.7 on inheritance,[20] the appellate judges argued that male and female heirs have equal ranking. According to these judges, the distant kindred are not foreclosed and, as the substitute heirs, they could inherit even with the presence of the Qur'anic heirs. The appellate judges further criticised the reference to Shafi'i legal jurisprudence:

> The twenty-five heirs as formulated in the classical Islamic jurisprudence is not necessarily applicable to the contemporary time. Imam al-Shafi'i himself did not always rely on his previous opinion when he found it did not match to the new conditions. As now people are much more aware of equality and they prefer to see it taking place in the relationship between men and women, the judges should pay more attention to this social norm of equality and fairness in order that people can see justice in their decisions.[21]

Secondly, the judges of the provincial sharia court disagreed with the opinion of the judges of the district sharia court, who viewed Article 185 of the KHI as applicable only to orphaned grandchildren. Since Article 185 does not elaborate on whether its application should be restricted to a vertical family tree, the provincial judges contended that the scope of the article is open to interpretation in a way that may include both vertical and horizontal family lineages.

Finally, to justify the extension of the principle of the substitute heir to collateral relatives, the provincial sharia court made a reference to the Qur'an on mawali,[22] as reinterpreted by Hazairin. This particular reference showed that Hazairin's theory influenced the judges' understanding of the provision of the substitute heirs in Article 185 of the KHI. Marluddin, one of the judges involved in the case, saw a connection between the Qur'anic term 'mawali' and the concept of heir replacement.[23]

In Aceh, as far as the extension of the substitute heirs to include collateral relatives is concerned, the decision of the Higher Sharia Court, above, was a novelty. Prior practice at the sharia courts in Aceh allowed the application of the substitute heirs only for orphaned grandchildren. It seems that a new legal jurisprudence had been established. In fact, an ensuing decision on the dispute of the substitute heirs confirmed the rights of collateral descendants to receive a share of the inheritance.[24]

Comparative Perspectives

Unlike in Indonesia, in a number of Muslim countries the entitlement for orphaned grandchildren is based on an obligatory bequest (Mahmood 1987; Welchman 1988; An-Na'im 2002). The obligatory bequest was introduced after the Second World War in Egypt, and was soon accepted in other Muslim countries, such as Syria, Tunis and Morocco. According to the Egyptian Law of Bequest (No. 71 of 1946), the *wasiyya wajiba* (obligatory bequest) would be given only to orphaned grandchildren and not to other relatives, and its amount was restricted to no more than one-third of the inheritance estate.

The principle of the substitute heir, used in Indonesia to entitle orphaned grandchildren to inherit the grandparent's estate, does not clearly refer to the obligatory bequest. The concept of obligatory bequest is, instead, used in the KHI only to grant an adopted child or adopting parent a share of inheritance. Despite this, several Indonesian jurists, and legal scholars generally, consider the obligatory bequest tantamount to the principle of the substitute heir (Manan 2008: 168). These two rules are seen as similar, because they function as a way of constituting a right of inheritance for those who are purportedly prevented from receiving a share of inheritance.

It becomes obvious that the logic of the obligatory bequest was employed for the purpose of justifying the principle of the substitute heir. By employing a logic parallel to that of the obligatory bequest, though illicitly, the drafters of the KHI sought to persuade Indonesian Muslims to accept this new legal interpretation of the substitute heir. Quoting Yahya Harahap, a member of the KHI drafters, Cammack (1999: 24) writes that 'the only basis on which the ulama could accept representation [replacement] of predeceased heirs was on the principle of an obligatory bequest'.

The question remains: why does the principle of the substitute heir, as found in Article 185 of the KHI, not clearly mention the obligatory bequest, as does the principle of the inheritance between adopting parent and adopted child? Article 185 made no reference to the obligatory bequest in the text of the KHI or in other related legislation, because in that way the amount of share would not be restricted to one-third of the estate and the beneficiaries of the obligatory bequest would not be limited to grandchildren. In fact, its lack of reference to the obligatory bequest would allow the judges to grant a substitute heir more than one-third of the estate and to extend the scope of the substitute heir to include children of collaterals, as discussed earlier.

The way in which the principle of the substitute heir is applied in Indonesia has some similarities with the practice in Pakistan. Pakistani legislation does not strictly refer to the Egyptian obligatory bequest, for the amount of share for an orphaned grandchild is not restricted to one-third of an estate. The 1961 Ordinance of Muslim Family Laws of Pakistan states:

> In the event of the death of any son or daughter of the propositus before the opening of succession, the children of such son or daughter, if any, living at the time the succession opens, shall *per stirpes* receive a share equivalent to the share which such son or daughter, as the case may be, would have received if alive. (As cited in Carroll 1998: 415)

Additionally, the entitlement of orphaned descendants in Pakistan has been accidentally stretched to the entitlement of the collateral descendants. As noted by Carroll (1998: 422–3), in one case, the Pakistani judges of the Lahore High Court annulled the lower courts' decisions to award the entire estate to a daughter of the predeceased son; instead, they granted half to the son of a predeceased brother. The extension of the replacement of the predeceased heir to collateral relatives at this Pakistani court has unique legal reasoning. The Lahore High Court founded its decision on a fiction that a predeceased son was deemed to be alive at the time of the death of the propositus. Thus, soon after the death of the propositus, the predeceased son would initially be notionally awarded the whole estate. This share would then be divided equally among two surviving heirs, namely, his daughter and the son of his predeceased brother (his nephew).

When this case reached the Supreme Court of Pakistan, the decision of the Lahore High Court was strengthened. The Supreme Court argued that the replacement by the granddaughter for her predeceased father does not mean that it can decrease the share of the other heirs or exclude the other legal heirs of the propositus (Carroll 1998: 422, 426). To some, this practice of the Pakistani courts has lawfully recognised the application of the replacement of the predeceased heir to the lineal descendants as well as children of the collaterals. But to others, the decision of those two appellate courts was exactly what the Qur'an stipulated: that is, half of the estate was allotted to the granddaughter and the remaining half to the nephew as a residuary heir.

What would be the outcome if the Pakistani case above is examined by the judges of the Sharia Court of Aceh? Would there be any difference due to dissimilar sources of law? Referring to Article 185 of the KHI, the most likely scenario for their decision would that the judges would grant the granddaughter the entire estate, for she replaced her predeceased father. As she occupies the position of the propositus' son as a residuary heir, the son of a predeceased brother is foreclosed. Even in the case where the brother or the uncle is alive, the legal standing of 'son' is still able to exclude the uncle from inheriting a share.

That the Aceh judges would decide the case in this way leads one to ask why they do not apply the replacement of the predeceased heir to collateral relatives. What is seen here is that the judges consider that the lineal descendants have a higher position than the collateral relatives. Indeed, some decisions of the Sharia Courts of Aceh, referring to the jurisprudence of the Indonesian Supreme Court, show that the sole surviving daughter, even with the presence of a brother of her deceased father, was awarded the whole estate.[25]

Finding the Other Half of Knowledge

The extent to which the predeceased heir can be replaced depends largely on what sources of norms and law are referred to in the inheritance division at any level of forum. In the foregoing discussion, we have seen how various legal references have been used to settle the inheritance disputes that involve the orphans of lineal descendants as well as of collateral relatives. These legal references include the custom of patah titi, Shafi'i inheritance law, the rule of plaatsvervulling, the theory of mawali, the KHI provision of the substitute heir, the Egyptian obligatory bequest (wasiyya wajiba) and the Pakistani principle of representation.

In these contested sources of norms and law what is at stake is the idea of justice and fairness vis-à-vis the close compliance with religious texts. For one group, since justice and fairness is the core of Islam, any means that produce justice and fairness are part of Islam. But for the other, the use of non-prescriptive means only eschews the core of Islam. For the former, the Islamic inheritance law develops continually and is not yet complete; for the latter, the law is beyond the finish line and no longer needs reform or correction.

That diverse cases were examined by judges at different courts and resulted in dissimilar outcomes shows that Islamic inheritance law is not yet conclusive. As Judge Marluddin has said:

> The inheritance law in Islam is not yet final. Should it be final, the Prophet Muhammad would not say that it is one half of the knowledge. A number of Qur'anic verses that deal with inheritance are only a half of the knowledge, and the other half has to be found outside those verses by our own thoughts.[26]

Given the plural decisions in inheritance disputes, the judges of Aceh's Religious Court seek to discover useful and full knowledge.

Notes

1. Refer to al-Ramli (1938/9), vol. 6, pp. 16–20.
2. Interview with Ernita Dewi (an Acehnese social worker who works to educate women about their inheritance rights), 31 March 2009.

3. Article 229 of the KHI states that 'in settling disputes brought before them, the judges are required to pay close attention to the living norms and law within the society, so their judgments are in accord with justice'.
4. Decision of the Religious Court of Selong, No. 111/Pdt.G/1997/PA.Sel.
5. Decision of the High Religious Court of Mataram, No. 04/Pdt.G/1998/PTA.MTR.
6. Decision of the Supreme Court, No. 354.K/AG/1998.
7. Qur'an 4.33: 'To (benefit) every one, We have appointed shares and heirs to property left by parents and relatives. To those, also, to whom your right hand was pledged, give their due portion. For truly God is witness to all things.' *The Holy Qur'an*, trans. Abdullah Yusuf Ali, Lahore: Sh. Muhammad Ashraf Publishers, 1938. All subequent references to the Qur'an are taken from this translation.
8. One example, among others, is Hazairin (1964).
9. Patah titi was especially observable in Aceh Besar and Pidie. Bowen (2003: 195) mentions that it was also a practice in the Gayo highlands of Aceh province.
10. According to Suparman (2005), the heir replacement under customary law has been sporadically practised in some districts of West Java province, such as Leuwiliang Bogor, Cileungsi, Banjar, Ciamis, Cianjur, Bandung, Pandeglang, Karawang, Indramayu and Bekasi.
11. Interview with Rosdiana, 24 May 2008.
12. Interview with Muzakkir Abu Bakar, 31 March 2009.
13. Interview with Muzakkir Abubakar, 31 March 2009.
14. Qur'an 4.8: 'But if at the time of division other relatives, or orphans or poor, are present, feed them out of the (property), and speak to them words of kindness and justice.'
15. Qur'an 4.10: 'Those who unjustly eat up the property of orphans, eat up a Fire into their own bodies: They will soon be enduring a Blazing Fire!'
16. Interview with Judge Marluddin, 7 April 2009.
17. The list of these heirs can be found in Majelis Permusyawaratan Ulama (2006).
18. Decision of the Sharia Court of Jantho, No. 103/Pdt.G/2007/Msy-Jth.
19. Decision of the Higher Sharia Court of Aceh, No. 13/Pdt.G/2008/MSy-Prov.
20. Qur'an 4.7: 'From what is left by parents and those nearest related there is a share for men and a share for women, whether the property be small or large, a determinate share.'
21. Decision of the Higher Sharia Court of Aceh, No. 13/Pdt.G/2008/MSy-Prov.
22. Qur'an 4.33: 'To (benefit) every one, We have appointed shares and heirs to property left by parents and relatives. To those, also, to whom your right hand was pledged, give their due portion. For truly God is witness to all things.'
23. Interview with Judge Marluddin, 7 April 2009.
24. Decision of the Higher Sharia Court of Aceh, No. 17/Pdt.G/2008/MSy-Prov.
25. Further details on these decisions can be found in Bowen (2003: 195–9). However, there has been a change of opinion on this issue among some judges in Banda Aceh, who recently returned from a short course in Saudi Arabia. It became apparent that these judges will no longer grant the whole estate to the sole surviving daughter, because this is considered a Shi'a practice and the majority Muslim population in Aceh subscribes to the Sunni belief.
26. Interview with Judge Marluddin, 7 April 2009.

Chapter 8

Insurance Benefits

I knew that the Prophet gave a portion of inheritance to the wife of the late Al-Sham al-Dibbi out of his blood money.

Dahhak ibn Sofyan al-Kilabi, a companion of the Prophet

Ibrahim, an employee of a big national company, died in the course of the tsunami that severely damaged Aceh in late December 2004. Having worked as its employee for many years, Ibrahim was insured by his company. His sudden death in the tsunami disaster attracted some payments, including life insurance, pension fund and other related mourning funds. As his wife and all three of his children were also victims of the disaster, his only surviving relatives were his mother and his brother. They both managed to obtain an order from the Sharia Court of Jantho confirming that they were legitimate heirs. With this order at hand, they were able to convince various insurance providers (such as the Jaminan Sosial Tenaga Kerja, or Jamsostek) that they were the only beneficiaries, and thus received the insurance benefits in the name of the deceased, Ibrahim. However, relatives of Ibrahim's deceased wife contested, and claimed a share of the payment on the grounds that it constituted a joint marital property between Ibrahim and his wife during their lifetime.

The inheritance dispute being examined here is whether insurance benefits (in the case of the death of the insured person) are a part of the bequest. Do they constitute property of the deceased and are therefore disbursable among legitimate heirs? Or are they entitlements given consecutively to nominated beneficiaries whose names are listed in the insurance policy or as stipulated in Indonesian national laws on insurance? The dispute was very intricate, since there are ambiguous and conflicting concepts of the estate of the deceased. Given that there are various forms of insurance schemes, and each form has a different concept of property – as either joint marital property or the separate estates of husband and wife, respectively – disputes on this particular issue become even more complicated.

Legal problems in this particular case were twofold: (1) whether insurance benefits are considered as joint marital property or as the separate property of the deceased; and (2) whether or not insurance benefits are inheritance that can be divided among the legitimate heirs. This chapter will explain what norms are often referred to and contested through the adjudicating process of the distribution of insurance benefits at the religious courts of Aceh. The chapter seeks to answer questions such as: how do judges draw on various interpretations of Islamic rules to deal with this particular matter? How much do they accommodate principles of local custom? Do national laws prevail in every dispute in similar cases? What happens if there is a conflict of rules between different national laws over this issue? Do the judges make any legal reference to international norms, and in what ways? By looking closely at courtroom discourse at different times and in different places, this chapter avoids being limited to examining disputes as something to be resolved at the local stage or between different interests of local actors, but sees local disputes as embedded in larger conflicts between different norms. For this purpose, the chapter will discuss court disputes concerning inheritance that took place in different Sharia Courts of Aceh, and in appellate courts both at provincial and national levels, from the early 1990s to the present.

While many accounts have been written of disputes concerning insurance benefits, they have mostly focused on the dispute between the insurance policy-holders and the insurance company. Attention to the question of whether insurance benefits are included in the estate of the deceased, and hence are inheritable, or whether they are excluded from inheritance is rare. Indeed, very few anthropological works have so far have looked at the dispute on insurance benefits in Muslim societies. This partly has to do with the fact that insurance itself, and life insurance in particular, remains a controversial issue in Islam. Most discussion (Billah 1998; Al-Ghadyan 1999) on this issue has been undertaken from a religious perspective, and has focused on whether insurance is *halal* (permissible) or *haram* (prohibited). The discussion of contested norms in the dispute over the inheritance of insurance benefits within Aceh's sharia courtrooms is, therefore, important not only because it attempts to fill the gaps, but also in order to shed a comparative light on the complexities of the relationship between customary law, Islamic jurisprudence, international values and modern positive law in Muslim contexts.

The next section briefly explains various forms of insurance benefits and how they are legally conceived in relation to inheritance disputes. Following that, a number of cases concerning disputes over insurance benefits that were settled in the early 1990s and similar disputes that took place in post-tsunami Aceh are presented. This discussion is important to demonstrate how different legal norms are in competition with each other in this particular case. Finally, the chapter concludes by highlighting a legal paradox in the implementation of sharia in the setting of Aceh's legal pluralism. Despite the fact that the implementation of sharia is now officially taking place in Aceh, many judges of Islamic courts continue to maintain a secular–national-based jurisprudence on the distribution of insurance benefits, rather than giving priority to a social norm, which is local as well as Islamic.

Disputes on Insurance Benefits in Indonesia

There are at least three general types of insurances in Indonesia, whose benefits are related to inherited property. The first is insurance and pension funds provided by an employer to its employees. This includes: (1) *Taspen* (insurance and pension fund for state civil servants); (2) *Asabri* (insurance and pension fund for army and police officers); and (3) *Jamsostek* (insurance and pension funds for workers in private companies). If an employee dies for one reason or another while she or he is still actively employed, her or his close relatives are entitled to this kind of compensation. This payment, which is similar to pension savings or superannuation, is paid in a lump sum at the time of the contributor's death. The second type is a life insurance. This is an arrangement by which someone could provide a legacy by making regular payments to an insurance company during a lifetime plan, in return for which the company pays a specific sum to the person's close family or nominees after the death of the insured. The third type is accident insurance. This is personal insurance against death caused by a traffic or vehicle accident, where the insurance policy-holder is a driver or a passenger of the ill-fated vehicle.

How and why could the distribution of these three benefits turn into a dispute following the demise of the insured? They become a matter of dispute especially in the absence of children as primary heirs, when the surviving heirs are usually spouse, biological parent and siblings of the deceased. The root of this dispute lies in the question of whether an insurance benefit is an inheritance. This is exacerbated given conflicting norms between, on the one hand, the Shafi'i jurisprudence of inheritance and the national Islamic inheritance law, as found in the KHI, and, on the other hand, the state regulations (Law 3 of 1992; Government Regulations 17 and 18 of 1965 and 25 of 1981), which stipulate the appointment of consecutive beneficiaries of insurance benefits. While both the Islamic jurisprudence and the KHI stipulate that each of the legitimate heirs would have a right to inherit the deceased's assets based on their respective places in the hierarchy and the proportions to which they are entitled, the state regulations on insurance suggest a singular entitlement based on consecutive ranks, where widow or widower are first in line, children second, parents third, and the rest of the family members, such as siblings, would be entitled only in the absence of all heirs whose rank is higher than theirs.

Baseran et al. *v.* Asmah

The court decisions issued in 1991 and 1992, by the district Religious Court of Tapak Tuan and the Appellate Court of Banda Aceh, respectively, illustrate how various norms were in contestation and sought to predominate over one another at different levels of adjudication.

The dispute began at the district Religious Court of Tapaktuan, South Aceh. The plaintiff, Baseran, was a younger sister of the deceased (Areh bin Bareh), while the defendant, Asmah, was the deceased's second wife. The deceased had no children. At stake in this dispute were some funds that resulted from Areh bin Bareh's death, which occurred while he was making a pilgrimage in Saudi Arabia in 1990. He died in the so-called 'Mina tragedy', where more than a thousand pilgrims were killed as a result of the overwhelming crowd of a million pilgrims congregating in a narrow tunnel. Indonesian pilgrims who died in this tragedy received payments from different sources, including the Saudi government, the Indonesian Ministry of Religion and life insurance companies. The plaintiff claimed that all these payments were inheritance, and therefore must be distributed to all surviving heirs according to Islamic laws of inheritance. The district Religious Court of Tapaktuan accepted this claim and divided the funds among the legitimate heirs.[1]

The judge who examined this case was Munizar Umar. He was the sole adjudicator. This was quite uncommon to Indonesian judicial procedure, where, usually, a panel of three judges appears in the courtroom to hear a case. In an interview with me at the Municipal Sharia Court of Banda Aceh in 2008, Judge Munizar, who was transferred to a position as a senior judge at this court, recalled that he accepted the plaintiff's claim based on evidence from, among others, a village elder who acted as a witness before the court. When asked by Judge Munizar about the case in question, this witness recalled the precedent of a similar case in the village in which donations and insurance benefits were distributed to all heirs. As cited in Effendi (2004: 242), the witness was reported as saying:

> Those funds, as far as I know, were given to heirs of the deceased and not to his wife alone. This [division] also took place last year when there was a

> similar tragedy that involved someone from Kuala Batee. The deceased was granted such funds because of that disaster, and they were distributed among heirs of the deceased, not only for a single person.

Although the defendant widow asserted that she was the only person who had a right to inherit the benefits, Judge Munizar took the plaintiff's evidence into account and distributed all funds equally among the heirs. Interestingly, what motivated Judge Munizar to reject the defendant's point was that the widow looked too greedy, as she wanted to receive all the funds without giving any portion to other legitimate heirs (a younger sister of the deceased, for example).[2]

The widow did not accept the decision of the district Religious Court of Tapak Tuan and subsequently made an appeal to the Higher Religious Court in Banda Aceh. The judges of the higher court found that Judge Munizar's decision had incorrectly applied the law. They corrected the lower court's decision by making a demarcation between monies from the donations of both the Saudi government and the Ministry of Religion, and monies from the insurance benefit payment. As donations, monies received from the Saudi government and the Ministry of Religion were not considered the estate of the deceased, and therefore should be distributed to all heirs in equal proportions. Meanwhile, the insurance benefit payment was regarded as joint marital property that both the plaintiff and the defendant must share equally.[3]

Despite now being entitled to a larger portion of the estate than had been granted to her by Judge Munizar a year earlier, the widow was not content with this outcome, and therefore made another appeal to the Supreme Court in Jakarta. The judges of the Supreme Court considered that neither of the lower religious courts had appropriately applied the law. According to the Supreme Court, that donation was intended exclusively as a gift to the wife and not to all heirs. As to the insurance benefit, the Supreme Court deemed it as something beyond inheritance property. In fact, in accordance with national regulations on life insurance, such an insurance benefit was considered as property under the possession of the beneficiaries nominated during the lifetime of the deceased; in this case, the beneficiary was the wife. Thus, in 1992, the Supreme Court issued a decision stating that life insurance benefits are not inheritance and that all payments should go to the surviving spouse.[4]

Many Islamic judges and Muslim jurists were not pleased with this ruling by the Supreme Court, but in spite of this a legal precedent (the Supreme Court decision 198K of 1992) on the dispute of inheritance of insurance benefits began to be established. Although Indonesia does not embrace the common law tradition whereby judges must apply rules created in earlier cases by other judges from a court of the same level as their own or higher, the Indonesian legal system acknowledges a similar concept, known as yurisprudensi tetap (consolidated jurisprudence). In a way, a legal precedent is an effort by the Supreme Court to organisationally unify the whole judicial system of Indonesia. To consolidate a legal precedent, the Supreme Court publishes a compilation of its decisions annually and disseminates it to all lower courts. The objective of these efforts is not only to present a compelling case for the new rule, but also to make legal enforcement in Indonesian pluralistic society much more integrated and unified (Bowen 1998a). However, as far as the application of Islamic law for Muslim citizens is concerned, one can argue that the Supreme Court's jurisprudence does not always comply with Islamic law. In fact, disagreements among judges and legal scholars persist.

A year after it was established, the 1992 legal precedent on insurance benefit payments was challenged by Aceh's lower courts. The judges in Aceh kept insisting on regarding insurance benefits as inheritance. Their main reason for wishing to distribute insurance benefits to all heirs was their understanding that those funds were joint *harta bersama* (marital property) between husband and wife during the marriage. As explained by Cammack and Feener (2008), joint marital property is an Indonesian customary practice that gained a place in the Islamic jurisprudence through the classification of marriage as a form of *sharika* (partnership) and of marital property as profits resulting from that partnership. In other words, the marital relationship involves an element of economic partnership. This concept was further incorporated into Indonesian laws, such as the 1974 Marriage Law and the Compilation of Islamic Law, or the KHI.

Joint marital property is understood as property acquired by husband and wife, either individually or together, regardless of which spouse formally holds title to the property. Marital property includes both tangible and intangible property, personal and real property, and rights and obligations. Judges of Aceh's lower courts categorised insurance benefits as part of joint marital property because premiums paid for the endowment policy were paid during the marriage. Thus, they thought, just because such insurance benefits could be claimed only after the death of the insured, that this did not mean the benefit was not owned by the deceased. In fact, property of this kind should be treated as if it were owned by the deceased during her or his lifetime. The case from Banda Aceh's Religious Court below illustrates this contention.[5]

Fatimah *v.* Aminah

The case started with a husband who travelled with two of his children in 1987. Tragically, they all died in an airplane accident. As they were insured airplane passengers, some payments of insurance benefits were available to their immediate family. The remaining family members were the widow (Aminah), two other children (Indra and Faradina) and the mother (Fatimah) of the deceased husband. According to Islamic legal jurisprudence each of these kin has a right to inherit. It has been the usual practice in Aceh that 100 days after a person's death the division of inheritance is undertaken and the lawful heirs receive their shares (Hoesin 1970). However, after more than five years the property left by the deceased, including insurance benefits, had not been divided. The widow who controlled the property did not want to distribute it to the legitimate heirs. Although the chief of the village where she was living had encouraged her to fulfil Islamic inheritance law, the widow was adamant and would not divide the estate.

In January 1992, the mother of the deceased husband (Fatimah) and the older son (Indra) registered their claim in the municipal Religious Court of Banda Aceh, asking for a decision that insurance benefits were part of the estate of the deceased, and for distribution of these payments to all legitimate heirs. As the defendant, the widow responded by refusing the plaintiffs' claim for a share of the insurance benefits. In her view, insurance benefits were not part of the estate of the deceased. To support her argument, the widow invoked Government Regulations 17 and 18 of 1965 on accident insurance benefits for passengers of public transportation. These regulations stipulated that the highest rank of beneficiary is the spouse of the deceased, who has the first priority to receive all kinds of payment. In the defendant's opinion, the insurance regulations have a nationwide jurisdiction that cannot be overridden.

Against the plaintiffs' claim and the defendant's refusal, the judges evaluated whether an insurance benefit could be considered a part of inheritance by reviewing the definition of *tirka* (the estate of the deceased). After consulting some Islamic legal textbooks and the KHI, the judges conceived tirka as the estate left by the deceased that consists of property and entitlements. With this definition, the judges decided that insurance benefits are to be considered part of the estate of the deceased. The judges cited the same regulation to which the defendant referred, but with a different understanding. The judges understood that because the insured person will be solely entitled to the insurance benefit, should she or he not die in an accident, this means that the insurance benefit is actually part of the estate of the insured person. Keeping this in mind, the judges concluded that the insurance benefit comes under the definition of tirka, above. Additionally, the judges held that the insurance benefit constitutes a joint marital property. This is because an entitlement to an insurance benefit was possible thanks to premiums that were paid by the deceased during his lifetime and during the marriage period. For the judges of Banda Aceh Religious Court, all this confirmed that such an entitlement is a joint marital property in which all lawful heirs should have a share.

With regard to the national regulations on insurance, the judges were of the opinion that just because there is a provision that mentions the widow or widower as the first nominee for receipt of the benefit, it does not mean that the widow or widower will be entitled to the whole benefit. It seems here that the judges sought to reconcile inconsistencies between what has been stated in the national regulation on insurance and Islamic legal jurisprudence. In the judges' view, the provision in the national regulations on insurance must be interpreted in a procedural sense that, first, the nominee would receive the insurance benefit on behalf of all legitimate heirs of the deceased, and, secondly, the benefit should be distributed between heirs in accordance with Islamic inheritance law.[6]

As the widow was unhappy with the decision of these judges and therefore made an appeal to the Aceh's higher court, it becomes apparent that the focus of this dispute is more on the definition of the estate of the deceased rather than the identification of the insurance benefits as either joint or separate marital property. This can be clearly seen in the provincial religious court's examination of the appealed case. The judges of the higher religious court reinforced the decision of the District Religious Court of Banda Aceh. The appellate judges further developed historical arguments from early Islam to strengthen the decision of the lower court that the insurance benefit is part of the inheritance. They made an analogy between insurance benefits and *diya* (blood-money or death compensation) and recalled the following story:

> The caliph 'Umar ibn Khatthab once said that the widow would not share any portion from [the] diya of her deceased husband because it belongs to the husband's clan. On hearing this statement, Dahhak ibn Sofyan al-Kilabi sent a letter to the caliph telling him that the Prophet Muhammad had given Asyyam al-Dibbi a part of her husband's diya. Having read the letter, the caliph 'Umar withdrew his earlier statement and said: 'If we had not heard this [Prophet's deed], we would have resolved it with a different decision.' (Effendi 2004: 373)

Drawing on this account, the judges of the provincial religious court considered that diya could be an inheritance, which could be distributed to the widow as well as to the immediate family of the deceased husband. Accordingly, the insurance benefit must be seen in similar vein and be divided proportionally among the heirs.[7]

The defendant widow was displeased with the decisions of both lower courts in Aceh, and, therefore, filed a cassation to the Supreme Court in Jakarta. There was no new counter-argument found in the defendant's second appeal, only the oft-repeated point that the government national regulation prevails over Islamic law in the dispute of insurance benefits. She challenged the decision of the provincial religious court, saying that, instead of paying attention to the law of insurance benefits currently applicable in Indonesia, Aceh's higher religious court ironically made a reference to a letter sent to Caliph 'Umar ibn Khatthab more than 1,300 years ago. According to the widow, Islamic inheritance law contravenes provisions of the national regulation on the disbursement of insurance benefits. The state regulation should become a guide that the provincial religious court has to take into account when examining disputes over insurance benefits. Referring to a legal precedent made in 1992, the judges of the Supreme Court who heard this case in 1995 accepted the widow's claim and annulled the decisions of both Aceh's lower courts.[8]

RESPONSES AND CRITICISMS

In Indonesia, jurisprudence, or earlier decisions made by the Supreme Court on a given case, has been influential in the decisions made by the judges at the lower courts. While not formally binding, those earlier decisions are, in practice, highly persuasive, and will often be followed by the lower courts when they are adjudicating subsequent cases that involve similar facts and situations to those of the case in which the jurisprudence was established. With respect to the importance of jurisprudence, Bowen (2003: 258) pointed out that past agreements often have an informal binding effect not only in village meetings, but also in the courtrooms of Aceh. While villagers should not violate past agreements, neither those amongst themselves nor those with third parties such as their ancestors, judges will take legal precedents into account when making decisions in a courtroom.

Despite the fact that the Supreme Court has twice – in 1992 and in 1995 – made the same decision on the dispute over insurance benefits, it is not easy for many judges at religious courts to welcome such a decision as jurisprudence. In their view, the substance of the national regulations on insurance simply cannot be reconciled with the Islamic inheritance law. Therefore, criticisms of, and resistance to, those regulations remained persistent, at least until 1997. Abdul Manan, who had a long career as religious judge and is now a Supreme Court judge, explained that many forms of insurance benefits can be classified as a joint property of husband and wife, including employment insurance, accident insurance and life insurance. Thus, they are inheritable (Manan 2008: 112–28). This point of view, according to Manan (2008: 127), was supported by the judges of the Islamic High Court from all over Indonesia who gathered in 1995 to attend special training in Bandung.

Satria Effendi, an Islamic jurist who graduated from King Abdul Aziz University at Mecca and served as a professor of Islamic law at the Syarif Hidayatullah State Islamic University, Indonesia, was of the same opinion, that insurance benefits are a part of inheritance (Effendi 2004). Effendi acted as a guest reviewer of an Islamic legal journal (*Mimbar Hukum*), which provided analyses and comments on the Supreme Court's decisions on various family legal issues for more than ten years (1990–2001). His thoughts on the estate of the deceased, in general, and on the insurance benefit, in particular, are worth describing here.

For Effendi (2004: 368), each of the four descriptions below fits the concept of tirka:

1. properties that come into a person's possession during that person's lifetime;
2. any entitlement that has an intrinsic value or measurable value;
3. a property which is acquired as a compensation payment for a person's death, such as diya;
4. properties that result from a person's particular activity, which will naturally lead to gains or profits even though these may come only after that person's death.[9]

Based on the above description of tirka, Effendi (2004: 369) criticised the Supreme Court's jurisprudence regarding the disbursement of insurance benefits to key family members of the deceased. He complained that the regulation on accident insurance was not in any way formulated based on Islamic legal jurisprudences (fiqh), but was then to be applied in religious courts. Effendi was discontented with this situation and sought to bring the practice, as stipulated in the insurance laws, in line with fiqh by proposing two Islamic legal concepts, gift (*hadiyya*) and bequest (*wasiyya*).

Of these two concepts, Effendi (2004: 369–70) saw that hadiyya has fewer similarities with the substance of the stipulated rules of insurance benefits. This is because hadiyya does not take into account either the meaning of *ganti rugi* (compensation) in the insurance laws or any of the definitions of tirka above. Additionally, hadiyya is not a kind of entitlement whereby the recipient can make a claim if the benefactor cancels the gift. This indicates that insurance benefits are not hadiyya in any real sense.

Having analysed legal literature from the different Islamic madhhab of Sunni and Shi'a, Effendi (2004: 370–2) was confirmed in his opinion that insurance benefits are comparable to wasiyya, with the following provisos. First, the insurance benefit should be envisaged in one of two ways: as property that accrues after one's death from an effort undertaken during one's lifetime; or as property that stems from the compensation payment for one's death. Secondly, since wasiyya cannot be given to a particular heir except with the approval of all other heirs, the appointment of a beneficiary to receive the insurance benefits must be dependent upon the consent of other legitimate heirs. Otherwise, it becomes unlawful. Thirdly, the amount of the insurance benefit must not exceed one-third of the whole estate of the deceased. With this kind of understanding,

Figure 8.1 The judges of the Sharia Court in Aceh hear a case of inheritance © Arskal Salim

Effendi was synchronising the contradictory norms of Islamic jurisprudence and state national regulation. In so doing, he sought to 'Islamicise' the national regulation on insurance so that, as a result, the decisions of the religious courts would not lose their Islamic character when referring to that secular regulation.

It is unknown to what extent to Effendi's analysis has been influential among Islamic judges in Indonesia. As Effendi's views were available in the *Mimbar Hukum* journal and almost all religious courts in Indonesia had access to this journal, one could speculate that some judges in Aceh might have read and understood, and even followed, Effendi's thought as such. However, this is very often not the case. There is not enough data to confirm whether or not the judges in Aceh referred to Effendi's view as outlined above. What we can do, perhaps, is to evaluate the extent to which post-tsunami Aceh's court decisions on inheritance cases have been in opposition to the jurisprudence of the Supreme Court, which gives the national regulation higher standing than Islamic jurisprudence in inheritance disputes, including disputes over insurance benefits.

Post-tsunami Disputes

In the aftermath of the disastrous earthquake and tsunami that hit the coastal areas of Aceh on 26 December 2004, which caused the deaths of more than 100,000 people, numerous legal problems emerged. Disputes mostly concerned inherited lands and properties whose owners were missing, or whose immediate heirs were not accessible. The disputes were not necessarily brought forward to the courts. Instead, many disputes over inheritance were settled within family meetings or with the guidance of a local teungku or the keuchik. This was partly because the Aceh government and religious officials encouraged heirs of the tsunami victims to first seek resolution at the village level, before coming to the sharia court (Salim 2006). Within the family or at the village meeting, settlement was reached mostly based on agreement among surviving heirs. According to the laws applicable in Aceh, heirs may agree to distribute the inheritance differently from the way that is stipulated as their lawful proportions.

However, on some occasions heirs appeared at the sharia courts applying for formal confirmation that they were the legitimate heirs. This was especially true for heirs who sought to access financial assets of the deceased, such as money held in bank accounts and benefits from insurance companies. The normal procedure of the sharia court is to first examine evidence from witnesses, to ensure that all heirs are included in the application, then issue a *penetapan* (an order) that identifies all legitimate heirs. However, due to case overload and the unstable situation during the first six months after the tsunami (January–June 2005), this procedure was not well implemented, and, as a result, a number of surviving heirs were not included in court orders, and, therefore, did not receive any portion of the inheritance. In such a case, an individual who believes that she or he is also a legitimate heir could sue the other heirs, who retain the legacy of the deceased. The following discussion on the dispute of the disbursement of insurance benefits at the District Sharia Court of Jantho will describe a case of this sort in detail.

Asmara et al. *v.* Rukiah et al.

An employee of the Indonesian Andalas cement company, Ali Musa, died in the tsunami. His wife, Haryani, and their three children were also victims of the disaster. Ali Musa's surviving heirs were his mother, Rukiah, and his brother, Dahlan. Both received an order from the sharia court confirming that they were legitimate heirs. With this order, they were able get some payments of insurance benefits from an insurance company, Jamsostek. Rukiah and Dahlan Musa did not communicate with the surviving heirs of Haryani, the deceased wife, let alone share the insurance benefits with them.

The heirs of the deceased wife (Haryani) were her two siblings: an older sister, Asmara, and a younger brother, Fikri. They sued Rukiah and Dahlan, who were both heirs of the deceased husband, and claimed a right to some portion from the estate of both deceased husband and wife. They asked the Sharia Court of Jantho to divide the estate, including the insurance benefit, on the grounds that it all was joint marital property. According to the plaintiffs (Asmara and

Fikri), the benefit must be equally shared between heirs of both the husband and the wife. To support their claim of joint marital property, the plaintiffs provided five witnesses to prove that: (1) the deceased husband was an employee of Andalas cement company; (2) heirs of the deceased husband (the defendants) received all payments of the insurance benefit; and (3) the plaintiffs were heirs of the deceased wife who received no share at all.

In addition, one witness from the Jamsostek insurance company was heard before the court with regard to the disbursement of the insurance benefit. This witness reinforced the position of the defendants. Before the judges, he confirmed the defendants' entitlement, mainly because a parent of the employee (in this case the deceased's mother) has a higher status than siblings of the employee's wife. The beneficiaries list for Jamsostek payments includes widow(er), mother and siblings of the employee. However, the wife's siblings are not part of this list, even though, from an Islamic legal point of view, they have a status as lawful heirs of their sister.

Judges: Did every employee of the Indonesian Andalas cement company who died in the tsunami receive the payment of insurance benefit?

Witness: Yes, that's right.

Judges: Who are beneficiaries that are entitled to that payment?

Witness: The insurance company refers to the Law 3 of 1992 on social insurance of manpower that the payment should go to the following hierarchy:

1. widow or widower of the employee;
2. children of the employee;
3. parent of the employee;
4. grandchildren of the employee;
5. grandparent of the employee;
6. siblings of the employee;
7. parent-in-law of the employee.

Judges: If all the above mentioned beneficiaries are no longer surviving, who will receive the benefit?

Witness: In that case, the insurance benefit will not be disbursed. Instead, the benefit will be given away to the state.[10]

The defendants were also heard to respond to the plaintiffs' claim. In their effort to refute the claim, the defendants presented a court order that they had received earlier confirming their status as the lawful heirs. Moreover, they argued that, based on consultation with local religious leaders who issued a fatwa based on Shafi'i jurisprudence,[11] the insurance benefit does not constitute a part of joint marital property. Instead, the defendants believed that the benefit solely belongs to the family of the deceased husband and should not to be divided among the respective heirs of husband and of wife.

Judges:	Why did you [think you are entitled to] receive the insurance benefit?
Defendants:	Because we are heirs of the deceased husband based on the court's order.
Judges:	Do you still remember the order?
Defendants:	Yes, I do remember. It was order number ninety-nine issued on 26 March 2005.
Judges:	Why did not you communicate [about the insurance benefit] with heirs of the wife?
Defendants:	Because, based on our consultation with some local teungku, that benefit is separate property and not a joint marital property.[12]

As can be seen above, three different norms were invoked to support the position of the defendants as the legitimate beneficiaries of the insurance benefits: (1) the national regulation on insurance; (2) the order of the sharia court that identifies the heirs; and (3) the legal opinion (fatwa) of local religious leaders. These legal references are not all mutually supportive. Instead, they may be conflicting. Each of these legal arguments was selectively utilised by the defendants to justify their control over the estate of the deceased husband. As far as all these arguments were concerned with the status of the deceased husband and his family kinship, the plaintiffs were certainly not beneficiaries. However, the result would be different if the marital relationship between the deceased husband and the deceased wife were taken into account.

The judges of the District Sharia Court of Jantho, who examined this case, considered this marital relationship, and, hence, decided that the insurance benefit was a joint marital property. The judges' decision referred to Article 35(1) of the Law 1 of 1974 on Marriage, which stipulates that property acquired during marriage shall become joint matrimonial property. An interview with one of the judges who adjudicated this case reveals that two unwritten arguments underpinned the decision of the District Sharia Court of Jantho. First, the endowment policy was present within the marriage period, thus it should be considered a joint marital property. For Zubaedah Hanoum, one of the few female judges in Aceh, who occupied a position as a vice chairman of the District Sharia Court, the issue was all about fairness and partnership between a husband and a wife.[13]

> We defend wives since husbands often say that they are the ones who are working, that they go to [a] workplace and to [the] rice-field. We refuse this

> [self-claim] and ask whether husbands pay attention to housing issues, look after the children. In Aceh, this is not easily applicable. In fact, local religious scholars deny [the concept of] joint marital property since it was not found in the Qur'an.[14]

Secondly, the judges understood that the insurance regulation about the disbursement to the listed beneficiaries was not necessarily undertaken in a hierarchical sequence. This understanding led the judges to think that, in the absence of a widow (because she had also died at almost the same time as her husband), heirs of the deceased wife should be regarded as auxiliary beneficiaries to a share, in particular, of the joint marital property. In an interview, Judge Zubaedah told me that she and her panel judge members already knew that if the case were to be appealed, the Higher Sharia Court of Aceh most likely would cancel their decision. Despite this, she and her colleagues were convinced and adamant that they should uphold justice by allocating a proportion of insurance benefits, which were considered a joint marital property, to heirs of the deceased wife.

According to Cammack and Feener (2008), the concept of joint marital property between husbands and wives has a long pedigree in Southeast Asian contexts. Although it is not acceptable to Shafi'i Islamic jurisprudence, to which the majority of Indonesian Muslims subscribe, for many centuries wives in Indonesia have not been prevented from actively supporting their spouses by working in the fields, cultivating land and harvesting rice, and selling food or garments in the market. This local tradition of economic partnership between husbands and wives has undoubtedly influenced the way the judges at the District Sharia Court examined and decided the case discussed here. As Bowen (1998b) pointed out in his study on law and property in Sumatran religious courts, Islamic law, in contemporary Indonesian jurisprudence, has been motivated and shaped by local social processes and social norms.

From one legal point of view, it appears that gender had become an analytical tool and was strongly articulated in these judges' legal reasoning. Although it was not explicitly stated in the consideration of the court decision, very few would deny that the judges employed gender analysis by making reference to Law 1 of 1974 on Marriage, a provision of joint marital property in particular. As an international norm, gender equality has certainly no blatant form in Indonesian inheritance practice. Despite this, as K. von Benda-Beckmann (2001b) pointed out, the role of international norms, such as gender equality and human rights principles, as influential elements in any given complex legal situation, has increasingly affected not only how contending parties approach their claims, but also the way the judges settle disputes.

The defendants were unsatisfied with the decision of the Jantho District Court that allocated some portions of the insurance benefits to the plaintiffs (heirs of the deceased wife). They therefore made an appeal to the appellate Sharia Court in Banda Aceh. The appellate judges who heard the case were all male. Yet this was not the main reason why they were not persuaded by the tone of gender equality in the decision of the lower court. In the view of the higher court, the insurance benefit cannot be regarded as part of a joint marital property, and its disbursement, therefore, must be conducted in accordance with the national law on insurances. Annulling the decision of the lower court, the appellate judges issued a new ruling that all insurance benefit payments belonged to the mother of the deceased husband, because the law lists the parent as the third nominated beneficiary. The appellate court neither accepted the legal reasoning of the lower court judges, allowing the heirs of the deceased wife to substitute for the position of widow in the first rank of nominated beneficiaries, nor recognised the plaintiffs' right to receive a portion of the insurance benefit as if it were a joint marital property.[15] The Supreme Court decision was once more cited to annul the ruling of Aceh's lower courts by restating that those insurance benefit payments could not constitute a part of the inheritance.

It becomes clear from this post-tsunami inheritance case that national insurance laws, which have been backed up by the Supreme Court's jurisprudence,[16] prevail in almost all disputes over inheritance that includes insurance benefits. Another post-tsunami case, from the District Sharia Court of Meulaboh, which was appealed at Aceh's appellate court in 2009, concluded with a similar decision to the one described above. Despite the Sharia Court of Meulaboh having decided that insurance benefits were part of joint marital property, this decision was corrected by the higher court, which stated that the disbursement of insurance benefits should follow the provisions of insurance laws as well as of the insurance policy.[17] The provincial higher court's decision referred to the Supreme Court's jurisprudence that clarifies that the insurance benefit is neither joint marital property nor the estate of the deceased husband. This decision once again demonstrates that the local religious concept of joint marital property was subordinate to the underlying secular norm, as stipulated in national regulations on insurance.

Conclusion

The preceding discussion has shown that different actors invoked various norms to justify a particular legal standpoint in court. In all the cases of inheritance disputes described in this chapter, Indonesian national law on insurance prevails. The law states that insurance benefit payments are not the type of funds that must be divided among all legitimate heirs, but are to be paid consecutively to the nominated beneficiaries, as listed in the endowment policy. Many Islamic jurists and judges consider that this provision overrides the Islamic inheritance law, which arranges the transfer of property and entitlements of the deceased to legitimate heirs. Likewise, in certain cases, where a husband and wife have died together, leaving no children, this provision has dispensed with the local norm of joint marital property, which emphasises the economic partnership of the couple during their lifetime by taking into account only the heirs of the insured spouse.

The fact that in Aceh's sharia courtrooms the national insurance laws remain more influential than Islamic inheritance law, as it is that they mostly determine the settlement of disputes over the inheritance of insurance benefits, has led to three ironies.

First, Aceh lost momentum for deepening legal change. After applying secular insurance laws for many years during the period before the region of Aceh was granted special autonomy in 2001, Aceh did not seek to end this situation when post-tsunami legal contexts (that is, the rigorous implementation of sharia) provided possibilities for change.

Secondly, Aceh reveals a legal paradox. Although officially the application of sharia has begun in Aceh, the sharia courts keep referring to a secular legislation. The Sharia Court of Aceh appears to apply an Islamic rule only as long as it is consistent with national law, even at the expense of a local religious norm.

Finally, the newly expanded jurisdiction of the Sharia Court of Aceh does not necessarily imply that any local religious norm will apply and prevail in a pure sense. Indeed, as pointed out by Lindsey *et al.* (2007), the final authority of appeal and the ultimate legal reference remain the jurisdiction of the Supreme Court in Jakarta, which could effectively overrule any decision of the Sharia Court of Aceh that it thinks departs from national secularist standards.

Notes

1. Decision of the religious court of Tapaktuan, No. 29/G/1991/PA-TTN.
2. Interview with Judge Munizar Umar, 7 January 2008.
3. Decision of the Higher Religious Court of Aceh, No. 49/G/1991/PTA-BNA.
4. Decision of the Supreme Court, No. 198/K/AG/1992.
5. A short description of this case is also available in Effendi (2004).
6. Decision of Banda Aceh Religious Court, No. 12/G/1992/PA-BNA.
7. Decision of the Higher Religious Court of Aceh, No. 35/Pdt/G/1993/PTA-BNA.
8. Decision of the Supreme Court, No. 97K/AG/1994.
9. For example, a deer trapped in a pit is considered as belonging to the person who prepared that pit, even if the deer became entrapped only after the person's death.
10. Records of this court examination can be found in the decision of the Sharia Court of Jantho, No. 24/Pdt.G/2006/MSy-JTH.
11. Of the four Sunni schools of law, the strongest rulings against the understanding that marriage is a partnership of labour are made by the Shafi'i school (Cammack and Feener 2008: 98).

12. Records of this court examination can be found in the decision of the Sharia Court of Jantho, No. 24/Pdt.G/2006/MSy-JTH.
13. Interview with Judge Zubaedah Hanoum, 7 January 2008.
14. Interview with Judge Zubaedah Hanoum, 7 January 2008
15. Decision of the Higher Sharia Court of Aceh, No.7/Pdt.G/2007/MSy-Prov
16. Decision of the Supreme Court, No. 2831K/Pdt/1996, maintains that: 'Insurance benefits must be paid to people whose names are listed in the insurance policy so as to comply with a maxim that each payment of insurance benefits has to consider what is stated explicitly in the insurance policy about who can legitimately claim the payment' . . . 'The payment of insurance benefits that deviates from what is written in the insurance policy is a tort act.'
17. See the appeal decision of the Higher Sharia Court of Aceh (No. 45/Pdt.G/2009/MSy-Prov) that corrected the decision of Meulaboh Syar'iyah Court (No. 147/Pdt.G/2008/MSy-Mbo). Additionally, on a similar case, the Higher Sharia Court of Aceh (No. 65/Pdt.G/2009/MSy-Prov) also cancelled the decision of the Lhokseumawe Syar'iyah Court (No. 211/Pdt.G/2008/MSy-Lsm).

Chapter 9

Triple Divorce

> The divorce is twice, after that, either you retain her on reasonable terms or release her with kindness . . . And if he has divorced her (the third time), then she is not lawful unto him thereafter until she has married another husband. Then, if the other husband divorces her, it is no sin on both of them that they reunite, provided they feel that they can keep the limits ordained by Allâh
>
> Qur'an 2: 229–30

In April 2009, an unmarried couple, Budiman and Wiwin (neither are their true names), were caught committing an act of intimate contact, known locally as 'khalwat', which is prohibited in Aceh. Leaders of a village in Lhoksukon, North Aceh, decided that the couple should be 'punished' by forcing them to marry. A small wedding ceremony was held two weeks later. When the solemnisation of the marriage was complete, the groom went up to a teungku and asked if he and the bride were now in a lawful marital relationship. The teungku confirmed this and said they were now husband and wife before God and the people. The groom then unexpectedly responded by pronouncing a triple divorce or talaq in a single breath: 'Tonight in front of the public I hereby declare that I divorce my wife three times.'[1]

Al Yasa Abubakar, a professor of Islamic law at IAIN Ar-Raniry, considered that a divorce like this was unlawful. In his view, since the couple had agreed to marry, the divorce pronounced immediately after their marriage was void. Referring to the Indonesian Marriage Law, Abubakar maintained that 'talaq becomes valid only if the husband pronounces it at a court with full consciousness'.[2] Given that the divorce was deemed illegal, there was certainly no need to save the marriage. This particular case turned out to be complicated as returning to the former marriage is unlawful after triple divorce, especially when the husband soon regretted his action and wished to return to his ex-wife.

However, Teungku Mandawali, chairman of the Ulama Council of the Lhoksukon sub-district, regarded this particular divorce as valid, although it dishonoured religion as well as custom. He suggested that if this couple wanted to reconcile or remarry, someone else had to act as a *muhallil* (an intermediary husband for the ex-wife). The ex-wife must be in this new marriage relationship for a specified time before being able to remarry her former husband. The return to the original marriage, Mandawali continued, could take place only if the intermediary husband had consummated the marriage and divorced the ex-wife, and her menstrual period had passed three times. Only then could the original couple remarry. This practice is popularly known in Aceh as '*cina buta*'.

'*Cina buta*'

The term 'cina buta' can be translated literally as 'blind Chinese', however, by custom, the term means 'a person who helps both ex-husband and ex-wife to remarry after triple divorce'. Its origin can perhaps be traced back to daily social life in the region. The story was told that a local man pronounced triple divorce to his wife in a single breath. Afterwards he was remorseful and wanted to revoke this divorce. Unfortunately, as the triple divorce had taken place, he was not allowed to rejoin his wife. As it was textually (mis)understood from the Qur'an, the only possibility for reconciliation after triple divorce was that his ex-wife must first marry another man, and then be divorced by this new husband. Only then would she be allowed to return to her former husband. However, the case would not be so simple. The ex-husband was afraid that the person who married his ex-wife would not divorce her because of her beauty and might, instead, want to remain in a permanent marriage with her. Aiming to avoid this unwelcome situation, the ex-husband decided to exploit a blind Chinese man who had just recently converted to Islam. It was thought that, because of his blindness, the man would not be able to see the beauty of the ex-wife, and the ex-husband was therefore confident that this intermediary husband would not retain his ex-wife and would divorce her soon after the marriage.

The practice of cina buta is quite well established in rural Aceh. It is driven largely by a popular understanding among the villagers, who subscribe to the opinion of some traditional religious leaders that the practice of cina buta is the only legitimate way to save the marriage after triple divorce. From time to time, local newspapers have reported that short-tempered couples still conduct this practice. In other Muslim contexts, this practice is known as '*halala*' and the person undertaking the role is called 'muhallil'. Very much like the practice of cina buta, halala can be a way in which a third party is involved to allow an ex-husband to return to his ex-wife in a lawful marriage.

Triple divorce in Islam has received attention from very few scholars. Existing works pay attention to historical as well as legal perspectives of divorce in Islam in general, and discuss the topic of triple divorce in a particular section or deal with this issue sporadically.[3] Of those rare works specifically on triple divorce, two accounts trace its social origin back to early Islam and even before Islam, and how the sources of Islam responded to it (Ahmad 1994; Hussain 2010). Other studies, such as that of Mahmood (1992), approach the concept of triple divorce from the point of view of legal reform, while Al-Azri (2011) looks at this particular topic in the context of prolonged and wide scholarly debates. However, an ethnographic study on the subject in question is almost non-existent, let alone one that employs a legal pluralist framework.

Using an ethnographic approach, this chapter examines four cases of triple divorce from different places in Aceh. The first case involves the role of a village religious teacher who provides services and facilities for the practice of cina buta to those couples who want to save their marriage after triple divorce. The second case concerns the discretion of a couple who look for a pragmatic solution to saving their marriage. Despite being similar to the practice of cina buta, their solution was unique. The couple made an agreement that each would marry another person for a particular period of time, and then divorce their respective new spouses and return to the original marriage. The third case deals with a couple who invited state religious authorities to save their marriage after triple divorce. This went against the consensus of the villagers, who believed that triple divorce had taken place and was irrevocable unless cina buta was practised. The final case shows the deliberation of village leaders who did not regard a triple divorce, if pronounced at the one time, as irrevocable, but counted it as a single divorce, thus allowing an ex-husband to return to his ex-wife without necessarily practising cina buta.

All four of these cases demonstrate the tension between state legality, on the one hand, and religious validity, on the other. These cases show that, while state legality has been fiercely challenged in Aceh, religious validity has more currency among Aceh villagers. The question of which authority has more legitimacy to validate (re)marriage has been dealt with by John Bowen (2003: 174), who asked: 'can a Muslim marry or divorce without the state?' and 'whose interpretation of scripture counts as definitive?' This chapter confirms Bowen's argument that religious validity supersedes state legality in certain cases. Yet this is not the only main point of this chapter. As discussed below, the chapter not only unveils the extent to which gender sensitivity has been observable among different actors, but also suggests a meaning and reasoning for why saving marriage after triple divorce by way of cina buta is imperatively crucial for some villagers.

Rules of Divorce in Islam

Before delving into each of the village cases, it is worth presenting a legal framework of divorce as derived from the Qur'an, Prophetic traditions and the classical Islamic jurisprudences.

Although Islam allows talaq or divorce to take place, it is considered the 'worst of all permitted things'. Thus, talaq is the last resort when all other means to keep a spousal relationship in harmony fail. A couple can dissolve their marriage by way of talaq if they both fail to fulfil the primary objectives of marriage in Islam. Throughout the history of Muslim societies, it has been conducted through different modes, by explicit or implied words, directly or through representation. In some situations the pronouncement of talaq is still seen as a privilege of power possessed by a husband, and it has been widely held within a number of Muslim communities that talaq occurs whenever a husband simply pronounces it, by saying to his wife 'you are divorced', or expressing it in any other verbal or written form, or clear sign, that indicates the same thing (Omar 2007; Al-Azri 2011).

Muslim jurists and others have classified talaq variously and with very detailed descriptions.[4] However, for the purpose of this chapter, a simple division of talaq into two types is preferable: revocable and irrevocable divorces. Revocable talaq is any talaq by which a husband can still return to his wife through the revocation of talaq before the expiry of the wife's waiting period (*'idda*), or by way of re-solemnisation if the waiting period has passed. This kind of divorce takes place only twice. A husband therefore has only two chances to take his wife back. The pronouncement of talaq for the third time is irrevocable talaq. It disallows a husband from reverting to or remarrying his repudiated wife (Hussain 2010). At this stage, the husband might remarry his ex-wife only after a quite complicated process, which will be discussed in the next sections, with reference to various case studies. As far as legal consequences are concerned, Al-Azri (2011: 280–1) has summarised the difference between revocable and irrevocable talaq as follows: 'Revocable talaq allows the husband to return to his wife during the waiting period without her agreement, and without a new marriage contract . . . [W]ith irrevocable talaq, a husband cannot reinstate his ex-wife unilaterally.' So while the revocable talaq is often identified with the first and the second talaq, the irrevocable talaq is mostly associated with the third divorce.

With regard to triple divorce, Muslim jurists have different opinions as to whether the pronouncement of the divorce formula three times on a single occasion is to be considered a single or triple divorce. As the primary source of

Islam, the Qur'an contains a statement that could imply diverse understandings. The Qur'an (2: 229–30) says:

> The divorce is twice, after that, either you retain her on reasonable terms or release her with kindness . . . And if he has divorced her (the third time), then she is not lawful unto him thereafter until she has married another husband. Then, if the other husband divorces her, it is no sin on both of them that they reunite, provided they feel that they can keep the limits ordained by Allâh.

While some have proposed that the Qur'an treats three talaqs pronounced on a single occasion as one, there are others whose interpretation of that pronouncement of talaq three times at the same time is that it should result in triple divorce.

In early Islam, from the Prophet's time to the reign of the first caliph, Abu Bakar, the practice of triple divorce in a single breath was not recognised, but when the second caliph, 'Umar ibn Khatthab, took power, he gave it validity. Caliph 'Umar declared that for any person who divorced his wife, that is, who uttered the formula of talaq three times, whether he seriously intended it or not, that divorce would take absolute effect, without retraction, reconciliation or remarriage (Rahman 1980). It was said that 'Umar's statement regarding the pronouncement of talaq thrice at one time as three divorces was meant as a response to the emergency situation in the specific circumstances following the wars of expansion of Islam. Later, a number of legal jurists accepted 'Umar's legal practice as a valid form of divorce and gave sanction to it (Ahmad 2003; Hussain 2010).

While the classical Islamic jurisprudences were of the same opinion, that triple divorce is irrevocable, they disagreed somewhat on its mode or procedure. If the Hanafi jurists regarded this kind of talaq as *bid'a* (innovation) or as not conforming to the Prophet's practice, the Shi'a scholars were, in general, against it, and, in fact, the Imamiya consider it not to be a divorce at all. It is a quite interesting that the Shafi'i school has a distinctive view on this. It holds that if a husband repeats three pronouncements of talaq only for emphasis, it will result in a single divorce. But if he pronounces talaq three times, with or without intending to do so, it shall result in irrevocable triple divorce. While the Hanbali jurists hold more or less the same view, the Maliki make a distinction between various expressions used in the pronouncement of talaq (Hussain 2010).

Following the disagreement outlined above, past and contemporary Muslim jurists have been in dispute as to whether or not triple divorce pronounced at the one time is irrevocable. According to an Andalusia Muslim scholar, Ibn Rushd (d. 1198), jurists who applied the rule of triple divorce at one time as irrevocable used the same legal reasoning as 'Umar had applied earlier. Another Muslim legal scholar, Al-Shawkani (d. 1834), criticised these jurists. In his view, jurists should adhere to the practice of the Prophet, who did not apply the rule of triple divorce at one time, rather than follow the practice of 'Umar (Al-Azri 2011). Despite this criticism, one can still observe current social practices of triple divorce, and the acceptance by some scholars of its validity. As will be discussed below, some village religious leaders in Aceh recognise and apply the rule of triple divorce at one time, mostly due to the strong influence of Shafi'i legal jurisprudences in this region.

Case 1: Facilitating Cina Buta

The practice of cina buta in rural areas of Aceh is possible partly through the presence of the so-called '*kadi liar*' (illegitimate religious functionary), who prepares both ex-husband and ex-wife for reconciliation after triple divorce and facilitates the process. I was told that the profession of kadi liar has a long pedigree in Aceh, even before Indonesia's independence in 1945. Its incidence significantly increased when the armed conflict between the Free Aceh Movement (GAM) and the Indonesian National Military intensified in the 1990s to early 2000s. This was because the GAM prohibited the Acehnese from going to the state marriage registrar of the sub-district religious office, or KUA. (Here and elsewhere in Indonesia, the KUA is a state institution that is responsible for ensuring marriages and reconciliations between couples are official and registered.) Instead, people were encouraged to deal with kadi liar when they had some problem related to marriage and family issues.[5] The deployment of kadi liar by the GAM can therefore be seen as a means of resistance against the Indonesian political structure.

My trip to Aceh in October 2010 enabled me to meet and talk to a person who fulfils this role as kadi liar. Let us say his name is Teungku Saiful. He is sixty-seven years old. I visited his house in Lhokseumawe on a Sunday morning. He was formerly a local businessman, but shut down his company due to security concerns in the early 1990s. His current occupation is as a village teacher who helps children recite and learn the Arabic letters or the Qur'an at his house. Apart from this, Teungku Saiful is also known as kadi liar who can reconcile and (re)marry couples who come to him for help. Usually, couples need Teungku Saiful's assistance because they cannot meet the terms and conditions required by the sub-district religious office, such as the presence of the guardian of the bride. Meanwhile, motivated partly by his wish to prevent the couple from committing adultery, Teungku Saiful is happy to facilitate the couple's requests.[6]

As I sat on a sofa in his guest room, Teungku Saiful showed me his two references justifying his action in conducting the solemnisation of remarriage between an ex-husband and his ex-wife after irrevocable divorce. The first was the Qur'an, which has a translation in Bahasa Indonesia by Mahmud Yunus. The second was an Indonesian version of a work on Muslim marriage and family issues. Teungku Saiful said that he had assisted many couples, including those who had been caught in the aftermath of triple divorce. I asked him how he helped a couple who wanted to reconcile after triple divorce. He explained that he has three local men who live nearby and are ready at any time to be called on to perform cina buta or to act as muhallil. These persons have, beforehand, given their implicit consent to marrying a divorced wife only for several days and not retaining her, however beautiful she is. This pre-scenario is important, for it is the reason that couples come to Teungku Saiful for help. According to Teungku Saiful, none of these muhallil is younger than fifty years of age. Otherwise, it would be difficult to ensure that they would divorce the ex-wife by pronouncing triple talaq after only a few days of marriage.

Usually, as Teungku Saiful further explained, the ex-wife comes alone to his house. Her ex-husband must not come with her. According to Teungku Saiful, this requirement for the ex-husband is to indicate that the marriage of his ex-wife to somebody else is beyond his knowledge, although, in many cases, it is he who expects and, in fact, engineers this practice of cina buta. As soon as the ex-wife conveys her intention to Teungku Saiful, one of those three local men is contacted and asked if he is free to be an intermediary husband. When the man comes into the house and meets the ex-wife face to face, Teungku Saiful asks both if they like one another and wish to marry. Should either of them find the other objectionable for whatever reason, Teungku Saiful would call another local contact to take the place of the first. Once both parties agree to go ahead with this kind of marriage, he then begins the process of marriage solemnisation. For Teungku Saiful, the presence of the bride's guardian, as formally required by Shafi'i legal jurisprudence, is not important. In fact, he regards himself as often serving the role of the guardian, particularly if the bride tells Teungku Saiful that her family lives far away (perhaps more than 175 km).

After the marriage solemnisation has taken place, Teungku Saiful asks both the new bride and groom to stay in his house for one or two nights to consummate the marriage. In fact, he provides the couple with a room if they want to have the required sexual contact. In the following days, the intermediary husband divorces the wife, as has been tacitly arranged. As soon as all these procedures for the shady marriage and divorce are completed, and the waiting period (usually three months) has elapsed, the former husband is then able to reunite with his ex-wife. Having gone through all these arrangements, Teungku Saiful produces his own certificates for the ex-wife: the first is a confirmation that a marriage with the intermediary husband has taken place; the second is proof that she has been divorced from her second marriage; and the last is a verification that the ex-wife has reunited with her original husband. According to Teungku Saiful, any couple holding these letters from him would be free to return to normal life in their village and their community would accept them as lawful wife and husband. They would not be disturbed or accused by the villagers of committing adultery.

Teungku Saiful acknowledged that, so far, he had conducted many ceremonies of marriage solemnisation and saved about ten (re)marriages associated with triple divorce. For organising all this, Teungku Saiful receives an amount of money from the ex-wife or her original husband. This money is then shared with the intermediary husband. Many whom I met in Aceh, from judges of sharia courts and chiefs of the sub-district religious offices to Muslim intellectuals, pointed to this financial reward as motivating kadi liar to conduct the (re) marriage of those divorced couples.

Case 2: Setting a Pre-agreed Scenario

Another case of saving a marriage after triple divorce took place in a small village where I stayed during my long fieldwork in Aceh. I was not aware of this story until a few days before I left the village in late May 2008. One of my informants incidentally mentioned it when I was reading a local newspaper that covered a similar issue in another district. He told me that Teungku Basir (not his real name), who lives in a house adjacent to a couple who had been through triple divorce, knew most of what had happened. This person was my source of information for the other disputed issue in the area (see Chapter 6 on land ownership disputes). As I had been with him on many occasions, not only in congregational prayers but also at many village events, I should have been able to spot the issue in question. Nevertheless, there was not even a single clue that I could detect on this very sensitive topic when we were engaged in conversation on a number of occasions.

I came back to the village and met Teungku Basir late one afternoon early in October 2010. When I started a conversation with him, it was quite difficult to get onto the topic of saving a marriage after a triple divorce. I was able to come to this very sensitive issue only by drawing on another similar case that I knew of from the newspaper. He eventually revealed the case when it was clear to him that what I wanted to discuss was a mode of reconciliation after triple divorce. Apparently, he did not consider the case as a *sengketa* (dispute), but rather as a *kejadian* (an occurrence).

Teungku Basir began telling me that the couple were his neighbours. He said that not many villagers knew the details of their story. From the vague story of my earlier informant, what I had in my mind was that two marriages were suffering the after-effects of triple divorce and that these two couples sought to resolve the problem by making an agreement between themselves to swap their ex-spouses for a certain period, after which both couples would be able to eventually return to their original marriages. As Teungku Basir told the story below, it became clear that my earlier understanding was incorrect.

The case involved a husband and a wife who had been married for more than ten years and who had four children. It was not quite clear to Teungku Basir how this triple divorce had taken place, whether pronounced at one time or three times on separate occasions. What became obvious was that the (ex-)husband and (ex-)wife could not be reconciled after this triple divorce unless an intermediary marriage took place between the ex-wife and someone else. The ex-husband, in order to be able to return to the original marriage, is not required to marry another woman. As described by Teungku Basir, the ex-wife and the ex-husband agreed to a unique idea for saving their previous marriage after triple divorce.[7]

Although this practice of saving a marriage after triple divorce is common among villagers in some parts of Aceh, the ex-husband was unhappy and felt uneasy when he discovered that his ex-wife would have to marry another man (even though this man would subsequently divorce her). For this reason, the ex-husband sought to marry another woman too, and went to Meulaboh, West Aceh, to marry a local woman there. During his second marriage, the ex-husband stayed in Meulaboh and had a child with his new wife. Meanwhile, the ex-wife and her new husband remained living in the village, but had no children. It was uncertain whether the new spouses of both the ex-husband and the ex-wife were aware of the 'pre-scenario' of the marriages they had engaged in. It is most probable that they had no idea about the agreement between the ex-husband and the ex-wife to treat them as intermediary spouses and that their marriages would only last for a limited period.

After more than a year, both the ex-husband and the ex-wife wished to return to their original spouses. It had been agreed at the outset of the scheme that the ex-husband and the ex-wife would divorce their present spouses and reunite in the renewed marriage that they both wished for. However, it was not easy for the ex-husband to divorce his new wife because they already had a baby. The ex-husband was quite reluctant to divorce his present spouse and, instead, planned just to remarry his ex-wife. Had he done this, he would have been in a polygamous marriage. The ex-wife did not want to find herself in this situation, and therefore raised objections to the earlier agreement should it lead to such a polygamous marriage. If her ex-husband did not want to divorce his new spouse, she preferred, instead, to stay with her new husband. Although it was difficult for the ex-husband to leave his new wife, he eventually divorced her to return to his previous marriage. The ex-wife did the same thing. She asked for a divorce from her new husband and, after the waiting period had elapsed, she was reunited with her former husband in the village.

Although these marriages and the remarriage were undertaken without the required state formalities, none of the villagers raised any objection to what the couple had done. The villagers probably did not follow in detail what had actually happened between the couple, but what they did know was that all the necessary religious mechanisms for the remarriage had been properly fulfilled. A few years after this reunion, the couple had a new baby, and, at least up to when I was in the village in early October 2010, they were living happily.

What do Aceh's prominent religious leaders say about the two cases above? Many approach these cases solely from a legal point of view. Gender analysis has been largely absent. While religious officials (for example, judges at sharia courts and sub-district religious officers) oppose this practice and consider it to be unlawful, local traditional Muslim teungku in Aceh have differing opinions. The issue here is whether a contrived remarriage, as such, is legitimate or not. According to Teungku Faisal Ali, a secretary general of the *Himpunan Ulama Dayah Aceh* (Association of the Rural Traditional Acehnese Ulama – HUDA), as long as there is no mention at the solemnisation of the marriage of a pre-nuptial agreement about the duration of the marriage (that is, that divorce will take place at a definite time in the near future), this kind of marriage is lawful.[8] In other words, the acquiescent arrangement made prior to the solemnisation of the marriage does not validate, or invalidate, the marriage itself. Another religious leader in North Aceh, Teungku Mustafa, shares this view, but with a different supporting argument. He regards this kind of marriage as valid, provided that a legitimate guardian of the bride is present during the marriage solemnisation.[9] For both teungku, since the terms and conditions of the marriage do not stipulate a certain period of time, the marriage is not a contracted marriage (*mut'a*) like the one in Shi'a legal tradition.

However, the former chairman of the Provincial Ulama Consultative Assembly of Aceh, Teungku Muslim Ibrahim, rejected this practice, saying that even if the couple do not pronounce it during the solemnisation, they have illicitly planned and agreed beforehand to play out a particular scenario. Although Teungku Muslim Ibrahim has a traditional background, he holds the view that the practice of cina buta, or any similar kind of practice is considered unlawful. Interestingly, he justifies his view by referring to one of the Islamic legal maxims: *al-qawaid al-fiqhiyya*: '*hukm al-qadi yarfa`u al-khilaf*' ('the decision of the judge eliminates the disagreements') (Ibrahim 2008). As the judges of the Aceh Sharia Court refer to the Indonesian Law on Marriage (1/1974) and the Presidential Instruction (1/1991) on the Compilation of Islamic Law, Teungku Muslim Ibrahim is undoubtedly advocating the state Islamic law rather than Shafi'i Islamic jurisprudence. This opinion, as put forward by Teungku Muslim Ibrahim, may not be in line with many of the district branches of the Aceh Ulama Consultative Assembly in the (sub-)districts of Aceh.

CASE 3: CONTESTING CINA BUTA

The third case took place in the other village of Lhoknga sub-district. Before their marriage in early 2000, the wife in the couple involved was a widow with two children and the husband was a widower with eight children. While the wife had been a resident of the village since her childhood, the husband lived in Banda Aceh, the capital of the province. When they married, the husband was fifty-four years old and the wife was forty-two years old. This couple had no children together, but this was not the reason for the tension between them. As the tension escalated, the husband declared triple divorce at the one time, witnessed by both the keuchik and the village *imeum meunasah* (religious leader). To confirm this triple divorce, the husband wrote a statement, dated 8 August 2006, and then left the village.

When I visited the village, the head of the village who had witnessed this triple divorce had been replaced. The new keuchik is Bukhari. Although he was not present when the divorce took place, Bukhari holds a copy of the signed letter relating to that divorce. He received this letter from the imeum meunasah who had kept the document. As this was triple divorce, which could not permit the couple to reconcile, the head of the village and the villagers were outraged to discover that the ex-husband had returned to the village and was re-uniting with his ex-wife. From the villagers' point of view, the triple divorce did take place, and, therefore, they did not want to see the ex-husband going back to his ex-wife without practising cina buta.

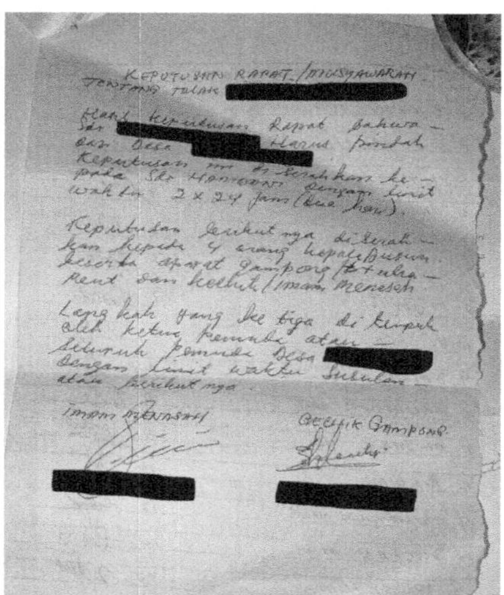
KEPUTUSAN RAPAT /MUSYAWARAH
TENTANG TALAK [redacted]

Hasil keputusan Rapat bahwa Sdr [redacted] dari Desa [redacted] Harus pindah
Keputusan ini di serahkan kepada Sdr [illegible] dengan limit waktu 2 x 24 jam (dua hari).

Keputusan berikutnya di serahkan kepada 4 orang kepala dusun beserta aparat gampong [illegible] dan keuchik / imam meunasah

Langkah yang ke tiga di [illegible] oleh ketua pemuda atau seluruh pemuda desa [redacted] dengan limit waktu sebulan atau berikutnya.

Imam Meunasah
[redacted]

Geuchik Gampong
[redacted]

Figure 9.1 A handwritten document detailing a decision by village leaders to evict a husband who divorced his wife by triple talak © Arskal Salim

In October 2007, the village organised a meeting in the meunasah. Seventeen village leaders and elders were at this meeting and agreed that the ex-husband would be expelled from the village and that his ex-wife must not see him again. Although they allowed the ex-wife to remain in the village, they consider her a widow. For them, there is no longer a spousal relationship between these two persons. The villagers hold the view that once a husband pronounces triple divorce at the one time, it becomes an irrevocable divorce.

Apparently the head of the village was aware of diverse legal views on this matter, but he, along with many other villagers, could not accept a view that allows the reunion of a couple after triple divorce in their village. The head of the village explained that if the ex-husband could not accept the village's decision and still wanted to get his ex-wife back based on another, different, opinion, he could go away and live in another village. Had the ex-husband wanted to return to live in this village with his ex-wife, the head of village said, cina buta must be carried out first. Otherwise, the couple would be committing adultery and thus disgracing the whole village.[10]

The couple nevertheless did not relent. They sought to challenge the village's decision. They made various efforts to claim that they remained, or could return to being, a lawfully married couple. First, they approached the Lhoknga sub-district religious officer, Zaini, and asked him to restore their marriage relationship. However, Zaini rejected their request. He told the couple:

> I have no authority to reconcile or remarry both of you since according to the state regulation your marriage is not yet dissolved. Why should I remarry you if you have no divorce? Both of you are still holding your marriage certificates. Had there been a divorce, all certificates would be cancelled. So, I cannot provide you with new marriage certificates . . . [Instead,] please go to the sharia court and let the court decide whether to dissolve your marriage. If the court decides to suspend it with a single talaq, please both of you come to my office again and I will reconcile you.[11]

Acting on this suggestion, the couple went to the Jantho Sharia Court. They expected to receive a court decision declaring the dissolution of their marriage so as to enable them to reconcile or remarry. When the judges began hearing this case and asked why the couple wanted a divorce, they discovered that they had been in a triple divorce outside the court. In most cases like this, judges in Aceh refuse to acknowledge the validity of such a divorce, especially since extra-judicial divorce is not recognised. The judges would only take account of those divorces that take place before the court. Thus, they would consider the three divorces only if the same couple brought their case to the court on three separate occasions.

The refusal by judges to apply the rule of triple divorce is based on the Indonesian Compilation of Islamic law (KHI), which consists of Muslim family issues and applies nationally. This compilation does not stipulate or deal with triple divorce pronounced in a single breath. As the existing regulation does not say anything about triple divorce, the judges were therefore hesitant to regard this case as a divorce lawsuit. In fact, since the couple actually sought a reunion, while there was not enough reason or strong evidence to suspend the marriage, the judges were inclined to settle this case by making a concord between the couple. In January 2008, the judges issued a *penetapan* (an order) that the couple agreed to a settlement and the wife thus withdrew her suit from the court's dossier. Finally, instead of receiving a single divorce certificate from the court, as required by the district religious officer in order for him to be able to remarry them, the couple came to a peaceful agreement (*perdamaian*). In the view of the judges, a confirmation of their (re)marriage in the form of a peaceful settlement would have been enough to reinstate their marital relationship. Nevertheless, the judges, paradoxically, requested that the couple meet the ulama council to receive a fatwa confirming the status of their marriage.[12]

The couple went to see the ulama council to obtain the fatwa declaring that they were able to remarry. With the fatwa in hand (although it was only in oral form), they both then visited the sub-district religious officer, Zaini, asking him to legalise their remarriage and issue a new certificate of marriage. The couple thought this step would at last end their marital problem and enable them eventually to go back to live in the village. However, this was not to be the case. Their request to remarry was denied. Zaini told them that, even though the ulama council had allowed them to remarry, he could not fulfil this request for three reasons. The first was that the chairman of the ulama council, who issued the fatwa, was not his superior. The second was that the fatwa had nothing to do with him as a religious officer. And the third was that the couple remained husband and wife before the state Islamic law, and thus they did not need to remarry. Zaini added that if they wanted to undertake an unofficial remarriage or practice cina buta, he would not say anything.[13]

Given the persistent efforts of the couple to achieve a reunion, why did the sub-district religious officer not simply remarry them? What made the issue in question so complicated? It appears that the major factor was social acceptance. When I posed this question, Zaini answered that he had to pay attention to what people in the village expected. With regard to this case, he was aware that the villagers would not allow the couple to reconcile unless they had practised cina buta. Zaini understood the complexity of the case, and he therefore thought himself unable to settle it. He was sure that he could not do something that was against the villagers' demands. Earlier Zaini had himself investigated the case by asking a person in the village: 'What do you think if I remarry the couple, what would happen?' This villager answered: 'Please don't ever do that. I heard people saying that if you would have remarried the couple, your career (as religious officer) would be ruined.'[14] Concerning his position, Zaini said frustratedly:

> I [still] ponder people's reaction and I finally came to a conclusion that I don't want to take care of, or sort out, this case anymore. I still hold the view that the couple's marriage is not dissolved yet. Why should I remarry them? If they want to reconcile through the 'cina buta' process, that's beyond my authority. [It was their fault] that they conducted divorce in this way. When the ex-husband made such a triple divorce, he did not ask my opinion, but now when the couple want to remarry, why they should come to me?[15]

One may wonder why the court order that the couple held was not effective. In the view of the villagers, this court order could not be accepted to justify the reunion after triple divorce, because it did not say anything about reconciliation or remarriage. What the head of village and other elders expected to read was a plain statement to the effect that the court had remarried the couple. However, the order only allowed the wife to withdraw her lawsuit, and gave an instruction to the court's registrar to remove this case from the court's dossier. The order did not deal with the status of (re)marriage at all, implying that the original marriage remained in place.

In some legal cases, the tension between the views of the villagers and those of the religious officials results in the officials relenting. In my interview with the judges of the Lhokseumawe Sharia Court, and the chiefs of the sub-district religious offices in North Aceh, in particular, they admitted that they were afraid people would be enraged if their decisions differed from what had been decided and accepted in the villages. This situation may answer the question of whether state legality is subordinate to religious validity or vice versa. It is apparent that social acceptance by villagers has been important in relation to decisions made either by the sharia courts or local religious authorities. Validation by the community, in the form of acceptance or resistance, has been the key factor that, oddly enough, determines almost all the outcomes of legal processes and judicial reasoning, particularly on the issue in question here.

Case 4: Undoing Triple Divorce

The fourth case took place in another village in the Lhoknga sub-district. This village was only five minutes away, by motorcycle, from the place where I stayed while conducting a long fieldwork in Aceh. I received information from one of the village elders that a young villager had declared triple divorce at the one time to his wife. Surprisingly, he had made this pronouncement through a mobile phone text message. Saleh, the husband, is Acehnese, while the origins of the wife, Weni, are East Javanese (these are not their real names). It was not clear what triggered Saleh's impulse to divorce his wife with a triple divorce, but it seemed that he soon regretted his action. As he wanted to clarify his relationship with Weni after sending her the divorce text message, Saleh informed the village leaders and asked their advice about what to do to resolve his marital problem.

The text-messaged divorce is no longer a new case. It has become more widespread in numerous Muslim countries. Although no study has been undertaken, it can be assumed that the majority of those who prefer to use this non-standard procedure of divorce are young men. This is not only because they tend to be husbands who are hasty in their decision making, and who later regret the decision, but these young men are also more used to working with smartphones than are older couples. Whether divorce via a mobile phone's short message is lawful or not remains debatable among different actors, such as religious figures, Muslim scholars, judicial authorities and feminist activists. Despite this debate, in July 2003, the Malaysian court ruled that it is lawful for a man to divorce his wife by sending her a text message, such as 'Am dvrcng u 3 times' or 'talaq, talaq, talaq'. For Malaysian judicial authorities, the text message serves as another form of writing (Wozniak 2003).

In the opinion of Mahdan, one of the village leaders in Lhoknga, such a pronouncement of divorce through a mobile phone message cannot be accepted as triple divorce because it is delivered hastily and in anger. The leaders of this village regarded it as being expressed by someone who is ill, a condition which should disqualify that person from performing a legal action. Furthermore, they distinguished between what was said by Saleh, the husband, and what was intended. The village elders emphasised that, although Saleh pronounced triple divorce, this could not have been a purposeful intent, especially in such an uncontrolled situation. Such a triple divorce ought to be regarded as a single divorce, revocable during the waiting period. For this reason, they did not hesitate to consider it a single divorce, and encouraged the couple to reconcile soon, before the waiting period of three months elapsed.[16]

I was fortunate that the head of the village invited me to participate in and observe this reconciliation process (*ruju'*) between a husband and a wife. Around eight o'clock in the evening, about ten to twelve people convened at the couple's house. Besides the couple, those present included village elders, neighbours, family members of the couple and me. All guests were sitting on the floor, making a circle in the living room. Having opened the meeting by reciting some verses of the Qur'an and the Prophet's tradition, Mahdan stated the purpose for which they were all in the couple's house that evening. He said that the meeting was to undo the triple divorce, to reinstate the marriage between the couple, and to witness that a required marital settlement did take place.

Although this village decision was in line with most practices of the Sharia Court in Aceh, which considers triple divorce at one time to be unlawful, the village leaders' decision had its own legal reasoning. Mahdan offered two reasons why the village leaders did not accept the triple divorce in this case and, therefore, allowed the husband to return to his original marriage without the cina buta process. The first was a hadith of the Prophet. It was narrated that a companion named Rakana delivered to his wife a pronouncement of three divorces at one time. When he came to the Prophet Muhammad to ask for a rule on this matter, the Prophet allowed him to retain his wife, because the divorce was not pronounced on three separate occasions. Interestingly, Mahdan knew, exactly, not only the content (*matn*) of this hadith, but also its chain of transmission (*sanad*), which began from Ibn Abbas. He also mentioned that this hadith can be found in *Musnad of Ahmad ibn Hanbal.*

The second reason mentioned by Mahdan was the opinion of Caliph 'Umar. It was said that 'Umar once stated: 'Human beings are always in a rush when making a decision. So if this rushed decision is considered valid, the human beings would certainly be failed or disadvantaged.'[17] Based on these Prophet and Companion traditions, the village leaders have been bold enough to disagree with the practice of the neighbouring villages, who deem triple divorce at one time to be irrevocable divorce. Interestingly, a controversial decision by Caliph 'Umar that enforced triple divorce at one time as equalling 'thrice' was not mentioned at all. It was unclear whether the village leaders were aware of this story. If they had already been informed of it, it may be speculated that the village leaders were selectively applying a preferred rule and discarding an undesired one.

Compared with the practices of saving a marriage after triple divorce that are prevalent in many parts of Aceh, where the practice of cina buta has been widely acknowledged, the decision of these village elders on the undoing of triple divorce was unusual. I was told that family issues or marital disputes that took place in this village were resolved by mutual consideration between the parties and the family members themselves. If this did not resolve the tension, the village leaders would take care of the problem. Nevertheless, only a very few family problems, excluding division of inheritances, reached the village leaders. As an illustration of this, one village elder pointed out the interesting 'fact' that not a single divorce had taken place in this village for the last five decades. I thought this was an exaggeration. When I asked how such a thing could not happen, I received the answer that such a practice is considered shameful in this village. A cross-check examination against the records of the District Sharia Court in Jantho is certainly needed to see if what was stated by the village leaders was true. It is likely that registered divorce does not exist in this village, but one can be sure that casual divorce outside the court, as in the case discussed here, has certainly taken place.

LAW AS LOCAL KNOWLEDGE: CONCLUSION

The cases presented in this chapter are not just about what sharia, classical Islamic jurisprudence, state Islamic regulation, religious court decisions and village consensus have prescribed for lawfully acceptable marriage and divorce. Yet the cases demonstrate how all these norms and outcomes have been understood and experienced by Muslim villagers, as well as by couples whose marital relationship has been in trouble. By comparing court adjudications and village practices on the issues of marriage and divorce, this chapter has not only discovered different ways of reconciling three-times divorced couples, but has also disclosed inconsistent legal reasoning for saving marriages after triple divorce.

For particular reasons, a number of couples had participated in the cina buta process, however unpleasant it is, to save their marriage after triple divorce. Although cina buta has been a popular and acceptable practice for some villagers in Aceh, a wide spectrum of criticism emerges against it. The criticism comes not only out of Islamic legal discourse, but also from socio-critical perspectives. The practice of cina buta was condemned because it has badly affected women's lives, physically and emotionally. In the aftermath of triple divorce, an ex-wife becomes trapped in a deep dilemma, without having much option. On the one hand, she has to go through this practice, often for her love of her ex-husband and for the sake of their children if they have any, or because of the ex-husband's insistence, or due to coercion exercised by her extended family, in order to return to her original marriage. On the other hand, she feels unhappy about having to marry and to have sexual intercourse with an intermediary husband, whom she does not know or love. Moreover, by engaging in this practice, the ex-wife becomes vulnerable to having an unintended pregnancy or a sexually transmitted disease from having sexual contact, without adequate protection, with a man who has probably been involved in many short-term marriages before.

For this reason, one may have argued that these cases of village legal settlements in Aceh do not take gender sensitivity much into account. Unlike some judges of the sharia courts, whose decisions have been shaped and influenced by gender equality (Bowen 2003; Salim *et al.* 2009), various village settlements in rural Aceh tend to marginalise female experience and maintain the male patriarchal structure. In light of this, Judith Tucker (2008) said that (Islamic) law often employs male norms to marginalise female experience. In her view, Islamic law often 'speaks in the voice of male experience', while 'female experience has often been a secondary consideration, hostage to male patriarchal priorities' (Tucker 2008: 29). But are these cases all about gender insensitivity, male norms and female experience?

Looking at these four cases from the way the villagers, as well as the couples themselves, sought to resolve the problems, it is perhaps acceptable to say that these cases reveal law in action within village communities. To recall Geertz (1983), law as local knowledge is not about the separate capacities of individuals, but something rooted in the collective resources of culture or people. It is true that law is about 'what is right'. But 'what is right' in the villages does not have to correspond to 'what is right' according to international laws or other norms. 'What is right' in these village case studies is simply about how one appropriately presents him- or herself in various relationships of communal life in the village, notwithstanding the fact that any other laws exist to contest or stipulate the contrary. A village legal tradition is not necessarily parallel to perceptions and judgements of Islamic scholars or jurists. This is because it founds its legitimacy and its normativity on the long experience or memory of repeated actions of a social ethnic group or in a specific location.

Notes

1. *Kontras*, 6 May 2009.
2. *Serambi Indonesia*, 25 April 2009.
3. Numerous works have studied modes of divorce pronouncement, and the legal implications in its aftermath, in Islam (Amira El Azhary 1996; Sonbol 1996; Ahmad 2003; Rapoport 2005; Omar 2007). Other similar works pay particular attention to divorce case studies at courts from different places and times (Layish 1991; Shaham 1994; Stiles 2003). In addition, there are several authors who examine formal mechanisms and the types of procedure required for a valid divorce in different Muslim contexts (Carroll and Kapoor 1996; Carroll 1997; Bowen 2003; Kusrin 2006; Nakamura 2006; Cammack *et al.* 2007).
4. See, for example, Kamali (1984); Haeri (1990); Amira El Azhary (1996); Omar (2007).
5. Interview with the head of sub-district Religious Office of Muara Dua, Lhokseumawe, 4 October 2010.
6. Description of this case is based on an interview with Teungku Saiful, 3 October 2010.
7. Description of this case is based on an interview with Teungku Basir, 7 October 2010.
8. Interview with Teungku Faisal Ali, 8 October 2010.
9. Interview with Teungku Mustafa, 4 October 2010.
10. Interview with the head of village, Bukhari, 3 June 2008.
11. Interview with the head of Sub-district Religious Office of Lhoknga, Zaini, 1 April 2008.
12. Interview with Judge Rosmawardani, who examined the case, 8 October 2010.

13. Interview with the head of Sub-district Religious Office of Lhoknga, Zaini, 1 April 2008.
14. Interview with the head of Sub-district Religious Office of Lhoknga, Zaini, 1 April 2008.
15. Interview with the head of Sub-district Religious Office of Lhoknga, Zaini, 1 April 2008.
16. Description of this case is based on my interview with village elders of Lampuuk, 13 April 2008, and my attendance at the marital reconciliation process of the couple on the same date.
17. This statement by 'Umar was quoted in Mahdan's remarks before the participants who were present at the couple's house on 13 April 2008.

Conclusion

When this Conclusion was written, Indonesia had just completed the April 2014 legislative election. The result of the election was officially released in mid-May 2014. It is highly relevant, as well as significant, to draw on this election result to look not only at changes, if any, within the political configuration of Aceh's legislative body in particular, but also to reflect on all discussions presented in the preceded chapters.

The questions being posed are: to what extent would the 2014 election result make changes, if any, to the future legal–political configuration in Indonesia, especially in Aceh? How would the reconfiguration of state elites influence the legislation of sharia in Aceh and its implementation regionally? In what ways would legal pluralism in Aceh be affected by this change, if any? Would there be immediate changes that the election result may usher into the plural legal constellation of Aceh?

I was able to visit Aceh in the first week of May 2014 and had discussions with some people with different backgrounds. Based on this, the following sections present some assessments and offer several key points that I hope will shed light on the future of sharia and legal pluralism in Aceh.

Changes in the Role of Law

For the last two centuries, especially since the emergence of nation-states, the role of law in society has been identified in multipolar ways. First, law safeguards members of society from each other or against anarchy by ensuring that no single person can abuse others. Law thus provides all members of society with equal rights, protects those who are physically and socially weaker and brings order to society. Secondly, law must reflect the sense of justice and moral ideas prevalent among the society. Law, therefore, can achieve its objectives only by sticking closely to the existing social norms. Thirdly, law becomes a tool for pushing forward changes in society. Law, hence, serves as a strategy through which transformation of society is designed.

While we can add other roles of law in society to those above, it is important to assert here that the role of law in society depends greatly on the particular characteristics of any given society. In the specific context of post-conflict and post-disaster recovery processes in Aceh, law plays at least three key roles. First, law decision making (that is, legislation and adjudication) appears as a site of contestation reflecting the unique conflicts brought about by multiple legal problems; secondly, it becomes a legitimate reference as Acehnese communities recover from hardship and calamity; and, lastly, it allows Aceh's legal pluralism to deepen within and beyond courtrooms. With all these changing roles, law in Aceh's particular condition is probably related to what Bourdieu (1987) described as the 'juridical field', in which it is a site of a competition between different actors and institutions for claiming the right to determine the law. In this case, the activity of legal interpretation has been a means by which players defend or try to secure and possess 'juridical capital'.

Changed and Unchanged

Thanks to various legislation and adjudication processes in the past decade, legal political transformations have emerged in post-tsunami Aceh in many ways. The Sharia Court of Aceh (Mahkamah Syar'iyah) not only experienced numerous changes in terms of its structure and jurisdiction, but it also brought several other changes. Village practice in inheritance division, such as patah titi, was cancelled whenever a case is brought before the sharia court. There has been a deep impression that the Mahkamah Syar'iyah defends women whose property rights were often denied in many villages in Aceh. That the Sharia Court of Aceh protects women's interests was earlier demonstrated in Bowen's work (2003). This book, however, pushed this further not only by looking at the ways in which the judges employed certain legal provisions that advantage women (as found in the KHI) in examining disputes, but also by pondering the programme of gender mainstreaming for judges of Aceh's sharia courts by international NGOs. Because of this programme, judges are more sensitive to gender equity and affirmative in upholding women's rights. They, for instance, were willing to appoint many female guardians for underage orphaned heirs in managing the inherited estates. They do not permit husbands to officially declare a divorce before the court if post-divorce payments are not yet settled.

Additionally, despite a long village inheritance practice that prefers uncles to their nieces, some judges began applying the jurisprudence of the Supreme Court that allocates all bequests to the only surviving daughter regardless of the presence of her deceased parent's siblings, who are considered guardian (*wali*) when this daughter gets married.

Despite some changes having being implemented, it must be noted, however, that there was resistance to some laws from both state institutions and various socio-political actors. Resistance included attempts at refusing changes in the (re)formulation of law as well as its actual implementation. The first part of this book demonstrated how the changes of the sharia court's jurisdictions met stiff resistance from the civil judiciary by still accepting and examining Islamic property disputes between Muslim parties. Most notably, initiatives by Islamic parties to bring changes by introducing more Islamic penal laws into the qanun were resisted, as shown in Chapter 5. In addition, as illustrated in Chapter 8, the Supreme Court opposed the discretion of some Islamic judges of the first instance courts in Aceh to make changes in distributing insurance benefits equally to heirs of both husband and wife. And last, as presented in Chapter 9, despite one village in Aceh having embraced legal change by undoing triple divorce, other villages persist in upholding the long-standing practice of triple divorce. In view of all this, the legal changes that have taken place depend very much on those who possess law-making authority, as well as on individual actors who have recognised capacity to construe facts, interpret legal texts and legitimise applicable norms.

To recall Starr and Collier (1989), the changed and unchanged legal constellations of Aceh in the past decade are the outcomes of certain major historical processes; the result of the interaction at different forums between diverse institutions, individuals and groups, including political and judicial powers, and the upshot of ordinary people's understanding about what they consider to be right, just and fair. Findings presented in this book reveal that in changing plural legal constellations, often particular historical circumstances and competing local actors and institutions (re)construct a new shape of law by acquiring legitimacy to claim and determine what right is and what law is about.

Future Changes

Although the official implementation of sharia in Aceh began in 2001 with the wholehearted support of the provincial government and reached its peak in 2005/6, changes of attitude towards rigorous implementation of sharia in Aceh began coming into the surface in 2007 when Irwandi Yusuf emerged as the newly elected governor. From then on, some leaders of Islamic groups in Aceh have become pessimistic about political support for the application of sharia in the region. In early 2008, direct control of the DSI over the Wilayatul Hisbah was transferred to the *Satuan Polisi Pamong Praja* (Municipal Police Unit). It was felt that this restructuring was part of a systematic effort by the government to weaken the implementation of sharia in Aceh, as indeed it has. In 2009, much to their great disappointment, Governor Irwandi refused to sign two qanuns on Islamic criminal law that contain the stoning to death penalty (see Chapter 5). In fact, during the period that Governor Irwandi was in office (2007–12), the number of offenders who were publicly caned overall in Aceh decreased, despite continued sentencing by the Mahkamah Syar'iyah in a number of districts. Governor Irwandi was reported to be unhappy with public caning being implemented in Aceh because it leads international audiences to discount Aceh as a destination for foreign investment (Salim 2009).

With the departure of Irwandi from the governorship position in 2012, it was hoped that the new governor (Zaini Abdullah) and his vice (Muzakkir Manaf), who was backed up by the ex-combatant party (Partai Aceh or PA), would give priority to the implementation of sharia in Aceh. This was especially true as during their election campaigns both leaders had highlighted the importance of strengthening Islamic values across diverse aspects of governance. Accordingly, the qanun on Islamic penal procedural law (*acara jinayat*) was passed by the legislature and approved by Governor Zaini in late 2013. In spite of this, many were doubtful that a non-religious party such as PA would vehemently support the enforcement of sharia in the region. There was dissatisfaction among proponents of sharia that only the qanun on Islamic criminal procedures had been passed, yet until mid-2014 the other qanun on Islamic criminal matters was not touched at all. Some Muslim leaders thus alleged that this particular legislation was a political move to entice Muslim voters towards the April 2014 legislative election.

The PA was not as successful in 2014 as they had been in the previous election in 2009. While the PA did very well in the 2009 election, gaining thirty-three (48 per cent) of the sixty-nine seats at the provincial legislature, in the 2014 election they were only able to obtain twenty-nine (35 per cent) of the eighty-one legislative members. Their attempt to persuade Muslim voters a couple of months before the election by passing one of the qanuns on Islamic criminal laws did not work well. It seems that some of their competitors that have a non-religious platform as well were able to attract significant number of voters. In the 2014 election, the PA shared votes with other new nationalist-secular parties, such as the NASDEM, GERINDRA and PNA (see Appendix II).

Despite the PA not being quite as successful in securing more seats as during the previous election in 2009, Aceh's political developments in the aftermath of the 2014 election would remain generally the same. As Islamic parties were not able to attain more voters (below 25 per cent), the direction of political energies towards the Islamisation of law in Aceh over the course of the next five years at least would not change much. This is because the nationalist-secular parties dominate the provincial legislature (about 75 per cent). Unless there is a strong political interest, these parties would not tend to introduce more aspects of sharia rules into the region.

In fact, the elites of the ruling PA have acted in a manner that could be interpreted as covert resistance to the implementation of formal sharia rules in Aceh. In mid-2013, the PA spokesperson, Hasbi Abdullah, suggested replacing the word 'sharia' with the '*Dinul Islam*', or religion of Islam. The PA argues that Dinul Islam has more historical legacy, and thus more significant implications, plus a broader scope for public social life than sharia. The conversion from the use of sharia to Dinul Islam has become official not only because the chairman of Islamic Sharia Bureau, Syahrizal, often uses Dinul Islam in important meetings and press interviews, but also because Governor Zaini reportedly keeps referring to it on many public occasions. The extent to which this recent conversion of terms will bring changes to the future of sharia in Aceh remains to be seen. One thing that is for sure, however, is that legal changes in Aceh will always be contested.

CONTESTED PLURAL LEGAL SYSTEM

As discussed in this book, social and political changes in Aceh during the past decade have contributed to rapid changes in Aceh's legal structure. While the official position of the sharia court was strengthened, its jurisdiction extended and sharia penal law officially enforced in all areas of Aceh, this does not mean that sharia is 'the only game in town'. Despite the increasing jurisdiction of the sharia court, several legal developments indicate that its jurisdiction remains contested by other authorities, such as the civil judiciary and traditional custom or adat.

Adat, or the 'living law' as practised by Acehnese community, as opposed to the 'law in books', continues to influence many legal aspects of people's lives. Even though the KHI has been the official reference for resolving family disputes in court, local religious leaders still rely on the legal opinions of traditional Shafi'i jurisprudence to resolve family law cases. In some penal cases, non-formal methods and social sanctions as directed by local leaders often counter formal legal procedures and sanctions stipulated in the qanun, and in fact these non-formal methods frequently lead to effective resolution of disputes. Above all, some qanuns stipulate that the first step in settling disputes have to be undertaken at the village level. This shows that dispute resolution at the village level should, in some ways, be more important than at the higher level. In other words, legal pluralism in Aceh allows people or disputants to have the opportunity to claim their rights and seek justice at a variety of (sub-) legal systems. This keeps each element of Aceh's plural legal system contesting one another.

Appendix I

The Population of Aceh based on Religious Affiliation, 2010

No.	*Cities/districts*	*Islam*	*Protestant*	*Catholic*	*Hindu*	*Buddhist*	*Confucianism*	*Total*
1	Banda Aceh	219,260	717	474	40	2,755	0	223,246
2	Sabang	32,260	170	140	20	312	0	32,902
3	Aceh Besar	350,159	17	73	0	30	0	350,279
4	Pidie	417,629	102	18	5	164	0	417,918
5	North Aceh	381,618	0	0	0	0	0	381,618
6	East Aceh	380,471	7	1	1	10	0	380,490
7	Central Aceh	176,786	490	144	11	206	0	177,637
8	West Aceh	179,194	37	23	5	101	0	179,360
9	South Aceh	213,975	36	12	0	98	0	214,121
10	Southeast Aceh	193,457	23,028	3,897	0	5	0	220,387
11	Simeulue	84,122	157	18	3	21	0	84,321
12	Singkil	89,501	11,493	1,752	3	4	0	102,753
13	Bireuen	389,820	93	117	13	144	0	390,187
14	Tamiang	260,549	101	74	1	1,376	23	262,124
15	Lhokseumawe	185,328	709	69	7	735	0	186,848
16	Langsa	180,228	665	43	52	759	29	181,776
17	Southwest Aceh	136,615	0	1	0	92	0	136,708
18	Nagan Raya	142,283	24	0	18	26	0	142,351
19	Aceh Jaya	81,580	4	0	0	0	0	81,584
20	Gayo Lues	70,546	0	0	0	0	0	70,546
21	Bener Meriah	120,571	37	10	0	5	6	120,629
22	Pidie Jaya	148,901	1	0	0	0	0	148,902
23	Subulussalam	65,241	1,924	239	0	3	0	67,407
Total:		4,500,094	39,812	7,105	179	6,846	58	4,554,094

Source: Provincial Office of the Ministry of Religious Affairs

Appendix II

The Result of the Provincial Legislative Election in Aceh, 2014

Nationalist secular parties 75.30%	Partai Aceh 35.80% 29 seats	Golkar 11.11% 9 seats	DEMOKRAT 9.88% 8 seats	NASDEM 9.88% 8 seats	Gerindra 3.70% 3 seats	PNA 3.70% 3 seats	PKPI 1.23% 1 seat

Muslim-based parties 9.87%	PAN 8.64% 7 seats	PKB 1.23% 1 seat

Islamic parties 14.81%	PPP 7.41% 6 seats	PKS 4.94% 4 seats	PBB 1.23% 1 seat	PDA 1.23% 1 seat

There were fifteen political parties participated in the 2014 legislative election in Aceh:

1. Partai Nasional Demokrat (NASDEM)
2. Partai Kebangkitan Bangsa (PKB)
3. Partai Keadilan Sejahtera (PKS)
4. Partai Demokrasi Indonesia Perjuangan (PDIP)
5. Partai Golongan Karya (GOLKAR)
6. Partai Gerakan Indonesia Raya (GERINDRA)
7. Partai Demokrat (DEMOKRAT)
8. Partai AmanatNasional (PAN)
9. Partai Persatuan Pembangunan (PPP)
10. Partai Hati Nurani Rakyat (HANURA)
11. Partai Damai Aceh (PDA)
12. Partai Nasional Aceh (PNA)
13. Partai Aceh (PA)
14. Partai Bulan Bintang (PBB)
15. Partai Keadilan Persatuan Indonesia (PKPI)

Two political parties (PDIP and HANURA) failed to obtain even a single seat at the Aceh provincial legislature.

Source: www.kip-acehprov.go.id.

Appendix III

Abbreviations and Glossary

The terms below are mostly Indonesian, although some of them are originally derived from Arabic words. Other terms are noted as Acehnese (Ac.), Arabic (Ar.) or Dutch (D.). Terms that only appear once or twice in the book, and always with translation, are not included.

adat	custom or tradition: it may include legal norms and practices of social life.
baitul mal	Islamic treasury: in Aceh this institution is present at multiple levels: village, sub-district, district and provincial governments.
BAL	Basic Agrarian Law (*Undang-Undang Pokok-Pokok Agraria*).
BPN	*Badan Pertanahan Nasional* (National Land Agency).
BPS	*Badan Pusat Statistik* (Central Statistics Agency).
BRR	*Badan Rekonstruksi dan Rehabilitasi* (Board of Rehabilitation and Reconstruction).
'*cina buta*'	a popular phrase in Aceh to describe a person who helps both ex-husband and ex-wife to remarry after triple divorce. He is also known as *muhallil*.
Darul Islam	'abode of peace': Islamic territory where Islamic law is in force.
dayah (Ac.)	Islamic boarding schools in Aceh; in Java they are known as *pesantren*.
diya (Ar.)	blood money or death compensation.

DPRA	*Dewan Perwakilan Rakyat Aceh* (Aceh's House of Representatives).
DSI	*Dinas Syariat Islam* (Bureau of Islamic Sharia). This state institution is available in both district and provincial governments in Aceh.
erfpacht (D.)	a right to fully enjoy the property belonging to others (usually adat communities or state) with the obligation to pay an annual tribute in the form of money, results or outcome to the owner.
fatwa	religious opinion issued by a competent scholar of Islamic law.
fiqh (Ar.)	Islamic jurisprudence: literally means 'understanding'.
GAM	*Gerakan Aceh Merdeka* (Free Aceh Movement).
gampong (Ac.)	literally means village: it is a legal community unit, which is the lowest government organisation in Aceh, led by a head of village.
hadith (Ar.)	Prophet's saying; collected traditions, teachings, and stories of the Prophet Muhammad, accepted as a source of Islamic doctrine and law second only to the Qur'an.
hak ulayat	a system of communal rights of an (ethnic) community to land based on tradition or custom of that community.
HGU	*hak guna usaha* (Rights to Cultivate).
HIVOS	*Humanistisch Instituut voor Ontwikkelingssamenwerking* (a Dutch aid organisation for development).
HUDA	*Himpunan Ulama Dayah Aceh* (Association of the Rural Traditional Acehnese Ulama).
hudud (Ar.)	fixed punishments for certain crimes, such as stoning to death for adultery and hand amputation for theft.
IAIN	*Institut Agama Islam Negeri* (State Institute for Islamic Studies).
'idda (Ar.)	legally prescribed period during which a woman may not remarry after having been widowed or divorced.
IDLO	International Development Law Organisation.
ikhtilat	derived from Arabic to indicate intimate behaviour by an unmarried couple in outdoor as well as indoor locations.
Jakarta Charter	the first draft of the preamble to the Indonesian Constitution and it contained what has since become a well-known phrase in Indonesia, consisting of 'seven words': *dengan kewajiban menjalankan syariat Islam bagi pemeluknya* (with the obligation of carrying out Islamic sharia for its adherents).

jinayat	Islamic penal laws.
kadi liar	illegitimate religious functionary, namely, the informal marriage celebrant who organises a solemnisation of marriage between a Muslim couple, but without having an authority to record the marriage according to the state law.
kelurahan	village: it is a particular name for a village in the municipal or city areas.
keuchik (Ac.)	a head of village.
khalwat	a close proximity between a male and female who have no marriage or kin relationship, in a place or situation where intimate contact is possible.
KHI	*Kompilasi Hukum Islam* (Compilation of Islamic Law).
KPA	*Komite Peralihan Aceh* (Aceh Transition Committee).
KUA	*Kantor Urusan Agama* (Office of Religious Affairs).
KOMNASHAM	*Komisi Nasional Hak Asasi Manusia* (National Human Rights Commission).
landraad (D.)	civil judicature in the colonial period.
madhhab (Ar.)	Muslim schools of law such as Hanafi, Maliki, Shafi'i and Hanbali. These schools of law refer to their founding fathers, respectively: Abu Hanifa (d. 767), Malik b. Anas (d. 795), Muhammad Idris al-Shafi'i (d. 820) and Ahmad b. Hanbal (d. 855).
Mahkamah Syar'iyah	derived from Arabic (*al-mahkama al-shar'iyya*). It is the name for the religious court of Aceh.
mawali (Ar.)	derived from Qur'anic word, this term in Hazairin's understanding means 'representative of heirs'.
meunasah (Ac.)	a multipurpose building set up in almost every village in Aceh, which serves not only as a centre of worship, but also as a meeting place for the local community.
millet system	a distinctive social system to organise and regulate religious diversity of people during the Ottoman era.
MPU	*Majelis Permusyawaratan Ulama* (Ulama Consultative Assembly).
muhallil (Ar.)	a man who acts as an intermediary husband, who marries a divorced woman and then divorces her soon afterwards only to enable the woman to remarry her previous husband.
mukim (Ac.)	a legal community unit of a number of gampong in Aceh headed by a leader called *Imeum Mukim*.
musyawarah (mufakat)	a traditional mechanism of mutual consultation to reach consensus or agreement among contending parties with the help of elders or third parties.

NGO	non-governmental organisation.
Pancasila	literally means 'five principles'. As the state ideology of Indonesia, it is located in the preamble to the 1945 Indonesian constitution and included (1) belief in One Almighty God, (2) a just and civilised humanitarianism, (3) national unity, (4) Indonesian democracy through consultation and consensus, and (5) social justice.
PDIP	*Partai Demokrasi Indonesia Perjuangan* (Indonesian Democratic Party Struggle).
PDS	*Partai Damai Sejahtera* (Prosperous Peace Party, a Christian-based party).
peunulang (Ac.)	a customary gift from the parents in the form of a parcel of land or a house and its yard to their daughter at the time of her marriage. This gift has been common practice in some parts of Aceh, especially Aceh Besar and Pidie.
PKS	*Partai Keadilan Sejahtera* (Prosperous Justice Party, an Islamic-based party).
plaatsvervulling (D.)	literary means 'of representation', it is a provision in an Indonesian Civil Code that provides the right to descendants, not to ascendants, to replace predeceased heirs. These descendants could act as successor in the same capacity and receive every right that would otherwise have been received by their predecessor.
PP	*Peraturan Pemerintah* (government regulation).
PPP	*Partai Persatuan Pembangunan* (United Development Party).
PUSA	*Persatuan Ulama Seluruh Aceh* (the Acehnese Ulama Union).
qanun	exclusively refers to regional regulations produced by the legislature of Aceh from the year 2002 onwards, whether or not relating to Islamic norms.
rajam	stoning to death: it is a capital punishment for adulterers.
Shi'i (or Shi'a)	a group of Muslims who consider Ali, the cousin of Muhammad, and his descendants as the Prophet Muhammad's true successors.
Staatsblad (D.)	a royal decree issued by the Netherlands during colonial rule in Indonesia.
Sunna (Ar.)	way or practice of the Prophet. It became one of the basic sources of Islamic law, based on Muhammad's words and deeds as recorded in the hadith. The *Sunna* complements and often explains the Qur'an.

Sunni	the largest group of Muslims, who believe in the traditions of the Sunna and accept the first four caliphs as rightful successors to Prophet Muhammad. This term literally means 'the people of the traditional way and of the congregation of believers'. It is often described technically as 'the people who follow the Prophetic Sunna and adhere to the largest mass of the Muslims beginning with the congregation of the Companions of the Prophet Muhammad'.
TAF	The Asia Foundation.
Tanzimat era	Ottoman governmental reforms that lasted from 1839 to 1876, largely during the reign of Sultan Abd al-Madjid.
ta'zir (Ar.)	a discretionary punishment for committing the prohibited acts or for omitting the obligatory acts. Although the legal texts of Qur'an and Sunna mention both prohibited and obligatory acts, there is no punishment specified therein. The punishment of ta'zir is left to the discretion of the ruler.
teungku (Ac.)	a title for Aceh's religious scholars. It is also used to identify a village religious leader.
tirka (Ar.)	the estate of the deceased.
ulama	religious scholars.
uleebalang	aristocrats or self-governing rulers in Aceh during Dutch colonial times.
UNDP	United Nations Development Programme.
USAID	United States Agency for International Development.
wakaf (Ar.)	religious endowments; a charitable trust dedicated to pious or socially beneficial purposes.
Wilayatul Hisbah	derived from Arabic (*wilaya al-hisba*), in the context of Aceh this term is defined as an institution whose task is to monitor and to advocate the application of qanun for the sake of promoting good and prohibiting evil (*amar ma'ruf nahy munkar*). It is sometimes inaccurately referred to as the 'sharia police'.
zina	adultery or fornication.

Bibliography

Abdurrahman (2006a). 'Hak ulayat masyarakat hukum adat', *Jeumala*, 20: 3–7.

Abdurrahman (2006b). 'Masyarakat hukum adat', *Jeumala*, 19: 17–21.

Abubakar, A. (2004). 'Peradilan Syariat Islam: Pengakuan perjuangan rakyat Aceh', *Jentera*, 2: 33–51.

Abubakar, A. (2005). *Sekilas Syariat Islam di Aceh*. Banda Aceh: Dinas Syariat Islam.

Abubakar, A. (2006). *Syariat Islam di Provinsi Nanggroe Aceh Darussalam: Paradigma, Kebijakan dan Kegiatan*. Banda Aceh: Dinas Syariat Islam.

Abubakar, A. (2007). *Kajian Undang-Undang Pemerintahan Aceh dan Essay Tentang Perempuan, Perkawinan dan Perwalian Anak*. Banda Aceh: Dinas Syariat Islam.

Abubakar, A. (2008). *Penerapan Syariat Islam di Aceh: Upaya Penyusunan Fiqih dalam Negara Bangsa*. Banda Aceh: Dinas Syariat Islam.

Abubakar, A. (2009a). *Bunga Rampai Pelaksanaan Syariat Islam: Pendukung Qanun Pelaksanaan Syariat Islam*, Banda Aceh: Dinas Syariat Islam.

Abubakar, A. (2009b). *Wilayatul Hisbah: Polisi Pamong Praja dengan Kewenangan Khusus di Aceh*. Banda Aceh: Dinas Syariat Islam.

Abubakar, A. and Halim, M. (2006), *Hukum Pidana Islam di Provinsi Nanggroe Aceh Darussalam*, Banda Aceh: Dinas Syariat Islam.

Ahmad, F. (1994). *Triple Talaq: An Analytical Study with Emphasis on Socio Legal Aspects*. New Delhi: Regency Publications.

Ahmad, F. (2003). 'Understanding the Islamic Law of Divorce', *Journal of the Indian Law Institute*, 45(3/4): 484–508.

Alfian (1985). 'The Ulama in Acehnese Society', in A. Ibrahim, S. Siddique and Y. Hussain (eds), *Readings on Islam in Southeast Asia*. Singapore: ISEAS.

Ali, S. S. and Naz, R. (1998). 'Marriage, Dower and Divorce: Superior Courts and Case Law in Pakistan', in F. Shaheed, S. A. Warraich, C. Balchin and A. Gazdar (eds), *Shaping Women's Lives Laws, Practices and Strategies in Pakistan*. Lahore: Shirkatgah.

Amira El Azhary, S. (1996). *Women, the Family, and Divorce Laws in Islamic History*. Syracuse, NY: Syracuse University Press.

Amiruddin, H. (2004). *Perjuangan Ulama Aceh di Tengah Konflik*. Yogyakarta: Ceninnets Press.

Angelino, A. de Kat (1931). *Colonial Policy*. The Hague: Martinus Nijhoff.

An-Na'im, A. A. (2002). *Islamic Family Law in a Changing World: A Global Resource Book*. London: Zed Press.

An-Na'im, A. A. (2008). *Islam and the Secular State: Negotiating the Future of Shari'a*. Cambridge, MA: Harvard University Press.

Ansori, M. H. (2012). 'From Insurgency to Bureaucracy: Free Aceh Movement, Aceh Party and the New Face of Conflict', *Stability: International Journal of Security and Development*, 1(1): 31–44.

Arabi, O. (1999). 'Early Muslim Legal Philosophy: Identity and Difference in Islamic Jurisprudence', Working Paper Series, UCLA Near East Center.

Aridi and Asnawi, N. (n.d.). 'Batasan kewenangan pengadilan dalam sengketa hak milik atas tanah', available at: http://www.badilag.net/artikel/14797-batasan-kewenangan-pengadilan-dalam-sengketa-hak-milik-atas-tanah-oleh--drs-h-aridi-sh-msi-dan-m-natsir-asnawi-shi--53.html, accessed 12 April 2014.

Aspinall, E. (2002). 'Sovereignty, the Successor State, and Universal Human Rights: History and the International Structuring of Acehnese Nationalism', *Indonesia*, 73: 1–24.

Aspinall, E. (2005). 'The Helsinki Agreement: A More Promising Basis for Peace in Aceh?', *Policy Studies No. 20*, Washington, DC: East West Center.

Aspinall, E. (2009a). *Islam and Nation: Separatist Rebellion in Aceh, Indonesia*. Stanford, CA: Stanford University Press.

Aspinall, E. (2009b). 'Combatants to Contractors: The Political Economy of Peace in Aceh', *Indonesia*, 87: 1–34.

Aswar, H. T. Raja Itam (2007). 'Penegakan nilai-nilai hukum adat bagi generasi muda dalam membangun keadilan hukum di Aceh', paper presented at Dialog dan Sosialisasi untuk Generasi Muda dan Mahasiswa mengenai Adat Istiadat dan Hukum Adat, Banda Aceh, 25 September.

Azra, A. (2006). *Islam in the Indonesian World: An Account of Institutional Formation*. Bandung, Indonesia: Mizan.

Al-Azri, K. (2011). 'One or Three? Exploring the Scholarly Conflict over the Question of Triple *Talaq* (divorce) in Islamic Law with Particular Emphasis on Oman', *Arab Law Quarterly*, 25(3): 277–96.

Baihaqi (1983). 'Ulama dan Madrasah Aceh', in Taufik Abdullah (ed.), *Agama dan Perubahan Sosial*. Jakarta: Rajawali.

Benda, H. J. (1958). 'Christiaan Snouck Hurgronje and the Foundations of Dutch Islamic Policy in Indonesia', *Journal of Modern History*, 30(4): 338–47.

Benda-Beckmann, F. von (2002). 'Who's Afraid of Legal Pluralism?', *Journal of Legal Pluralism*, 47: 38–82.

Benda-Beckmann, F. von (2006). 'The Multiple Edges of Law: Dealing with Legal Pluralism in Development Practice', in World Bank (ed.), *The World Bank Legal Review: Law, Equity and Development*. Washington, DC: World Bank, vol. 2, pp. 51–86.

Benda-Beckmann, K. von (1981). 'Forum Shopping and Shopping Forums: Dispute Processing in a Minangkabau Village in West Sumatra', *Journal of Legal Pluralism*, 19: 117–59.

Benda-Beckmann, K. von (2001a). 'Legal Pluralism', *Tai Culture*, VI(1/2): 18–40.

Benda-Beckmann, K. von (2001b). 'Transnational Dimensions of Legal Pluralism', in W. Fikentscher (ed.), *Begegnung und Konflikt – Eine kulturanthropologische Bestandsaufnahme*. Munich: C. H. Beck, pp. 33–48.

Benda-Beckmann, K. von (2009). 'Balancing Islam, Adat and the State: Comparing Islamic and Civil Courts in Indonesia', in F. von Benda-Beckmann, K. von Benda-Beckmann and A. Griffiths (eds), *The Power of Law in a Transnational World: Anthropological Enquiries*. New York: Berghan Books, pp. 216–35.

Benda-Beckmann, F. von and K. von Benda-Beckmann (2001). 'State, Religion and Legal Pluralism: Changing Constellations in West Sumatra (Minangkabau) and Comparative Issues', Working Paper No. 19, MPI for Social Anthropology, Halle.

Benda-Beckmann, F. von and K. von Benda-Beckmann (2006a). 'Changing One is Changing All: Dynamics in the Adat–Islam–State Triangle', *Journal of Legal Pluralism and Unofficial Law*, 53/4: 239–70.

Benda-Beckmann, F. von and K von Benda-Beckmann (2006b). 'The Dynamics of Change and Continuity in Plural Legal Orders', *Journal of Legal Pluralism and Unofficial Law*, 53/4: 1–44.

Benda Beckmann, F. von and K. von Benda-Beckmann (2013). *Political and Legal Transformations of an Indonesian Polity: The Nagari from Colonisation to Decentralisation*. Cambridge: Cambridge University Press.

Biezeveld, R. (2004). 'Discourse Shopping in a Dispute over Land in Rural Indonesia', *Ethnology*, 43: 137–54.

Billah, M. M. (1998). 'Islamic Insurance: Its Origins and Development', *Arab Law Quarterly*, 13(4): 386–422.

Boediarto, A. (2000). *Kompilasi Abstrak Hukum Putusan Mahkamah Agung Tentang Hukum Waris*. Jakarta: Ikatan Hakim Indonesia.

Bohannan, P. (1957). *Justice and Judgment among the Tiv*. London: Oxford University Press.

Boland, B. J. (1982). *The Struggle of Islam in Modern Indonesia*. The Hague: Martinus Nijhoff.

Bourdieu, P. (1987). 'The Force of Law: Toward a Sociology of the Juridical Field', trans. R. Terdiman, *Hastings Law Journal*, 38(5): 814–53.

Bowen, J. R. (1993). *Muslims through Discourse: Religion and Ritual in Gayo Society*. Princeton, NJ: Princeton University Press.

Bowen, J. R. (1998a). 'Qur'an, Justice, Gender: Internal Debates in Indonesian Islamic Jurisprudence', *History of Religions*, 38(1): 52–78.

Bowen, J. R. (1998b). '"You May not Give it Away": How Social Norms Shape Islamic Law in Contemporary Indonesian Jurisprudence', *Islamic Law and Society*, 5(3): 382–408.

Bowen, J. R. (2003). *Islam, Law and Equality in Indonesia: An Anthropology of Public Reasoning*. Cambridge: Cambridge University Press.

Bowen, J. R. (2008). 'Intellectual Pilgrimages and Local Norms in Fashioning Indonesian Islam', *Revue d'études sur le monde musulman et la Méditerranée*, 123: 37–54

Bowen, J. R. (2013). 'Contours of Sharia in Indonesia', in M. Künkler and A. Stepan (eds), *Democracy and Islam in Indonesia*. New York: Columbia University Press, pp. 149–67.

Bräuchler, B. (2009). *Reconciling Indonesia: Grassroots Agency for Peace*. London: Routledge.

Braude, B. (1982). 'Foundation Myths of the Millet System', in B. Braude and B. Lewis (eds), *Christians and Jews in the Ottoman Empire: The Functioning of a Plural Society*, vol. I. New York: Holmes & Meier.

Brown, N. J. (1997). 'Shari'a and State in the Modern Muslim Middle East', *International Journal of Middle East*, 29(3): 359–76.

Burns, P. (2004). *Leiden Legacy: Concepts of law in Indonesia*. Leiden: KITLV Press.

Buskens, L. (2000). 'An Islamic Triangle: Changing Relationship between Shari'a, State Law, and Local Customs', *International Institute for the Study of Islam in the Modern World Newsletter*, 5.

Cammack, M. (1999). 'Inching toward Equality: Recent Developments in Indonesian Inheritance Law', *Women Living Under Muslim Laws*, 22: 7–31.

Cammack, M. (2003). 'Indonesia's 1989 Religious Judicature Act', in A. Salim and A. Azra (eds), *Shari'a and Politics in Modern Indonesia*. Singapore: ISEAS, pp. 96–124.

Cammack, M. (2008). 'Islamic Inheritance Law in Indonesia: The Influence of Hazairin's Theory of Bilateral Inheritance', in T. Lindsey (ed.), *Indonesia: Law and Society*, 2nd edn. Sydney: Federation Press, pp. 329–45.

Cammack, M., H. Donovan and T. B. Heaton (2007). 'Islamic Divorce Law and Practice in Indonesia', in R. M. Feener and M. Cammack (eds), *Islamic Law in Contemporary Indonesia: Ideas and Institutions*. Cambridge, MA: Harvard University Press, pp. 99–127.

Cammack, M. and M. Feener (2008). 'Joint Marital Property in Indonesian Customary, Islamic, and National Law', in P. Bearman, W. Heinrichs and B. G. Weiss (eds), *The Law Applied: Contextualizing the Islamic Shari'a: A Volume in Honor of Frank E. Vogel*. London: I. B. Tauris, pp. 92–115.

Carroll, L. (1997). 'Muslim Women and 'Islamic Divorce' in England', *Journal of Muslim Minority Affairs*, 17(1): 97–117.

Carroll, L. (1998). 'Orphaned Grandchildren in Islamic Law of Succession: Reform and Islamization in Pakistan', *Islamic Law and Society*, 5(3): 409–47.

Carroll, L. and H. Kapoor (1996). *Talaq-i-Tafwid: The Muslim Woman's Contractual Access to Divorce*. London: Women Living under Muslim Laws.

Chiba, M. (1986). *Asian Indigenous Law in Interaction with Received Law*. London: KPI.

Cribb, R. (2010). 'Legal Pluralism and Criminal Law in the Dutch Colonial Order', *Indonesia*, 90: 47–66.

Davidson, J. and D. Henley (eds) (2007). *The Revival of Tradition in Indonesian Politics: The Deployment of Adat from Colonialism to Indigenism*, Abingdon: Routledge.

Dijk, C. van (1981). *Rebellion under the Banner of Islam: The Darul Islam in Indonesia*. The Hague: Martinus Nijhoff.

Donovan, D. A. (1998). 'Codification in Developing Nations: Ritual and Symbol in Cambodia and Indonesia', *University of California Davis Law Review*, 31(3): 693–733.

Effendi, S. (2004). *Problematika Hukum Keluarga Islam Kontemporer: Analisis Yurisprudensi dengan Pendekatan Ushuliyah*. Jakarta: Prenada Media.

Escovitz, J. H. (1982). 'The Establishment of Four Chief Judgeship in the Mamluk Empire', *Journal of the American Oriental Society*, 102(3): 529–31.

Fasseur, C. (1994). 'Cornerstone and Stumbling Block Racial Classification and the Late

Colonial State in Indonesia', in R. Cribb (ed.), *The Late Colonial State in Indonesia: Political and Economic Foundations of the Netherlands Indies 1880–1942*. Leiden: KITLV Press.

Feener, R. M. (2007). *Muslim Legal Thought in Modern Indonesia*. Cambridge: Cambridge University Press.

Feener, R. M. (2013). *Shari'a and Social Engineering: The Implementation of Islamic Law in Contemporary Aceh, Indonesia*. Oxford: Oxford University Press.

Firdaus, U. (2009). 'Studi Analisis Terhadap Kewenangan Absolut Pengadilan Agama Sidoarjo tentang Hak Kepemilikan Tanah dalam Perkara No. 1430/Pdt.G/2006/Pa.Sda', undergraduate thesis, IAIN Sunan Ampel, Surabaya.

Fitzpatrick, D. (1997). 'Disputes and Pluralism in Modern Indonesian Land Law', *Yale Journal of International Law*, 22: 171–212.

Fitzpatrick, D. (2005). 'Restoring and Confirming Rights to Land in Tsunami-affected Aceh', *UNDP/OXFAM Report*, 14 July.

Fitzpatrick, D. (2008). 'Managing Conflict and Sustaining Recovery: Land Administration Reform in Tsunami-affected Aceh', *Asia Research Institute Working Paper No. 4*, Singapore, April 2008.

Geertz, C. (1983). *Local Knowledge*. New York: Basic Books.

Gerber, H. (1999). *Islamic Law and Culture 1600–1840*. Leiden: Brill.

Al-Ghadyan, A. A. (1999). 'Insurance: The Islamic Perspective and its Development in Saudi Arabia', *Arab Law Quarterly*, 14(4): 332–8.

Gluckman, M. (1955). *The Judicial Process among the Barotse of Northern Rhodesia*. Manchester: Manchester University Press.

Griffith, J. (1986). 'What is Legal Pluralism?', *Journal of Legal Pluralism and Unofficial Law*, 24: 1–56.

Gulliver, P. (1963). *Social Control in an African Society*. London: Routledge & Kegan Paul; Boston, MA: Boston University Press.

Gulliver P. (1969). *Tradition and Transition in East Africa: Studies in the Tribal Factor in the Modern Era*. London: Routledge & Kegan Paul; Berkeley, CA: University of California Press.

Grigorovich, J. (2009). 'Social Change in the Wake of Disaster: The Tsunami and Humanitarian Response in Aceh Province Indonesia', *Attaché Journal of International Affairs*, Special edition, pp. 150–77.

Hadi, A. (2004). *Islam and State in Sumatra: A Study of Seventeenth-Century Aceh*. Leiden: Brill.

Haeri, S. (1990). *The Law of Desire: Temporary Marriage in Islam*. London: I. B. Tauris.

Hallaq, W. B. (2004). 'Juristic Authority vs. State Power: The Legal Crises of Modern Islam', *Journal of Law and Religion*, 19(2): 101–16.

Hallaq, W. B. (2005). *The Origins and Evolution of Islamic Law*. Cambridge: Cambridge University Press.

Hallaq, W. B. (2009). *Shari'a: Theory, Practice, Transformations*. Cambridge: Cambridge University Press.

Hassan, K. (2006). 'Employment Dispute Resolution Mechanism from the Islamic Perspective', *Arab Law Quarterly*, 20(2): 181–207.

Hazairin (1964). *Hukum Kewarisan Bilateral Menurut Al-Qur'an dan Hadith*. Jakarta: Tintamas.

Al-Hibri, A. (1992). 'Marriage Laws in Muslim Countries: A Comparative Study of Certain Egyptian, Syrian, Moroccan, and Tunisian Marriage Laws', *International Review of Comparative Public Policy*, 4: 227–44.

Hirsch, S. F. (1998). *Pronouncing and Persevering: Gender and the Discourses of Disputing in an African Islamic Court*. Chicago, IL: University of Chicago Press.

Hoesin, M. (1970). *Adat Atjeh*. Banda Aceh: Dinas Pendidikan dan Kebudayaan Propinsi Daerah Istimewa Atjeh.

Hooker, M. B. (1975). *Legal Pluralism: An Introduction to Colonial and Neo-colonial Laws*. Oxford: Clarendon Press.

Hooker, M. B. (1984). *Islamic Law in South-east Asia*. Kuala Lumpur: Oxford University Press.

Husain, F. (2007). *To See the Unseen: Scenes Behind the Aceh Peace Treaty*. Jakarta: Health & Hospital Indonesia.

Husnaini (2007). 'Sengketa milik dalam proses beracara di PA: Sebuah dinamika hukum', available at: http://www.badilag.net/data/ARTIKEL/WACANA%20HUKUM%20ISLAM/sengketa_milik%20artikel.pdf , accessed 27 May 2013.

Hussain, S. (2010). 'Triple Talaq: A Socio-legal Analysis', *Indian Law Institute Law Review*, 1(1): 129–50.

Ibrahim, M. (2008). 'Cina Buta, Islamic Consultation Rubric', *Serambi Indonesia*, 4 April.

Ichwan, M. N. (2007). 'The Politics of Shari'atization: Central Governmental and Regional Discourse of Shari'a Implementation in Aceh', in M. Cammack and M. Feener (eds), *Islamic Law in Contemporary Indonesia: Ideas and Institutions*. Cambridge, MA: Harvard University Press, pp. 193–215.

Idria, R. (2010). 'Muslim Theological Perspectives on Natural Disasters: The Case of Indonesian Earthquakes and Tsunami of 2004', Master's thesis, Leiden University.

International Council on Human Rights Policy (2009). *When Legal Worlds Overlap Human Rights, State and Non-State Law*. Versoix: Atar Roto Press.

Ismuha (1978). *Penggantian Tempat dalam Hukum Waris Menurut KUH Perdata, Hukum Adat dan Hukum Islam*. Jakarta: Bulan Bintang.

Ismuha (1980). 'Pengadilan Agama/Mahkamah Syariah di Aceh, dahulu sekarang dan nanti', in I. Suny (ed.), *Bunga Rampai tentang Aceh*. Jakarta: Bhratara Karya Aksara, pp. 232–81.

Ismuha (1983). *Sejarah Singkat Majelis Ulama Propinsi Daerah Istimewa Aceh*. Banda Aceh: Sekretariat Majelis Ulama Propinsi Daerah Istimewa Aceh.

Jackson, A. R. and D. A. Gozdecka (2011). 'Caught between Different Legal Pluralisms: Women Who Wear Islamic Dress as the Religious "Other" in European Rights Discourses', *Journal of Legal Pluralism and Unofficial Law*, 64: 91–120.

Jackson, S. A. (2006). 'Legal Pluralism between Islam and the Nation-state: Romantic Medievalism or Pragmatic Modernity?', *Fordham International Law Journal*, 30: 158–75.

Kamali, M. H. (1984). 'Divorce and Women's Rights: Some Muslim Interpretations of S. 2:228', *The Muslim World*, 74(2): 85–99.

Kamali, M. H. (2003). *Principles of Islamic Jurisprudence*. Cambridge: Islamic Texts Society.

Karpat, K. H. (1982). 'Millets and Nationality: The Roots of the Incongruity of Nation and State in the post-Ottoman Era', in B. Braude and B. Lewis (eds), *Christian and Jews in the Ottoman Empire: The Functioning of a Plural Society*. New York: Holmes & Meier.

Kell, T. (1995). *The Roots of Acehnese Rebellion 1989–1992*. New York: Cornell Modern Indonesia Project.

Kuran, T. (2004). 'The Economic Ascent of the Middle East's Religious Minorities: The Role of Islamic Legal Pluralism', *Journal of Legal Studies*, 33: 475–515.

Kusrin, Z. M. (2006). 'Conversion to Islam in Relation to Divorce in Malaysian Family Law', *Islam and Christian–Muslim Relations*, 17(3): 307–15.

Layish, A. (1991). *Divorce in the Libyan Family: A Study Based on the Sijjls of the Shari'a Courts of Ajdabiyya and Kufra*. New York: New York University Press.

Lazarus-Black, M. and S. F. Hirsch (eds) (1994). *Contested States: Law, Hegemony and Resistance*. New York: Routledge.

Lev, D. (1972). *Islamic Courts in Indonesia: A Study in the Political Bases of Legal Institutions*. Berkeley, CA: University of California Press.

Lindsey, T. (2012). *Islam, Law and the State in Southeast Asia, vol. I: Indonesia*. London: I. B. Tauris.

Lindsey, T., M. B. Hooker, R. Clarke and J. Kingsley (2007). 'Shari'a Revival in Aceh', in R. Feener and M. Cammack (eds), *Islamic Law in Contemporary Indonesia: Ideas and Institutions*. Cambridge, MA: Harvard University Press, pp. 216–54.

Lubis, N. A. F. (2003). 'The State's Legal Policy and the Development of Islamic Law in Indonesia's New Order', in A. Salim and A. Azra (eds), *Shari'a and Politics in Modern Indonesia*. Singapore: ISEAS, pp. 48–75.

Lukito, R. (2006). 'Religious ADR: Mediation in Islamic Family Law Tradition', *Al-Jami'ah*, 44(2): 325–46.

Lukito, R. (2012). *Legal Pluralism in Indonesia: Bridging the Unbridgeable*. London: Routledge.

Mahmood, T. (1987). *Personal Law in Islamic Countries: History, Text, and Comparative Analysis*. New Delhi: Academy of Law and Religion.

Mahmood, T. (1992). 'No more Talaq, Talaq, Talaq: Juristic Restoration of the True Islamic Law on Divorce', *Islamic and Comparative Law Review*, 12(1): 1–12.

Majelis Permusyawaratan Ulama (2006). *Modul Tatacara Penyelesaian Hak Waris/ Pembagian Harta Warisan dalam Masyarakat Aceh*. Banda Aceh.

Manan, A. (2007). *Etika Hakim dalam Penyelenggaraan Peradilan: Suatu Kajian dalam Sistem Peradilan Islam*. Jakarta: Kencana.

Manan, A. (2008). *Aneka Masalah Hukum Perdata Islam di Indonesia*, 2nd edn. Jakarta: Kencana Prenada Media.

Mashhour, A. (2005). 'Islamic Law and Gender Equality: Could there be a Common Ground? A Study of Divorce and Polygamy in Sharia Law and Contemporary Legislation in Tunisia and Egypt', *Human Rights Quarterly*, 27(2): 562–96.

Matrais, S. (2008). 'Kemandirian Peradilan Agama dalam Perspektif Undang-Undang Peradilan Agama', *Jurnal Hukum*, 15(1): 121–44.

Melchert, C. (1997). *The Formation of the Sunni Schools of Law, 9th–10th Centuries* CE. Leiden: Brill.

Menski, W. (2006). *Comparative Law in a Global Context: The Legal Systems of Asia and Africa*. Cambridge: Cambridge University Press.

Menski, W. (2010). 'Fuzzy Law and the Boundaries of Secularism', *Potchefstroom Electronic Law Journal*, 13(3): 30–53, available at: http://ssrn.com/abstract=1752910, accessed 15 February 2014.

Menski, W. (2011). 'Flying Kites in a Global Sky: New Models of Jurisprudence', *Socio-Legal Review*, 7(1): 1–22.

Merry S. E. (1990). *Getting Justice and Getting Even: Legal Consciousness among Working-Class Americans*. Chicago, IL: Chicago University Press.

Miller, M. A (2009). *Rebellion and Reform in Indonesia: Jakarta's Security and Autonomy Policies in Aceh*. London: Routledge.

Mills, K. (2006). 'Indonesia', in M. Pryles (ed.), *Dispute Resolutions in Asia*. Frederick, MD: Kluwer Law International, pp. 165–200.

Moore, S. F. (1978). *Law as Process: An Anthropological Approach*. London: Routledge & Kegan Paul.

Moore, S. F. (1986). *Social Facts and Fabrications: 'Customary' Law on Kilimanjaro, 1880–1980*. Cambridge: Cambridge University Press.

Moore, S. F. (ed.) (2005). *Law and Anthropology: A Reader*. Oxford: Blackwell.

Moors, A. (1995). *Women, Property, and Islam: Palestinian Experiences 1920–1990*. Cambridge: Cambridge University Press.

Morris, E. E. (1983). 'Islam and Politics in Aceh: A Study of Centre–Periphery Relations in Indonesia', PhD dissertation, Cornell University, Ithaca, NY.

Muhammad, R. A. (2003). *Revitalisasi Syari'at Islam di Aceh: Problem, Solusi dan Implementasi*. Jakarta: Logos.

Nakamura, H. (2006). 'Conditional Divorce in Indonesia', *Occasional Publication*, 7, Islamic Legal Studies Program, Harvard Law School.

Nurlaelawati, E. (2010). *Modernization, Tradition, and Identity: The Kompilasi Hukum Islam and Legal Practices of the Indonesian Religious Courts*. Amsterdam: Amsterdam University Press.

Omar, S. (2007). 'Dissolution of Marriage: Practices, Laws and Islamic Teachings', *Policy Perspectives*, 4(2): 92–117.

Peletz, M. G. (2002). *Islamic Modern: Religious Courts and Cultural Politics in Malaysia*. Princeton, NJ: Princeton University Press.

Quataert, D. (2000). *The Ottoman Empire, 1700–1922: New Approaches to European History*. Cambridge: Cambridge University Press.

Rabo, A. (2005). 'Family Law in Multicultural and Multi-religious Syria', in G. Collste (ed.), *Possibilities of Religious Pluralism*, Linköping Studies in Identity and Pluralism, No. 3. Linköping: Linköping University Electronic Press, pp. 71–87.

Rahman, F. (1980). 'A Survey of Modernization of Muslim Family Law', *International Journal of Middle East Studies*, 11(4): 451–65.

Al-Ramli, S. M. (1938/9). *Nihaya al-Muhtaj ila Sharh al-Minhaj fi al-Fiqh 'ala Madhhab al-Shafi'i*. Cairo: al-Mustafa al-Babi al-Halabi, vol. 6.

Rapoport, Y. (2003). 'Legal Diversity in the Age of Taqlid: The Four Chief Qadis under the Mamluks', *Islamic Law and Society*, 10(2): 210–28.

Rapoport, Y. (2005). *Marriage, Money and Divorce in Medieval Islamic Society*. Cambridge: Cambridge University Press.

Rashid S. K. (2004). 'Alternative Dispute Resolution in the Context of Islamic Law', *Vindobona Journal of International Commercial Law and Arbitration*, 8(1): 95–118.

Reid, A. (ed.) (2006). *Verandah of Violence: The Background to the Aceh Problem*. Singapore: Singapore University Press.

Ricklefs, M. (2001). *History of Modern Indonesia since c. 1200*, Stanford, CA: Stanford University Press.

Rosen, L. (2000). *The Justice of Islam: Comparative Perspectives on Islamic Law and Society*. Oxford: Oxford University Press.

Rosen, L. (2006). *Law as Culture*. Princeton, NJ: Princeton University Press.

Saby, Y. (2001). 'The Ulama in Aceh: A Brief Historical Survey', *Studia Islamika Indonesian Journal for Islamic Studies*, 9(1): 1–54.

Sait, S. and H. Lim (2006). *Land, Law and Islam: Property and Human Rights in the Muslim World*. London: Zed Books.

Saleh, S. (2005). 'Pembagian harta warisan praktek di *Mahkamah Syar'iyah* Nanggroe Aceh Darussalam', paper presented at the Workshop on Joint Marital Property, Determining Heirs and Guardianship in Acehnese Society, Banda Aceh, 20 May 2005.

Salim, A. (2003). 'Shari'a in Indonesia's Current Transition: An Update', in A. Salim and A. Azra (eds), *Shari'a and Politics of Modern Indonesia*. Singapore: ISEAS, pp. 213–34.

Salim, A. (2004). 'Shari'a from Below in Aceh (1930s–1960s): Islamic Identity and the Right to Self-determination with Comparative Reference to the Moro Islamic Liberation Front (MILF)', *Indonesia and Malay World*, 32: 80–96.

Salim, A. (2006). *Praktek Penyelesaian Formal dan Informal Masalah Pertanahan, Kewarisan dan Perwalian Pasca Tsunami di Banda Aceh dan Aceh Besar*. Banda Aceh: IDLO.

Salim, A. (2008). *Challenging the Secular State: The Islamization of Laws in Indonesia*. Honolulu: Hawaii University Press.

Salim, A. (2009). 'Politics, Criminal Justice and Islamisation in Aceh', *Islam, Syari'ah and Governance Background Paper Series*, 3, University of Melbourne, Australia.

Salim, A. and A. Azra (2003). 'Introduction: The State and Sharia in the Perspective of Indonesian Legal Politics', in A. Salim and A. Azra (eds), *Shari'a and Politics in Modern Indonesia*. Singapore: ISEAS, pp. 1–16.

Salim, A., E. Nurlaelawati, L. Marcos and W. Sayuti (2009). *Demi Keadilan dan Kesetaraan: Dokumentasi Program Sensitivitas Jender Hakim Agama di Indonesia*. Jakarta: Puskumham UIN and The Asia Foundation.

Sarjono, C. M. (2011). 'Analisis hukum putusan pengadilan agama yang memutuskan sertipikat hak milik atas tanah tidak berkekuatan hukum (Studi kasus: Putusan Pengadilan Agama Tebing Tinggi No. 52/Pdt.G/2008/PA-TTD jo. Putusan Pengadilan Tinggi Agama Sumatera Utara No. 145/Pdt.G/2008/PTA-MDN)', Master's thesis, Universitas Sumatra Utara, Medan.

Sarong, H. (2002). '*Mahkamah Syar'iyah* dan kewenangannya di Nanggroe Aceh Darussalam', in F. M. Nur (ed.), *Syariat di Wilayah Syariat: Pernik-Pernik Islam di Nanggroe Aceh Darussalam*. Banda Aceh: Dinas Syariat Islam, pp. 212–20.

Schröter, S. (2010). 'Acehnese Culture(s): Plurality and Homogeneity', in A. Graf, S. Schröter and E. Wieringa (eds), *Aceh: History, Politics and Culture*. Singapore: ISEAS, pp. 157–79.

Shaham, R. (1994). 'Judicial Divorce at the Wife's Initiative: The Shari'a Courts of Egypt 1920–1995', *Islamic Law and Society*, 1(2): 217–57.

Shahar, I. (2008). 'Legal Pluralism and the Study of Shari'a Courts', *Islamic Law and Society*, 15: 112–41.

Shaw, S. J. (1976). *History of the Ottoman Empire and Modern Turkey*. Cambridge: Cambridge University Press, vol. I.

Smith, A. (2002). 'Conflict in Aceh: The Consequences of a Broken Social Contract', *Harvard Asia Quarterly*, 6(1): 47–55.

Sonbol, A. (1996). *Women, the Family and Divorce Laws in Islamic History*. Syracuse, NY: Syracuse University Press.

Stange, G. and R. Patock (2010). 'From Rebels to Rulers and Legislators: The Political Transformation of the Free Aceh Movement (GAM) in Indonesia', *Journal of Current Southeast Asian Affairs*, 29(1): 95–120.

Starr, J. (1992). *Law as Metaphor: From Islamic Courts to the Palace of Justice*. New York: SUNY Press.

Starr, J. and J. F. Collier (eds) (1989). *History and Power in the Study of Law: New Directions in Legal Anthropology*. Ithaca, NY: Cornell University Press.

Stiles, E. E. (2003). 'When Divorce is Divorce? Determining Intention in Zanzibar's Islamic Courts', *Ethnology*, 42(4): 273–88.

Sufi, R. (2002). *Hukum Adat Pertanahan: Pola Penguasaan Pemilikan dan Penggunaan Tanah Secara Adat Aceh Tempo Doeloe dan Masa Kini*. Banda Aceh: Pusat Dokumentasi dan Informasi Aceh.

Sugiono, S. (1999). 'Islamic Legal Reform in Twentieth-century Indonesia: A Study of Hazairin's Thought', MA thesis, McGill University.

Suminto, A. (1985). *Politik Islam Hindia Belanda*. Jakarta: LP3ES.

Suparman (2005). *Hukum Waris Indonesia dalam Perspektif Adat, Islam dan BW*. Bandung: Refika Editama.

Syahrizal (ed.) (2003). *Kontekstualisasi Syariat Islam di Nanggroe Aceh Darussalam*. Banda Aceh: Ar-Raniry Press.

Syahrizal (2004). *Hukum Adat dan Hukum Islam di Indonesia: Refleksi terhadap Beberapa Bentuk Integrasi Hukum dalam Bidang Kewarisan di Aceh*. Banda Aceh: Nadiya Foundation.

Syahrizal (2007). 'Pelaksanaan Syariat Islam di Aceh dalam Kerangka Sistem Hukum Nasional', in Syahrizal (ed.), *Dimensi Pemikiran Hukum dalam Implementasi Syariat Islam di Aceh*. Banda Aceh: Dinas Syariat Islam, pp. 2–13.

Syamsuddin, N. (1985). *The Republican Revolt: A Study of the Acehnese Rebellion*. Singapore: Institute of Southeast Asian Studies.

Taji-Farouki, S. (1996). 'Islamic State Theories and Contemporary Realities', in A. S. Sidahmed and A. Ehteshani (eds), *Islamic Fundamentalism*. Boulder, CO: Westview Press.

Tucker, J. (1998). *In the House of the Law: Gender and Islamic Law in Ottoman Syria and Palestine*. Berkeley, CA: University of California Press.

Tucker, J. E. (2008). *Women, Family and Gender in Islamic Law*. Cambridge: Cambridge University Press.

Turner, B. (2006). 'Competing Global Players in Rural Morocco: Upgrading Legal Arenas', *Journal of Legal Pluralism and Unofficial Law*, 53/4: 101–40.

Vikør, K. S. (2000). 'The Shari'a and the Nation State: Who can Codify the Divine Law?', in B. O. Utvik and K. S. Vikør (eds), *The Middle East in a Globalized World*. Bergen: Nordic Society for Middle Eastern Studies.

Vikør, K. S. (2005). *Between God and the Sultan: A History of Islamic Law*. London: Hurst.

Welchman, L. (1988). 'The Development of Islamic Family Law in the Legal System of Jordan', *International and Comparative Law Quarterly*, 37: 868–86.

Welchman, L. (2000). *Beyond the Code: Muslim Family Law and the Shari'a Judiciary in the Palestinian West Bank*. The Hague: Kluwer Law International.

Wierienga, E. (2010). 'God Speaks through Natural Disasters, but What Does He Say? Islamic Interpretations in Indonesian Tsunami Poetry', in A. Graf, S. Schröter and E. Wieringa (eds), *Aceh: History, Politics and Culture*. Singapore: ISEAS, pp. 313–33.

Wignyosoebroto, S. (1996). *Tanah Negara: Tanah Adat yang Dinasionalisasi*. Jakarta: Elsam.

Woodman, G. (1999). 'The Idea of Legal Pluralism', in B. Dupret, M. Berger and L. al-Zwaini (eds), *Legal Pluralism in the Arab World*. The Hague: Kluwer Law International, pp. 3–20.

Wozniak, L. (2003). 'Digital Divorce', *Foreign Policy*, 1 November, available at: http://www.foreignpolicy.com/articles/2003/11/01/digital_divorce, accessed 28 October 2013.

Yilmaz, I. (2005). *Muslim Laws, Politics and Society in Modern Nation States*. Aldershot: Ashgate.

Zubaida, S. (2003). *Law and Power in the Islamic World*. London and New York: I. B. Tauris.

Index

EU Authorised Representative:
Easy Access System Europe Mustamäe tee 50, 10621 Tallinn, Estonia
gpsr.requests@easproject.com

Printed and bound by CPI Group (UK) Ltd, Croydon, CR0 4YY
14/09/2026
02216780-0004